MIXED
FEELINGS

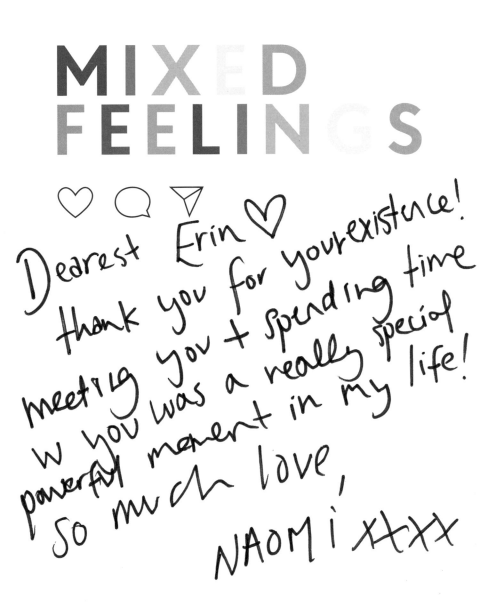

Dearest Erin ♡
thank you for your existence!
meeting you + spending time
w you was a really special
powerful moment in my life!
So much love,
          NAOMI xxxx

MIXED FEELINGS

EXPLORING THE EMOTIONAL IMPACT
OF OUR DIGITAL HABITS

NAOMI SHIMADA + SARAH RAPHAEL

Hardie Grant

QUADRILLE

Publishing Director Sarah Lavelle
Commissioning Editor Susannah Otter
Copy Editor Gemma Wain
Designer Katherine Keeble
Cover Design Claire Rochford, Katherine Keeble, Christine Geiger
Production Director Vincent Smith
Production Controller Nikolaus Ginelli

First published in 2019 by Quadrille,
an imprint of Hardie Grant Publishing

Quadrille
52–54 Southwark Street
London SE1 1UN
quadrille.com

Cataloguing in Publication Data: a catalogue record for this book is
available from the British Library.

ISBN: 978 1 787133983

Printed in Italy

Here's to seeing
each other
as we really are

Contents

INTRODUCTION

♡ ◯ ◁

SARAH

The people in my life who talk most enthusiastically about social media are teenage girls and my dad. The girls say that it makes them feel unattractive and unpopular and causes arguments and ruins their sleep, but that it's also made their generation far more open-minded because they're exposed much earlier than my generation were to body diversity and the LGBTQ+ community and beauty bloggers who wear the hijab. Statistically, teenage girls feel the negative effects of social media most directly, but they're also the group most likely to appreciate a window into the exciting world beyond their classrooms and bedrooms.

At 66, my dad spends over an hour a night in bed catching up on his WhatsApp groups, where he shares political memes, YouTube videos and jokes that make him cry with laughter with some Egyptians he grew up with in Cairo and found on Facebook years after losing touch. He finds it all so wondrous. I wish I could see it the way he does, without all the layers of crap, but as one of the millions of millennials with an anxiety disorder and a job that involves being on the internet all day, I'm much too aware of the dark side.

For the last 10 years, I've worked as an editor and journalist at very fast-paced digital media companies, from Vice to Refinery29. My entire career to date has consisted of sitting at a desk, essentially inside the internet, observing how people behave, what they expect, what makes them feel bad, good, angry, satisfied. My job requires me to be analytical about why people click on posts and where those clicks take them, yet my own behaviour online (as a highly sensitive, jealous Cancerian with Scorpio rising) is frenzied. I've always existed in the strained place between self-control and impulsive desires. I used to sit in assembly at school – with an unnerving level of poise for a 12-year-old – thinking about what would happen if I screamed, and then being worried that I would in fact scream, because although it would be really embarrassing to scream in assembly, the idea felt very thrilling to me. I think most people have these kinds of impulses, ones that don't quite match up with the personality they show the world, and the internet is where these impulses find an outlet. It's where people go to watch a girl roll her face in bread or where they kick back with some animé porn after a hard day at the office. When asked what he's learned in his years as a journalist interviewing those on the fringes of society, Louis Theroux brought up these opposing forces within us: 'We are all much more complicated than we let on, and we go around judging people and stigmatising people but, actually, if we opened up our minds like cabinets, you'd see so much weird stuff in there, stuff that would be deeply embarrassing and hard to justify ... We're full of these contradictory impulses, some of which are quite dark' [*Desert Island Discs*]. It's that tension between the character traits we project to the outside world and the character traits we feel inside ourselves that I wanted to explore in this book.

A lot of people say that social media is neither good nor bad – it's just a reflection of what's happening in society. I struggle with this view because I think people behave online in a way that they wouldn't in real life. I think society on social media has a different value system. In the outside world, vanity is a deadly sin, narcissism is a cautionary tale, charity is supposed to be humble, and basic morality means not bragging about your successes, expensive clothes and nice holidays. I know that makes me sound like a nun, but I'm speaking from the position of having done the opposite online hundreds of times: I've only posted photos of myself where I either look the best I've ever looked or I'm doing something that demonstrates my popularity, physical fitness, charitable nature or professional success. Half my Instagram feed is a humble work brag captioned with phrases like 'So honoured to have taken part in ...' and 'So humbled to have been asked to ...' But what I know from working in the media industry is that most people who appear narcissistic and vain online aren't like that when you meet them in real life – in fact they often seem insecure; and most people who brag about their work successes online aren't pleased with themselves at all – they're too busy worrying about the next thing. The truly pleased-with-themselves aren't posting, because they don't need the boost.

Asked why she doesn't use social media, the actor Olivia Colman said: 'I just find it distasteful. I just don't know why I'd have to show everyone what happens every day – what I'm eating or me with a filter. There's a level of vanity which is accepted that used to be mocked. If anyone caught you looking in a mirror ... I'd have been embarrassed as a teen, whereas now you see youngsters all the time on a bus or anywhere holding their phone up, filming themselves, looking at themselves. It's weird' [*David Tennant does a Podcast with ...*]

It's very weird, and what's even weirder is that we don't talk about how weird it is, we just get on with the business of doing it – taking photos of ourselves while we're looking in a mirror. Social media makes us behave in such strange ways: we give in to impulses online that we would never give in to in real life; we share things with strangers we've never said out loud; we desire the very same things we resent.

My intention for my part of each chapter in this book was to explore an uncomfortable feeling or dark impulse I had while using social media – an impulse that most people could relate to in some way. Then, with the help of psychologists, social media experts, teenagers, activists, journalists, drag queens and plastic surgeons, to try to get to the other side of that uncomfortable feeling. I didn't seriously expect anything about the way I used social media, or the way I was as a person, to change in writing this. But by working through the dark feelings – the judgements I made about other people online, the way I compared myself to everyone, the digital paranoia I felt in romantic relationships – I found the light.

Based on her Instagram account, I thought Naomi only existed in the light side, and I thought that made us the perfect pair for this project: me with my dark impulses at the back end of the internet, and Naomi with her rainbow-bright worldview at the front end. But what I realised is that her light is the result of overcoming various dark experiences. She's taught me to slow down, calm down and look at a feeling from the outside with compassion before letting it rule me, both on- and offline.

While we knew we could offer a good balance of perspectives between us, our experiences of social media are limited to the specifics of our jobs and own lives, and we wanted to do more than explore our own feelings. So we cast the net wider and asked the women in our networks – and outside of them – what their uncomfortable feelings were about social media, and how it affected their work, leisure time, relationships and self-image. Each time we read a new contribution, we gained a new perspective. Technology and society change fast, and tomorrow will bring another set of stories, but for a greasy slice of time, this is how it felt to us.

NAOMI

I have earned a living working as a model in the fashion and advertising industries for almost 15 years, but for me the moment that everything changed, as for so many others, was the advent of social media.

My life on the internet felt like it started to escalate when many years ago I started voicing my concerns about the fashion industry's reluctance to use more varied body types in their ads and campaigns. At that moment in time, 'diversity' in fashion was still very much a new conversation. As I look around now, I can see that a lot has changed since then. But these new changes have given birth to fresh challenges. As someone who's been prevalent on social media, I have benefited

Does social media impact how you spend your free time?

Yes, my neck hurts from hunching over a phone, so now my free time is spent at the chiropractor's.

CELIA BURTON, 29, MAKE UP ARTIST

greatly from its invention. I have been privileged enough to earn a somewhat-decent stable living, to travel the world and I've met so many wonderful people online – some of whom I've had deep connections with offline too. But as social media has grown to become the dominant way of communicating and the background noise of our daily lives, we cannot deny its side effects on our emotional well-being. When social media companies have literally a thousand engineers working on making you addicted to their products for financial gain, it's no wonder we are caught in an infinite scroll. These apps are built to tap into our natural human cravings for validation and we need to understand how they affect us.

Even though 'the attention economy' is still a fairly new term, it's something most of us who use social media are already severely affected by, one that speaks of human attention as a now rare commodity. Our attention is a resource and the fact is, we all only have so much of it. The longer we spend on the apps the more it becomes an effective marketing and advertising space.

Because of the commodification of social media, the lines between my 'work self' and who I am as a person in my own life started to feel increasingly blurred. Last year, this triggered a total existential breakdown that forced me to start to reassess my relationship to social media, and thus my relationship to myself.

Just as how decades ago it was thought that watching TV was rotting our brains, we're now afraid the internet is doing the same – but as it stands, the emotional price we are paying already seems a lot more drastic. The internet is so new, and there's still so much long-term research that needs to be done to really know how it's affecting us, but we cannot deny the change that it has already brought into our lives. From the way we work, to how we look at our bodies, to how we travel and how we love – so much of our inner workings have been vastly affected by social media, and so many of us can now barely remember the world without it.

Over the last couple of years, wherever I seem to go, whoever I talk to, every conversation I overhear, everywhere and anywhere, people are having, and expressing, mixed feelings about social media. I see it in the lives of my friends and the people I follow online – so many of them are struggling with feelings of animosity, anxiety and loneliness. As individuals, what we project outwards and what we're actually feeling inside can often be vastly different. But while we've been presenting curated versions of ourselves since before the dawn of social media, the internet has truly magnified this tendency of ours.

Working with Sarah on this book was everything. Before this, I had barely written anything since I was at school, and my imposter syndrome and fear of failure have often felt like a physical paralysis. Sarah gave me a priceless gift; her supportive nature and her loving, kind energy helped me believe I could actually do this. Even though we are very different people, our spectrum of human experiences binds us together in the most soul-enriching of ways.

We came up with the idea for this book because, even though we work on opposite sides of the media – I'm usually front-facing and as an editor Sarah works behind the scenes – when we'd meet as friends we had so many stories to share concerning our very mixed feelings about social media. We both felt a complex mix of confusion, guilt and discomfort regarding the things we were putting out into the world, and we were both trying to figure out how to fix it. Our mixed feelings connect and bind together so many of us.

We didn't want to just write a book about how social media is bad for us. For so many of us, leaving and deleting the digital world that we're a part of just isn't viable right now. But we were curious to try to find out if balance was possible. We wanted to explore the relationship between those two worlds we now all straddle. We wanted to swim down into the depths to discover what that inner world really looks like, and not just our inner world, but the inner world of others too; which is why we knew we wanted to have more than just our voices in this book.

Having been forced to put my own relationship with social media under the lens, I feel like I'm coming out of this book a fairly changed person. The process of thinking about the effects of the internet encouraged me to not only put my phone down, but also to think about how I could use it more responsibly when I picked it back up again. The irony was I had to take time off social media to write a book about social media, and by doing so I started to find a new perspective. Through examining my own online behaviour and seeing it for what it was, I'm now trying to cultivate a new relationship with social media. And by spending so many hours indoors alone at my computer, writing, it also really brought home the importance of stepping outside and back into the real world – as well as back into my body – in a way that I am truly grateful for. I found that so many of the answers I had been yearning for (you know, all the classic existential ones: Who am I? What makes me happy? What do I want from life? What do I define as success?) lay within me, and I just needed space and time off the internet to find them and feel them out. To discover what was right for

Do you feel pressure to match your online appearance in real life?

People are always surprised when they meet me because I am the exact same person. Of course there's always the pressure that if I run into someone and don't look great that day, that person's gonna be like 'ohh I met her and she's ugly!' But I've grown up on the internet, it's never not been a part of my life. Personality-wise, I'm exactly the same too, which is another thing I didn't realise; that people masquerade as completely different on the internet. Having alternative personalities is so wild to me.

SANAM, 28, CREATIVE DIRECTOR

me personally, instead of being trapped in a very loud echo chamber that was deafening me to my own thoughts and affecting my POV in a way that wasn't always best for me.

This process has taught me to look beyond the image, and think about all the things we can't see from a post. It's all the things left unsaid that speak to me most now.

When we started this book, I thought we were writing about social media, but what became very clear very quickly was that by trying to write about our experiences on social media, we were actually exploring the depths of the human experience. The internet reflects a new, heightened version of the old human condition. It just augments everything that we already are. We felt this was an important thing to write about, but then I started to literally live the subject matter. During the writing process, I experienced so many things that directly related to the book and that changed my perspective. Things I used to think were really significant started to fall by the wayside. In a world where there is such an emphasis on work and status, I began to question not just my relationship with social media but my entire existence. And boy, did I spiral. Hard.

But I wouldn't change a thing about this process. I've never spent so much quiet time alone, and it shows! I needed to really self-reflect and ask myself some vital questions: What do I really want out of life? What kind of person do I want to be? What's really important to me? What does my heart want? As Meister Eckhart wrote so beautifully: 'Many people wonder where they should be and what they should do, when in fact they should be more concerned about how to be.'

I still don't have all the answers, but I think I understand myself well enough now to know I don't need all the answers. That I can live life without having to define it all the time. And that's been the most liberating part of all of this – it's allowed me to sit into the mystery of life. This book gave me a chance to re-evaluate my goals, to write them out, to take a step back and be able to really unpack my thoughts. As Sarah and I began to write and plan together, we realised that social media isn't like two women having a chat behind closed doors. It's more like a sea – no, a deep vast ocean – of so many people and so many voices. We wanted the book to reflect that. We wanted to hear from a broad spectrum of perspectives, ages, and racial and socio-economic backgrounds, to understand each other's vast experiences and learn about the things that unite us. We wanted to speak to people we felt had new ideas, who are proposing ways of using social media that are helpful, supportive and exciting. We wanted to speak to women with huge online followings, as well as ones with next to none, so we could encourage each other to step off the pedestals that social media often forces us to put each other on. I would like to believe that when you send out goodness by sharing the things that make you happy or the things that feel good within you, it comes back to you in all kinds of ways; that when you come from a place of love, there is no competition for attention. Social media at its best can be a powerful entry point to finding great teachers, and we wanted this book to reflect that. I've learned so much from every one of the excerpts, interviews and essays that follow, and I am honoured to have all these voices speaking.

We never set out to write a book that had all the answers – we just felt like our collective experiences were a simple yet powerful place to start. We are very much students; our only goal is to share our findings, and we hope that by doing so a handful of people might feel less isolated. Sometimes a heart emoji in the comments section just isn't human enough, and often we're left yearning for more.

There were so many nights I woke up in a sweat thinking of other things we 'needed' to cover in this book. But there came a moment where I had to accept the fact that it was just too big a subject, and we would have to think of what we were doing as a drop in the ocean of online experiences. That because the scope of our online lives is so big, there was no way we'd ever be able to cover everything! That we had to look at this book as an anthropological slice of what's going on in this moment in time – a collection of stories that spoke to us. No matter who we are, to be alive in the world and have a smartphone tends to mean you, too, will have mixed feelings.

It feels like there is a universal sentiment at the moment: that we can't go on like this, as things are, forever. There is a feeling of unfulfillment, of restlessness, as if we're just waiting to see what's around the corner, that there has to be more. A sense that as human beings we not only want to connect, we need to connect to stay alive. But how can we stay connected online and do so responsibly? How can we collectively explore ways of being mentally balanced in a world where social media's presence and influence continue to grow? Temporarily deleting apps isn't a permanent solution.

Working on this project has given me a lot of hope that there is a way to have a healthier relationship with the online world, but it has also shown me that we have to be responsible for the way we manage that shift. If we want the internet to grow up, we first have to try to grow up ourselves. And while I've been struggling to make sense of it all, one thing is for certain: I know I'm not alone.

Authors' Note

We want this book to be read by anyone and everyone who wishes to dive in and explore how social media has affected the inner workings of our lives. The topics we're discussing affect so many of us, regardless of where we see ourselves on the gender spectrum, but just as a heads up, this book mostly features the voices of women. When we use the word women, we mean all people who choose to identify as women (including cis, trans and anyone else who identifies with the word).

The correct way to speak about people, gender and identity is constantly evolving, so if you're reading this at a time when terminology has advanced, please bear in mind that we did our best to communicate respectfully.

Because of how quickly the landscape of social media and technology changes, we also had to surrender to the fact that some of the ideas, studies and references would date quickly. We hope that because we are writing about and exploring what it means to be human, through the lens of social media, the meaning and depth of this book will continue to be relevant.

As a side note, you don't have to read it all in the order presented to you. If there are certain themes that you're more curious about, read them first! Take what works for you and leave what doesn't.

How Does Instagram Affect Your Well-being?*

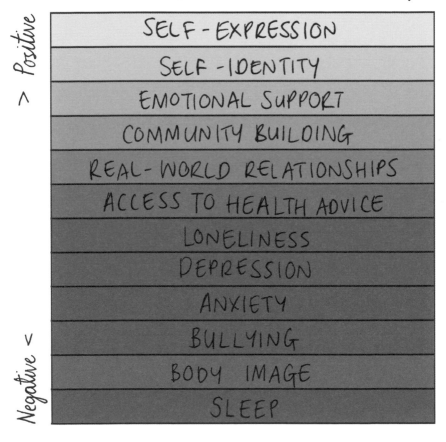

> Positive

SELF - EXPRESSION

SELF - IDENTITY

EMOTIONAL SUPPORT

COMMUNITY BUILDING

REAL - WORLD RELATIONSHIPS

ACCESS TO HEALTH ADVICE

LONELINESS

DEPRESSION

ANXIETY

BULLYING

BODY IMAGE

SLEEP

< Negative

*Answers from 1,479 people age 14-24

by Mona Chalabi

SOCIAL MEDIA +

BODIES

♡ ♡ ◁

NAOMI

Our bodies often feel like vessels looking for acknowledgement. We put them out into the world, and how people react to them can affect us to our core. So much of how we think about our bodies comes from the cultures we're born into and grow up around and no matter where we're from, every culture has an aspirational beauty ideal that women are conditioned to aim for at all costs.

The internet was where, for the first time, I felt like I could put all the different parts of me together in one place and have them make cohesive sense. I felt like I was putting myself and my body out there, and I was supported by a legion of strangers who, for the most part, made me feel good. The internet has made me in so many ways, but in particular it has heightened my awareness of my body, what it does, what it can do and what it can mean.

In the summer of 2014, I took a trip to Japan to see my Japanese family. It was the first time I had been there in four years, which was the longest I had ever gone without seeing my beloved, nearly centenarian grandmother, Fumiko. I had been going back more regularly in the past but life had got in the way and not a single day had passed since then without me going to sleep worrying about whether or not I would make it back to Japan in time to see her again. My guilt and sadness at not having been around to take care of her, alongside the worry that I hadn't spent enough time with her, plagued me constantly.

Since my father passed away when I was 9 years old and we moved from Japan to Spain in search of a fresh start a few years later, there had been a rift between my mom and his family, and we'd not really kept in touch regularly over the years. The Japanese people albeit being well known for being kind, like many other cultures often struggle to communicate, especially emotionally. To pick up the phone and say 'I miss you' just isn't in our cultural language. The after-effects of a death can often lead to consequences that, as a child, are hard to understand. I tried to keep in touch, but it was hard to connect on the phone. I realised that the only way I could have even a smidge of the kind of kinship I yearned for was to just turn up and share space with them. So I started going back as regularly as I could, at least every 2 years or so, when I could afford it, but time had slipped by, and it had been twice as long since my last visit and so there I was, back home, in the place of my birth, on a mission to reconnect. I used the bright green payphone in the lobby of the stark business hotel I was staying in to let my family know of my arrival.

A few days after that call, I found myself walking into a Japanese-Korean barbecue restaurant in a very nondescript suburb of Tokyo. The thick smell of grilled meat overwhelmed my senses and anxiety closed in around my throat. My palms were sweaty, and I suddenly felt as if all my clothes were too small. I was nervous. I had thought about what this reunion would be like hundreds of times.

As soon as I arrived, I felt everyone's eyes laying into me from across the restaurant. I was dressed all in pink, like a bubblegum-coloured highlighter, so not exactly hard to miss. We examined each other, trying to see what we could recognise and remember in one another. My grandmother was wearing the violet cashmere twinset I had bought for her on my last trip. It was hard to tell if she had aged since then. Those kind eyes and the warm face that always had a glow about it looked the same, though her wrinkles were maybe a little more deep-set. She seemed even smaller – no more than four feet tall. At almost 100 years of age she had finally been forced to slow down, and the legs that had served her for so long – through war, displacement and famine; the births of her four children and her nine grandchildren; death, joy and heartbreak – had finally given up. Now she was struggling to walk at all.

I had come to Japan on my last pay cheque, totally confused as to what I was doing with my life. I was feeling a little shaky and all over the place. I was newly single and living out of a suitcase, temporarily homeless. That's obviously not what my traditional Japanese, somewhat conservative family wanted to hear after not having seen me for four years. I knew that they wanted to hear that I had job security, a nice solid man on lockdown and some babies on the horizon. I had absolutely none of those things, but I didn't want to worry them more than they would already be worried about me, so I took a deep breath and mentally prepared myself to smile and ham it up.

'Ohisashiburi desu-ne!' (What a long time it's been!) I said in what used to be my native tongue. Before she could even muster a 'Konnichiwa!' my auntie – looked me up and down with a look of disgust and blurted out, 'You got . . . so fat,' her face tinged with shock at the changes she saw in my body. After I had waited so long for this moment, her words were like a stab in the chest. I felt winded and could sense the tears building forcefully in my eyes. I excused myself and ran to the bathroom, where I sat on the heated Toto toilet seat and let tears that were so big they felt like raindrops flow down my face, wetting the neckline of the fresh T-shirt I was wearing.

By this time, I had been a public voice in what is now known as the 'body positive' movement for a few years, and although I had made peace for the most part with my ever-evolving body, I was not immune to hurtful comments about it. I was used to my body being picked apart by strangers on social media, but when it came to an IRL comment from a family member, it temporarily broke me. I was upset that, even after all this time, after all the lessons I'd learned and everything I'd accomplished, I had been cut down to a (too-big) size by my father's sister – someone I wanted to care about me, to feel connected to in some way, in the hope of feeling connected to him – and that hurt.

In Japan, where I had spent the early part of my childhood, you can't help but be hyper-aware of your size from the moment you're born. Standards of beauty there are ruled by oh-so delicate thinness and petiteness, above everything else. I remember from a very young age being conscious of how 'fatness' was spoken about, and it scared me. Being fat was made to sound like the ultimate shame on a family. Being big – whether that was tall, fat, chubby or however you want to phrase it – often made you feel unwelcome. Early on in my life, I made a mental note to not get 'fat', because the societal ostracisation just seemed like too big a price to pay.

The journey to self-acceptance of our own bodies is an everyday battle, wherever we live. This is a world where we're constantly bombarded, from every angle, by society's white-centric, capitalistic patriarchal messaging that women's bodies are not good enough simply as they are in the present version of themselves. You can walk out into the street and feel like you've got to grips with it one day, and then go on Instagram, see bodies that you've been conditioned to think are 'right', and feel like you're totally falling apart the next.

It's not our fault we're susceptible to these mind games, as we live within a system that thrives by making us feel that our bodies are not what they are 'supposed' to be – and it's a system which has been extra bolstered by the internet. For anything to really change the way we view and live in our bodies, we need to keep reminding ourselves that our body size doesn't dictate the state of our health. It's impossible to really know how healthy someone is just by looking at them, which means we have to stop thinking that 'skinny' equates to 'healthy'. It doesn't, and we have to stop listening to the messages that tell us that it does.

I was at my unhealthiest, by far, when I was at my thinnest. As I reached my twenties, my body began to change and I evolved from the gangly little string-bean I had been for much of my youth. In order to try to keep working as a model, I had to lose the weight I'd put on. Except it wasn't just weight, because my bones had changed. My hips had widened; the arch between my legs looked different. Purely out of the need to keep a roof over my head, I madly convinced myself that I could find a way to effectively shave my bones down.

Barely eating enough to survive, my body and mind started to deteriorate. My mood, my memory and my daily functionality were at an all-time low. I had been dieting and trying every magic 'treatment' – pills, teas, personal trainers, 'detoxing' – and I had never felt more empty, bored and hollow. And the darkest part was that people were constantly commenting on how 'great' I was looking. I remember going to a party at my sickest, when I hadn't eaten a solid piece of food in 10 days, and it seemed as if every guy I had ever had a crush on congregated around me at once, flexing over who was going to take me out first. I was too delirious to actually do anything about it, but I remember feeling intoxicated by the sudden awareness of a desire for me that I could almost smell on them. I wondered if they in turn could smell my overpowering desperation to be thin.

Looking back, it all feels very surreal, because I was actually in a nightmare. I was losing weight all right, but I was also losing my mind. I no longer had the ability to hold an interesting conversation and I didn't want to be judged for my decisions around food, so I found myself pulling away from my good friends and instead resorted to only hanging out with other models who were doing the same thing as me. With them, I didn't have to pretend there was anything on my mind other than losing weight.

Then there came a moment when I couldn't even remember the last time I had heard myself laugh, and I was filled with an immeasurable sadness. I started grieving for the person I used to be. After a humiliating day of being totally shamed and then thrown off a job in front of 20 other people for not fitting the clothes, I ran out of the studio and into the bathroom of the closest train station as fast as my skinny (but not skinny enough) little legs could carry me. As I washed the makeup off my sad face, as clichéd as it sounds, I had an awakening. A voice seemed to boom all around me, telling me that this life, as I was living it, wasn't for me anymore, that I couldn't continue like this any longer. I had ground myself and my bones down as far as I could.

I left my agency the next day, got a job bartending at a very unremarkable salsa bar next to my apartment, and decided to take stock. After a couple of months of trying to reconfigure myself, I slowly started to feel human again. I made an immense effort to eat properly and enjoy food in a way that I had forgotten. I reached out to people I loved and had missed. I slept, went swimming, read books by Naomi

Klein and learned how to salsa from drunk customers at the end of my shift every night. I don't really remember what my internet life was like at this time – I think it was fairly minimal. Maybe a little bit of Facebook usage between friends and family from around the world; I didn't feel as if my life was on the internet.

One afternoon at the public pool in the spring of 2011, I ran into a makeup artist I had worked with a few times on set. She asked me what I was up to, and I told her I was taking some time out of the modelling game. She said she'd been working with a lot of plus-size models and clients, and that it was a growing market and I should maybe look into it. The words 'plus' and 'size' came out of her mouth as if in slow motion, as she looked me up and down. It made me feel so vulnerable as I stood there, cold and wet, in my frayed bathing suit that now felt too small for me. Was she mocking me? I couldn't decide. I could make out that she was saying, 'You look so great like this!' but I couldn't register it properly.

Just so we're clear, I'm not offended by the term 'plus-size' – and nor was I back then. I was just acclimatising to 'thin' not being my MO after years of being forced to think that it was the thing I should want to define me. And I was uneducated about what the term even meant. I was unaware then that, in industry terms at the time, anything above a UK size 10 (US 6) was considered plus-size. Now that industry standards have finally started to shift, this is thankfully nowhere near as prominent anymore but at the time, just as 'normal' designers used models at the smallest end of the spectrum, plus-size brands used models who were an 'aspirational' size 12 – rather than shooting models sized 18 and up, which was their actual market. So, at the size I was that day at the pool, I would have already been categorised as 'plus'.

It was true that my body had changed. I had spent years heavily policing everything that went into my mouth, and my poor darling body – now that I was finally letting it be – was beginning to settle into the weight that it was supposed to be, and I was still trying to make peace with how I looked. None of my clothes fitted me anymore, so my temporary uniform while I figured out how to dress my new body was a pair of shiny black American Apparel leggings and an oversized black T-shirt.

Playing around with fashion has been my favourite form of self-expression for as long as I can remember. Ever since I could walk and point at what I wanted, I demanded to dress myself. And I've always been experimental. When I was two years old, it was Hawaiian shirts and chinos; at four it became T-shirts and tutus and ribbons worn as chokers. (I have the photos to prove it.) Throughout my life I've turned to clothes for a sense of support and to be a crutch when I've needed one. I think what we wear can be an extension of us – a message we put out into the world about how we want to be seen, and a coat of armour to shield us when we need that extra protective layer.

So at that point in my life, with my body having changed, I wanted to find joy in dressing again. I recall desperately looking at magazines, movies, TV and the street for inspiration. I just wanted to see *one* other young girl who had a body that looked like mine and was dressed in a way that made me feel excited and inspired. But while I would sometimes spot a girl out in the real world, it saddened me that when I looked to the media there was no one I felt like I could connect to.

The sadness about the lack of visibility for women like me quickly turned to frustration and then rage. Why was it that, no matter how accomplished a woman was in her career – whether she was an actor, scientist, author or mother – to gain recognition and be deemed socially acceptable, she generally had to be thin? Other than the occasional funny looks and comments every time I went back to Japan about what was considered a 'giantess' height, up until this point I'd had the privilege, for the most part, of having a body that was shaped in a way that didn't make me feel isolated from the masses, so I hadn't really had to think about the world from this perspective before. I now felt wide awake to this reality, and it sent the strongest electric-like shocks through my body. It was as if I had been struck by lightning, because I had a sudden urge to try to change that narrative forever, and this need burned in me like nothing before.

I thought about the tools I had that could make a difference: I had a body and a mind, and I wanted to use them both. Going back into modelling with this new perspective and purpose had the potential to be really powerful. I felt refuelled and inspired to go out there and be the person I had been wanting to see.

I took the makeup artist's advice and decided to give it a shot. I approached a plus-size modelling agency the following week, by sending in a couple of photos of myself alongside a description of my current situation. I didn't really have any expectations but they then asked me to come in, which I did as soon as I could, and they signed me on the spot. The makeup artist had been right: something was starting to shift.

I started seeing more articles about plus-size models in newspapers, and I even saw a handful of plus-size models on the runways at London Fashion Week. There were Tumblr pages dedicated to bigger bodies and

How does social media make you feel about your body?

It makes me feel weird about my body. It has helped me immensely in some ways; seeing bodies like mine was helpful in confronting deep body image issues. While representation is undeniably empowering, I still think this focus on appearance is not the way to lasting peace with ourselves and our bodies. Being beautiful is not a moral imperative; showing your body online isn't either. I can't help but think that the end goal in cultivating a better relationship with ourselves cannot simply be for us to aspire to be beautiful — we are limiting ourselves dangerously, and mitigating other really powerful things we have inside of us if that is the only thing we are striving towards. Sometimes it feels like I'm doing myself a disservice by letting myself be bombarded with all these images, no matter how positive the place they are coming from is, because it shifts my focus outwards instead of inwards.

AMANI AL KI, 27, JEWELLER AND MAKER

bigger models. Change was slow – it definitely wasn't going to happen overnight – but it was something. There was a sense of excitement brewing and a sense of curiosity in the air. Then, before I knew it, I started seeing images of myself being circulated on the internet. To my surprise, someone even started one of those 'Fuck Yeah!' Tumblrs about me. I was both shocked and honoured by this stranger's dedication!

My new sense of perspective allowed me to feel invigorated in every aspect of my life. To be allowed on to a set at the size that I was – and to show up without being nervous and waiting for the penny to drop with whoever was in charge that the measurements on my model card were a total lie – was a refreshing thrill. I could go to work with pride. I felt like I walked the streets differently; I finally felt like I had permission to take up space. But there was a flipside. The only brands and clients I could work for were making clothes that looked like they were meant to dress women at least three times my age. Why weren't they making clothes in bigger sizes for younger women in cooler styles? Why did it feel like they wanted bigger women to get dressed in the 'special section'? Looking at the range of clothes that were available in plus-sizes, it seemed like they wanted bigger women to hide themselves. These clothes existed for them to be able to leave the house but they definitely weren't about making them shine, and that made me so mad!

I was surprised that, even at a very average size, I found it difficult to find clothes that fitted, let alone looked good on me. It felt like everything I tried on in my size was two sizes too small. This forced me to get more creative with the way I dressed. I mixed in random pieces of swimwear, equestrian wear, menswear and all kinds of jewellery. I shopped on eBay and in charity shops, and trawled local markets. I wanted to find my jam.

I started wearing and photographing myself in outfits I felt good in. I reignited my Blogspot account and started posting the images on there, alongside mixtapes and favourite recipes I had been trying. I was a fan of other blogs and people started following mine and before I knew it I had a little fan base. But when social media got upgraded to a more clean-cut aesthetic and Instagram became more dominant, I closed down the blog. I was embarrassed by what suddenly felt like 'juvenile' images, and I didn't want anyone to be able to find them. I thought they looked like my angry teen phase, except they were in the public domain and the bandanas of my youth had been replaced with a million 'cool' bangles. I wish I still had the site to look at now; I wish I had saved it. It was an age of innocence that helped me cut my teeth in terms of online self-expression.

After shutting down the blog, I moved on to Instagram as my internet source du jour but posted the same kinds of images, ones that had a similar sentiment. (I never want to use the word 'content' for my own images – I feel like it sucks the soul out of them!) I shared things I was inspired by, meals I'd cooked, outfits that made me feel good and the people I loved! It was all very natural to me – these were things that gave me a sense of pleasure and that pleasure is what I truly wanted to share. The internet had provided me and my body with a home in a world that hadn't accepted us as a whole person. What I had been craving to see were girls my age and my size and of varying ethnicities, who dressed cute and did fun stuff. Just like me! It seems silly now, because we have in some ways come so far since then. But it was a big deal for me then. Being from the modelling world, I felt like the parameters of what you could be were so limited, and my work hardly ever allowed me to express myself fully. Modelling is a job in which you have to be what someone else – i.e. the brand or art director – wants you to be that day. The internet was the first place I was able to express myself as me. Instagram quickly became a means of regaining my sense of self. It was exciting and fun! The tiled images helped me see so many different parts of myself come together. Clothes and how I dressed became an even bigger part of my identity than they had been before.

One of the most positive things about social media is the platform it has created for other kinds of bodies to not only be more visible but also more celebrated. Depending on who you choose to follow, and thus the echo chamber you create for yourself, social media can be a celebration of all bodies. And it should be. Have you ever judged someone else's body? Thought something unpleasant about them in your head and felt guilty to have entertained such a notion? It's okay, you're only human, and these thoughts only serve as reminders of how deep society's conditioning goes and how hard we have to work to unlearn it all. Studies show that by simply being exposed to different body types, you become more accepting of them. Despite social media being a place where a lot of unrealistic body ideals are promoted, it can also be an important tool in the unlearning process. We now have access to a huge range of different people, of all ages, ethnicities, body types, abilities, sexualities and genders – all by typing in your search box.

We have to be able to see all types of bodies in order to normalise them. Because the more we regard other bodies with kindness, the more we can view our own bodies with the same. And we all have to be mindful and careful to do this despite any other messages we might be

Do you think the 'plus size' movement could have happened without the internet?

No. Obviously these were conversations that were happening all the time in the past, but there was no way for us to come together and speak loudly as a collective. The internet was the opportunity and tool to activate that. It gave us the power to come together and realize that there are a lot of us. We can now use our voice to make each other feel safe and comfortable, and to tell brands to make clothes that fit us. It's given us the opportunity to bring forth power as a whole.

GABI GREGG, 32, FASHION DESIGNER AND BODY POSITIVE INFLUENCER

hearing or receiving. And yes it's an everyday battle.

I have been labelled as 'body positive' many times during my career, but over the last few years it's a term I have really started to move away from, for my own personal reasons. When I first started publicly voicing my opinion on the importance of representing more body types in fashion, I had never heard the term 'body-positive'. By standing on my soapbox and advocating for the importance of diversity, I was branded as 'body positive', simply for being bigger than the average model. Of course, I not only stand for the ideals around body positivity, I live by them. But the term has been hijacked by capitalism and added to every ad campaign, which means that the forces of white supremacy, anti-blackness and fatphobia have taken over a space that used to be a safe and important space for not only fat black women and femmes, but also other marginalized bodies. These same oppressive forces have made it into what can often feel like a very commercialized and actually fatphobic space.

I think it's confusing when something like 'body positivity' becomes an internet buzzword that gets repeated: so often its messaging gets watered down and ends up taking the meaning out of the original phrasing, because we become so desensitised to it. I just hope that people are really soaking up the intention and feeling beyond what the commercialised capitalist version is trying to sell us; that your body is worthy of being here *no matter what*.

In the past, I have also often been labelled as plus-size, which is also a term I personally don't identify with, as I have never actually been a plus-size woman, so being asked to talk about being one is something that I don't want to do. I don't want to speak for women whose experiences I haven't actually shared, especially at a time where there are so many prominent plus-size voices in the public sphere whom they could ask instead. I started out on this journey speaking out about the importance of size inclusion in fashion because of my own exposure to the prejudices of the industry, and through that I became an inadvertent talking head for the body-positive movement. But while I was referred to as plus-size in fashion because of the fashion world's narrow-minded view of what 'plus-size' actually is, it didn't mean that I was plus-size in the real world.

Thin privilege is undeniable, and it is everywhere. I am very aware that I benefit from the privilege of being 'thin enough'. Being in a bigger body changes your everyday experience. Everything from air travel, to getting dressed, to just being able to sit in a restaurant with someone you love, is more difficult. So as each day passes, I feel more and more like it's not my place to speak out about body image. As a conventionally attractive, able-bodied, racially ambiguous and average-sized person, it's clear to see how I have benefited from the system and how I continue to do so. For the most part, I can walk into a store and buy something in my size. I do not encounter discrimination in the way that so many other bodies do. By any standard real-life measures, I am of 'palatable' size. As someone that currently fluctuates between a UK 12–14 (US 8–10), I am the average size in UK – the entry point on the size diversity scale. And because of that being labelled 'body positive' doesn't feel right to me anymore. That term, at least for me personally, should be saved for those with bodies that have been marginalised, and who need it to keep carving out their place in the world, for their bodies to be able to have the absolute minimum they deserve: just to be acknowledged.

The internet was the place where I initially felt I could just let myself *be* for the first time – but now it often acts like it doesn't actually want me to just *be* anymore. That sense of freedom is now tinged with something more complex. As someone who came up through social media talking about bodies, there seems to be a kind of ownership that people feel over my own. If you type my name into Google, one of the top searches that comes up is 'Naomi Shimada before and after' or 'Naomi Shimada skinny'. It's still weird to see people commenting on my body as if it doesn't belong to me. As if my head doesn't come attached to it, along with a heart, soul and a lot of feelings too. It's especially weird when the lens that people look at me through is so magnified, and they see things that I hadn't even noticed about myself. A new freckle, a fly on my shoulder, a bruise. People look at me so scrupulously sometimes but, at the end of the day, it's hard to know what to think when I'm the one who's chosen to upload these images in the first place.

It always makes me think about whether there is a more responsible way we can be using social media. Are there boundaries we can collectively choose not to cross? Things we can agree not to comment on? Can we opt to respond with more love and kindness? I often struggle with the dichotomy that can result from uploading images of our own bodies onto the internet. Our intention may be to celebrate and empower, but we can't always control what happens to such images or how they are perceived by others. In uploading them we make ourselves so much more vulnerable, and there is often a price to pay for this self-expression.

Last year I posted a picture of myself on Instagram. I loved everything about it. I looked really happy, I loved the background, I loved my outfit, and at the time I was in love with the person who had taken the photo. After uploading it, I went about my day, not thinking any more of it. Because I had turned off notifications on my phone, I didn't see all the activity it was attracting. In the caption, I had mentioned that I was feeling 'very grateful' that day. In the picture, my belly was popping out a little. And it was popping out a little because that's what my belly does naturally if I'm not sucking it in or wearing two pairs of Spanx – and on that day, I had simply forgotten to suck it in. But I hadn't cared, because I was overjoyed by all the other things going on in the photo.

Even though I was used to people sporadically commenting on photos asking me if I was pregnant, this was the first time (because of the somewhat confusing caption that accompanied the photo) that people assumed that it was an official pregnancy announcement. There were so many comments from people congratulating me, telling me that I was going to be a 'wonderful mother' and how I was 'going to have such a beautiful baby'. And not only were the comments coming in on social media, but I was getting multiple texts and calls. Even from family members and close friends! I quickly glanced at the photo to re-examine it myself. I looked at my round stomach, and for a second I felt a pinch of shame and thought about deleting it. Then I stared at it for a minute longer and decided to change the caption instead, to alert everyone to the fact I wasn't pregnant: I was just relaxed and having a lovely time, so, everyone, please don't panic!

I decided to laugh about it. But it was a good example of how unaccustomed we are to seeing real bodies. By deleting the picture, I would have once again been complicit in furthering the narrative of 'acceptable' body types. I feel like even when the word 'curvy' is used, it tends to conjure up big boobs, big hips and a big butt – but you'd better not even think about a visible stomach being attached to those other body parts! We're so quick to jump the gun on how we perceive and comment on each other's bodies. I try my utmost to never comment on anyone's body, as I don't feel it's my place to – especially being someone who is often on the receiving end of such remarks.

But it works the other way too. After a really bad episode of anxiety forced me to get my diet and exercise routine right, I lost some weight. I then received multiple DMs and comments from strangers, as well as people I knew. Most of these messages had a tinge of concern: 'Hey, I don't mean to be nosy but ... have you lost weight? You still look great, but you know, I just wanted to ask?' Some of them rang a little angrier: 'I just wanted to say that I feel disappointed in you. I thought you were supposed to be body positive!' It's as if those two things – health and changes in your body – can't go together. If taking care of my body because I love and appreciate it doesn't mean self-love, then I don't know what does.

To my absolute dismay, a couple of months ago an old photo of me in my underwear was used on a Murdoch-owned, right-wing news site to illustrate a story for an agony-aunt column about men who love to sleep with 'fat' women. The title read 'I had sex with fattest girl I know and loved being smothered by her body, but fear mates will mock my passion', and my face and my body had been used to illustrate this abhorrent tale of misogyny, body-shaming and all-round hatred. I was hit by a wave of emotions that started with shock and within seconds turned into blood-boiling, shaking anger, followed by big tears. I felt naked and violated like never before. For my face and body to be used in such a disgusting piece, on such a despicable news site that was responsible for so much hate being shared in the world, felt like a violation of not only my body but my soul and my entire sense of being. A photo that had been taken with pride and love now served as a harsh reminder of how an image can be taken out of context and used without your consent to misrepresent you. I eventually got it taken down, but the experience left a very bitter taste.

The problem is, we aren't always sharing responsibly on social media: neither as individuals nor as organisations. We aren't asking people who view our images and our bodies online to sign non-disclosure agreements or contracts to view with gentleness, care and compassion. One upload, one screenshot, one forward – and that's it, the image is out of our hands. From all my years of modelling, I am used to having images of me circulated in a way I have no control over; the lack of ownership is part of my job and I've often just seen it as the price I pay for this being my trade. But the agony-aunt incident felt like it had crossed a line.

How can we share our bodies while keeping them protected? Is any kind of shield even possible? By using these apps, we literally sign ourselves and our precious bodies away. Our bodies can be taken away from us as if they don't belong to us, and we're just supposed to make peace with that as something that might happen in the name of online sharing? Is this what we're forced to sacrifice in the fight to promote the visibility of different kinds of bodies? I try to keep the bigger picture in mind – that there are always ramifications that come with pushing for change; that there will always be opinions we don't agree with and people trying to take us down – but I can't deny that, as time goes on, these experiences make me weigh up what's more important, and they definitely make me think twice about how I continue to share images of myself and this body of mine with the digital world.

In our culture, we have a tendency to monitor what our bodies look like, but not what they feel like. When was the last time you really touched base with yourself and tuned in to how you're feeling? In recent years, thinking back to my childhood experiences has made me more conscious of the state of my health. When my father's cancer was found, it was too late for any medical intervention to make a difference. Within months, the disease had spread throughout his body. He passed away at the age of 41. A mere decade from the age I am while writing this book.

My father passing away at such a young age has made me distinctly aware of the privilege of having a well-functioning, living, breathing body. It just makes me think: if he had been checking in with his body a little bit more, would he have passed away? If he had taken the time to listen and taken better care of his body, would he still be alive? If he hadn't been part of a toxic male narrative that makes men feel like they can't divulge their pain and forces them to think they have to work through it, would he still be by my side?

If there was ever a sobering thought to stop me being so hard on myself for the superficial things I want to change about my body, it's that. Because I know that I look and feel my best when I've been taking care of myself. I prioritise exercise and sleep now as if my life depended on it, because I've realised it actually does. For years, I thought that exercise wasn't for me. I thought exercise was for smug, skinny people in yoga pants on the weekend, who I saw and rolled my eyes at when I was crawling to the shop hungover to buy a block of cheese and a can of Coke. Now, no matter how busy I am, I move my body in whatever way I can. My love of dance will keep coming up in this book, but I can't emphasise enough the way it's changed my life! Dancing helped me feel comfortable in my body, in a way that no outfit, boyfriend or material thing ever could. To connect to my body, to see it in motion, to see it grow strong, to see it live and breathe freely has been the biggest gift I could ever give myself. And if I can't get to dance or the gym, I run around the block or go for a bike ride, or dance around my bedroom. Whatever I can do to break a little sweat, I do it.

Exercise was something I originally started in order to 'get in shape' after not having done any physical exercise since my teens. But when I began to view exercise as an essential to my life as eating, breathing and sleeping rather than a weight-loss tool, I finally began to surrender to it and to benefit from it. We all know it's 'good' for us, but there are so many negative feelings of shame and failure that surround it. I actively choose to move my body because I can feel how good it is for me. Whether I'm having a great or terrible day, it helps me to stay calm enough to navigate and handle things. Life is messy, and exercise gives me the tools to deal with it. I cannot urge you enough to do the same – deciding to exercise or to move around (if your body is able to) is never a bad decision. Ever!

But I never want to shame anyone into physical exercise, as I have a lot of mixed feelings about wellness culture on Instagram. Being able to take care of yourself doesn't have to mean SoulCycle and a green smoothie; it can mean different things to different people, and that's okay, because we're all different and so are our needs – and we need to learn to listen to those needs. Not to mention our differences in socio-economic access that also determines how we can serve those needs. All I'm saying is let's just do what we can, whatever that may look like to you. In this day and age, when we're stuck in a mind-bending cycle of the never-ending scroll, we are trapped in our heads and cut off from our primal senses that are trying to get us to pay attention to them. Often we are completely guilty of ignoring our needs, but for our bodies to be on good form, we all need to rest, eat and move.

In my day-to-day life, I no longer really think about my weight. Most of my clothes are elasticated. I don't own scales. I try to live a balanced life and to gauge and listen to what my body is trying to say to me. Despite most advertising having conditioned us to think we don't deserve food, we do. We REALLY do. Most of the time, I don't eat meat, but sometimes, while I am on my period, I fantasise about eating burgers and steaks at the same time, on top of each other. So, if I feel like it, I'll eat one – or three. Recently, I've found myself needing a lot more sleep than I used to. I was fighting it, but now I'm surrendering to it. I figure my body is doing some deep repairing, some deep healing, and just needs more rest. So I've forced myself, after a lifetime of being a night owl, to go to bed earlier.

Listening to your body can sometimes mean re-evaluating the relationships with the people you have around you. That can be tricky, especially when it comes to family or other people you love who aren't always good for you. Are you spending time with someone your body is rejecting? Is there an energy vampire in your midst that might need to avoid? Ask yourself these questions, because the body you're in is the only one you have – and it's trying to tell you things!

As a final point, one we hear all the time, nothing is more important to remember than the fact that **perfection is not real**! We feel the pressure to be perfect from the day we're born, and the idea of perfection is magnified on social media because – let us never forget – it's a curated version of all of our lives. All the nice bits! But just like perfection online isn't real and we know it, perfection IRL isn't real either; it's a fallacy created to keep us down. I know it's hard! Trying to remember and remind ourselves of these things – let alone learning to live by them – is a daily process. That's the reality of our lives. I know, it's a conflicting feeling – wanting to truly accept our bodies as they are, right now, and also wanting (or needing) to change a lifetime of conditioning about what are 'good' bodies. But what's also real is discrimination against any bodies that don't conform, and this inequity is killing us. Literally. Eating disorders are killing more people than any other kind of mental illness, and they affect more than 1.6 million people in the UK alone. It's not just our bodies we have to learn to love. It's our minds, and it's ourselves – on bad days as well as good. We need to learn how to cut through all the noise, for the sake of ourselves.

Actively deciding not to compare your body to the backdrop of anyone else's so-called perfect-looking body is a conscious practice that of course isn't as easy. As a very simple start, if you choose to engage with social media, follow people that make you feel good. There is a plethora of breathing, magnificent bodies of all types on social media; that's what makes the online world so rich. Fill your feed with them. And then, even more importantly, look out into the world around you – on the bus, in the supermarket, wherever you are. Lift your eyes from your phone. Bodies of every size, shape and colour: they're out there, just living. Every day I walk out onto the street and feel invigorated by the women I see going about their daily lives who exude a magical something. Don't fall into the trap of looking at versions of what you think your body should look like. This means unfollowing or muting people who make you feel ashamed about yourself, and looking instead to the world around you and the people who make you feel joy. We all have our own personal triggers, so listen to yourself and figure out what they are, and try not to choose to actively consume them.

I recently read a passage on beauty from the Irish poet and philosopher John O'Donaghue that I found really helpful: 'In our time, we mistake glamour for beauty. But glamour only shines for a very limited time, while beauty invites harmony and unity. Beauty fulfils the deepest needs of your soul, so that you'll feel at home in the world.'

He also wrote that: 'Only you decide if you find something beautiful or not, because tastes differ. But if you start looking in a different manner, beauty will surround you.'

His words are a gentle reminder to me that opening myself up to more beauty in the world will allow me to see more beauty in myself – as an imperfect, messy student of life. That I have to see myself through my own eyes, not the ones of my family back in Japan, nor by comparing myself to someone else on social media. Each of us is the only one who can truly re-examine our relationship with our own body, and we need to approach this with love and kindness. Discovering and accepting my own body is when I finally began to feel like I was starting to discover the deepest depths of my soul.

Do selfies boost your confidence?

Sometimes – they are always the most liked posts.
However, I get so, so self conscious taking them.
Filters in a way soothed that – they can be so fun.
I think the motifs and angles of selfies are worrying.
I hate watching people take them. I'm always
concerned if I look young or thin enough in them.

**FRANCESCA GAVIN,
WRITER AND CURATOR**

'Do not read beauty magazines, they will only make you feel ugly'

BAZ LUHRMANN, 'SUNSCREEN'

SARAH

My therapist is called Valerie. She's so chic, I feel bad I'm her only audience. She looks like an actor playing a therapist in a French film where the costume designer is someone very revered. Valerie has cat-eye-shaped glasses, a stunning earring collection and perfectly manicured nails in a range of sophisticated shades. Her hair has just the right amount of volume to balance her features, which individually aren't perfect but work well together. Even though the therapy sessions are conducted in her flat, Valerie wears a tasteful midi-heel at all times, which I suspect she leaves by the door and steps into gracefully just before I ring the bell. If she wasn't my therapist, I would tell Valerie how fantastic she looks all the time, but the nature of our relationship prevents me. We're not there to talk about how fab she is; we're there to talk about my obsession with perfection. To my mind, either I do a perfect job or I fail completely. Either I'm all or I'm nothing. This translates to every area of my life but particularly to my appearance, which in an image-obsessed world where the average millennial will take 25,000 selfies in their lifetime, is more of an issue than perhaps it should be at my age.

I first went to see Valerie during a six-month period of insomnia and depression a few years ago when all the little things I didn't like about myself – which get called 'imperfections' – were going round my head on a loop as I walked to work or lay awake in bed. I would stare at other people's selfies, listing all the ways I didn't measure up (your lips are horrible compared to hers ... your hair is horrible compared to hers ... your nose is horrible compared to hers). The obsessive thoughts I was having when scrolling through Instagram started to interrupt me in real life and I became so self-conscious that, when I spoke to people, I'd feel very aware of how my face looked as I was talking. Had they noticed the hair on the side of my face? Did speaking make my lips look thin? When I shared these thoughts with Valerie in therapy, embarrassed about how they sounded out loud, her expression was somewhere between a raised eyebrow and a frown. 'I understand that's how you feel about yourself,' she said, 'but the person you are describing is not the person sat in front of me.' I later realised it was the person I saw in the reverse camera on my phone.

It feels passé to be talking about Instagram making people feel insecure in 2019, because we're all supposed to have gotten over it by now and moved on, into a vinyasa. But I still feel weak under the pressure of digital perfection, which has become the new normal. According to Dr Helen Sharpe, a clinical psychologist and a specialist in adolescent body image, not everybody does get over insecurity. 'Body image issues are often viewed as a young person's problem – "a bunch of silly girls who need to get over it" – but the reality is that it carries on, it's not just a passing phase,' she told me over the phone. Dr Sharpe recently worked with a group in the US who have collected data on young women from the middle of high school right into their thirties. 'One of the things that's really depressing about this data,' she said, 'is that if you look at the trajectories of body image difficulties over time, they are incredibly stable. Meaning that if young people are struggling with body image difficulties in their teens, chances are they will still be struggling with them when they're in their thirties.'

For those still struggling, social media presents several contradictory solutions. On the one hand, it tells us to love our 'imperfections' – our curves, our curls, our body hair, whatever is on the list of things we carry in our heads, formed over a lifetime of comments and experiences. And on the other hand, it gives us the option of editing out all the things we don't like using filters and apps, while bombarding us with images of beautiful women that get millions of likes and adverts for self-improvement products and fitness plans. Embrace your imperfections! Strive for perfection! Both messages are powerful.

'I worry that this generation have gotten used to living with a low-level noise, and for some women it's more acute, the "I'm not good enough" noise,' the activist, writer and diversity professor Caryn Franklin MBE told me recently. 'I never felt that when I was growing up. We didn't have social media, so I was only looking locally and I was only looking live. I was never going to see a whole load of women in bikinis because I was walking down my street. I try to help my daughters understand that this is a modern thing.'

I recently asked a group of eight teenage girls aged 13 to 18, who attend a youth group I volunteer at, to raise their hands if they felt happy with the way they looked. Just two of them did. Having known these girls for over a year, I suspected one of those raised hands was bravado. The other belonged to a 15-year-old who is the recipient of constant compliments from the rest of the group. When I take photos of them as a group, many pout, contorting their faces into what they clearly feel is the most attractive arrangement, while the girl who's always complimented just smiles sweetly. 'Argh, you're so pretty it's not fair . . . Why do you always look so pretty?' the rest of the group say to her after looking at the photos and criticising various aspects of themselves; criticisms which make no sense to me, because they are all beautiful. As a former fashion editor, I see outstanding beauty in all the things they find fault with. The compliments haven't made this girl vain – she is the sweetest – but they have made her feel confident, or at least like she is enough. Official stats on a much bigger scale (a Girlguiding survey of 1,000 girls across the UK) have found that 66 per cent of girls feel they're 'not pretty enough', 61 per cent feel they 'need to be perfect' and 37 per cent often compare themselves to celebrities. A third of the group surveyed said that they specifically worry about how they look in photos.

Last year I interviewed the actor and singer Lola Kirke (*Mistress America, Gone Girl, Mozart in the Jungle*), and the conversation got on to the pressures social media puts on young women, a theme she explores in the music video for 'Sexy Song'. I guess I expected, being a beautiful Hollywood actress and all, that Lola would be one of those who feels good about herself on social media. But even she has mixed feelings.

'We totally live in a culture that promotes narcissism. And it's a disease! It's a mental illness!' she said in between mouthfuls of pickled onion crisps. 'There's a great quote that's floating on the internet . . . "In a culture that profits from your low self-esteem, liking yourself is a radical act." I think the culture of social media advocates for you to like and dislike yourself at once. It's a very confusing time to . . . be alive.'

It seems the reality is that very few people are self-confident enough to avoid being affected by negative comparison online. It's hard for teenagers, for adults, for Hollywood actors; it's even hard for born-again Christians. I mentioned this chapter on beauty and body image to the people on a course I attend on Wednesday nights about religion and the meaning of life. For some reason, I assumed that because they all believe in God – who made humans in his perfect divine image and who asks that we treat our bodies like temples – they wouldn't care what they looked like in selfies. But when I brought it up, the most fist-pumping Christian of the lot pulled his chair close to mine and started telling me how he wanted to get cheek implants and pec implants and maybe the bump in his nose removed. He started showing me photos of his friends on Instagram who had had work done. Turns out, striving to see your body like a temple made in the image of God does not make you impervious to the earthly temptations of… looking good in selfies. Those things are not mutually exclusive.

The best of social media in the context of body image and beauty is that marginalised groups who were previously shut out of mainstream beauty conversations have a voice. Instagram, YouTube and Snapchat have heralded a vital beauty revolution that celebrates difference in terms of body size, ethnicity and gender presentation. As a consequence of this revolution, big brands are being called out for misrepresentation in their ad campaigns and, slowly, diversity is moving up the agenda. That's the best of it. But there is also a worst of it. And the middle of it is that we're scrutinising ourselves in a way that's never happened before. Or rather, it's happened to models – who've long had to deal with intense scrutiny as their faces have been blown up and photoshopped and plastered around cities with taglines like 'Because you're worth it' – but not to the majority of young people. It's only recently that a majority of young people have felt compelled to take close-up photos of their own faces and bodies using 12-megapixel phone cameras with the intention of posting them on public forums.

I started taking selfies the same time everyone else did, when selfie culture was exploding in 2014. Looking at the images didn't just confirm the things I already knew I didn't like about myself, they actually inspired new insecurities. I felt I looked like Picasso's Weeping Woman in all the pictures I took – something in the eyes. Worried there might actually be something wrong with my eyes, I asked my optician at my next routine appointment, who said, 'Ah yes, your left eyelid is fatter than your right, and always has been.' It had just taken me 25 years and the birth of selfies to notice. For a short, ridiculous while, I tried to open my left eye wider than my right in photos, eventually coming to the conclusion that selfies would not be part of my personal branding online. I resolved instead to post pictures of the panels I was hosting on female empowerment for work. Oh, the irony.

In *The Whole Woman*, published in 1999 when the author was still a popular feminist, Germaine Greer wrote:

Every woman knows that, regardless of all her other achievements, she is a failure if she is not beautiful. She also knows that whatever beauty she has is leaving her, stealthily, day by day. Even if she is as freakishly beautiful as the supermodels whose images she sees replicated all around her until they are more familiar than the features of her own mother, she cannot be beautiful enough. There must be bits of her that will not do ... However much body hair she has, it is too much ... If her body is thin enough, her breasts are sad. If her breasts are full, her arse is surely too big.

Feminism has come a long way since 1999, and with each passing year we're seeing more movements challenging patriarchal systems and the expectations they place upon women. But despite progress in the workplace, in the hard-fought right for Irish women to choose to have an abortion and in the collective power of #MeToo, the pressure on women to be beautiful is more suffocating than ever on social media. Yes, there are now more individuals defying Greer's theory online, such as the body-positive activists who post photos of their bodies as they are and their body hair as it is. And that's powerful, it's helped, but there's still a majority 'liking' those inspirational pictures, thinking 'yay' for women, and then privately dissecting their own body parts according to a totally different set of rules: bum not round enough, lips not pouty enough, face not pretty enough.

As a social media manager for a women's media company, Sadhbh O'Sullivan spends her days immersed in this world. I asked her why, when there are thousands of positive messages out there, so many women still feel mired in the old ideals of conventional beauty and body ideals. She was quick to draw a distinction between body positive activists and 'self-love influencers'. *(PTO)*

How does social media make you feel about your body?

Terrible. There are no other words. Looking back at pictures of myself is just gut-wrenching. Mostly because I don't think I photograph particularly well. On the rare time I like a photo of myself, it'll be for my face, not my body because social media has made it so that normal bodies aren't in anybody's consciousness or maybe more accurately, social media has skewed what 'normal' really is.

Do selfies boost your confidence?

Not really because I am fully aware any pic I, or anybody else, puts up, is usually a lie. I don't use Facetune or anything like that so it doesn't go that far for me but I have tried not to have my confidence tied to anything as fleeting as a selfie.

LYNETTE NYLANDER, 29
WRITER, EDITOR AND CREATIVE

Sadhbh O'Sullivan, 26
Social media manager

Do you think the self-love messages on Instagram get through?

Yes and no. The idea of loving yourself propagated by influencers is good, but it's quite banal. It feels quite superficial when the motivation is not ... beyond yourself feeling good in a photo. That is important! It's hugely important! But that can't be the only purpose, because it's just so individualistic, focusing entirely on yourself and your own position in the world. There are lots of influencers promoting self-love who should recognise their privilege of just ... being hot all the time, and that being their job, when there are other people – like fat activists and body-positive activists, who are part of a political movement because their bodies were actively hated – whose messages might have more political relevance, but who get left behind. I follow a couple of body-positive activists but I don't immerse myself in that self-love influencer world. I mainly just follow my friends and some funny accounts.

How do you feel when you take a photo of yourself? What makes you think 'that's a good photo of me'?

A lot of it is acne-dependent. Four years ago it was all self-love, blah blah blah, and I thought, 'Hell yeah! I wanna look good! I wanna join in.' But then I got really bad acne – late cystic acne that a lot of people get – and I just felt really shit. That's when it became important to me to document what I actually looked like – to see those deep red scars and reconcile myself to them instead of hiding them, so the kind of self-love that actually has a point as opposed to just feeling like you look pretty. When you're a femme lesbian, the way we communicate how we present is haircuts and the way we wear makeup. I think a good photo of me is one that communicates my identity.

When Instagram started it wasn't about selfies or even beauty, it was about art, photography and design. Why do you think it changed?

It changed because we got the reversing camera. But before that it was Facebook selfies and MySpace selfies and stuff.

How does your feeling about yourself differ when you're on social media?

It differs hugely. What has helped me is . . . this is obvious . . . but recognising that it's not reality, it's only a snapshot. The reason everyone hates photos of themselves is because you never actually look like that! My wife hates photos of herself, but she was on a work trip and someone took a video and she was in the background, and she said, 'Oh, is that what I look like?' I was like, 'Yes, babe, you're fucking hot!' and she was like, 'Oh! Oh, I like that.' You can't ever capture someone's charm, or the little movements in their face, or their moods.

Are you glad Instagram didn't exist when you were growing up?

Yes, definitely. Instagram would have made my anorexia so much worse. It started when I was 17 but I wasn't diagnosed until I was 18. Eating disorders never really go away, the voice is always there – it's just that your power to shout it down strengthens. You have to accept that when you're overexposed to certain images, you will start to desire them and see them as the ideal, even if you think you're above it. Just last week I was feeling shit and I went down a #weightloss hole. I knew it was bad for me, and eventually, after half an hour, I stopped and ate a cookie. I recovered from anorexia at 22, which was four years ago. Now I'm well into my recovery, I can stop myself when I go down that destructive pathway, but had I had access to those hashtags at the height of my illness, it would have been bad. Had I been born three years later, it would have been much worse for me, not in terms of how far I went, but in how long it took me to get back.

What about the women sharing their recovery photos, do you think that's inspirational?

I think @bodyposipanda is great, and she was anorexic. But more often than not, it's the thin people who've recovered that you see. You never see fat people with eating disorders – they are there but you don't see them.

You said the other day that you were 'off to another influencer event to stare at everyone's lip fillers'. Tell me about that!

Yeah! It's really interesting because you often can't tell if someone's had lip fillers in an Instagram photo because the photo is angled a certain way, but you can tell in real life. It's like when you see contour from the side – and the elements are much more obvious. People get surgery for Instagram and lips are the priority, which I find fascinating. It's so interesting that it's so clearly a fetishisation of what black women have been demonised for for years – now bigger lips are the trend. I follow this Tumblr account called Kardashian Kolloquium that analyses the Kardashians, and I was hungover on a weekend and reading it in bed and someone submitted this theory that Kylie had the baby so that she'd have enough fat to transfer to her hips and her bum. It can't be true . . . but maybe?! I've been comfortably outside heterosexuality and heteronormativity for a while now, so these trends are not seen as desirable by the people I desire and they're not seen as the epitome of beauty in my community. I'm just an observer, and honestly I'm fascinated by them. I don't condemn or judge anyone who has surgery, I think it's cool you can change your body.

Back in 2014, the American Academy of Facial Plastic and Reconstructive Surgery reported that selfies were 'having a huge impact on the facial plastic surgery industry', with one in three surgeons noting 'an increase in requests for procedures due to patients being more self-aware of [their] looks on social media'. Dr Edward Farrior, a plastic surgeon in Florida, commented that 'social platforms like Instagram [and] Snapchat . . . which are solely image based, force patients to hold a microscope up to their own image and look at it with a more self-critical eye than ever before'.

Brazilian butt lifts, described as 'the most dangerous cosmetic procedure to undergo' [*BBC*] with a 1-in-3,000 death rate, have increased by 134 per cent in the last five years. In the 'Butt Lifts for Likes: The Instagram Booty Effect' episode of Vice's *Plastic Planet*, Dr Ashkan Ghavami spoke scathingly about the consumerist effect of Instagram on his profession:

'Once Instagram came it allowed for a propagation of just people at home who don't have a career, aren't models, don't have connections in Hollywood that became Insta-famous because of their bodies. And with that came the Kardashian craze – people would come in with six or seven screenshots of Instagram models . . . talking about what they like from each, as if it's a menu at McDonald's.'

This desire to edit yourself not just with filters or by knowing your angles, but through risky surgical procedures in order to create a better image of yourself – where the photograph of your face is the desired outcome, rather than the face itself – is a new type of body dissatisfaction. I can look in the mirror and feel satisfied with my reflection, and then spiral into a self-hate hole after looking at a selfie a minute later. New research suggests there is actually a reason for this – it's because photos taken at arm's length distort features, making noses look 30 per cent bigger than they actually are [*Guardian*]. Barely anybody realises this, though, and so we have a generation of young people effectively looking in distorted mirrors, being hypercritical of their features and then daydreaming about or actually going through with cosmetic surgeries.

Image-editing apps like Facetune (endorsed by Khloé Kardashian) offer a temporary solution – the chance to change everything about yourself and your selfie that you don't like, as well as all the things you didn't even realise you didn't like until you saw the options available in the edit bar, such as 'eyebrow lift', 'eye tilt' and 'nose tip'. Created in 2013 by a group of Israeli computer-science PhD students, Facetune was named Apple's most popular paid app in 2017, and using it has become standard practice for teens posting selfies.

'Everyone uses photo-editing apps,' Lesley, 18, confirmed to me over text. 'To make their face look bronzed, their thighs look bigger, their nose look smaller and straighter, their lips bigger. If you don't have money, you use apps.' 'Money for what?' I asked. 'For plastic surgery,' she replied. 'If you can't afford surgery, you use apps so you can seem "perfect".'

'Girls judge each other for posting heavily edited selfies,' Lesley continued, 'but I don't understand why, because everyone does it.' Another teenager I spoke to – 15-year-old Joy – says the only person she would send an unfiltered or unedited selfie to is her best friend.

It's easy to sigh and think, 'Kids these days have it so hard, I'm so glad that wasn't available when I was their age,' but the desire to edit yourself extends way beyond the teenage demographic. I read an article about a group of women in their late thirties who circulate group photos from nights out on WhatsApp. Each person edits her own appearance in the image using apps before sending it on to the next person. Only when everybody in the picture has edited themselves to their satisfaction is the photo posted online.

How do you feel about yourself in photos?

I never thought of myself as particularly attractive when I was a teenager — although I've always tried to be, so I've always been quite insecure. As a person and in my work, I'm extremely into details, and online that translated into me taking apart my whole appearance and putting it under scrutiny. I was learning to use Photoshop to edit my work, and I started using it to edit photos of myself for my blog. It was only when I started taking pictures on my iPhone that I started posting unedited ones. Now there's apps like Facetune that girls use, and it's heartbreaking to see how many people feel like they need to edit themselves. Instant gratification, algorithms and insecurities you haven't overcome are a dangerous mix for anybody using the internet.

INDIA ROSE, 26, ARTIST

In his BBC Radio 4 podcast series *Hacking Happiness*, Leo Johnson talks about the social media generation's obsession with content optimisation – where the content is you. 'We are expected to think about ourselves as individuals to be optimised,' he says. 'And there are no limitations to what you could improve.'

I'd never used Facetune before writing this chapter, but once I'd seen what my nose looks like smaller and with a pointier tip, what my eyebrows look like with a slight lift, what my skin looks like when it's totally smooth, and what my lips look like wider and plumper, it was bitterly disappointing to swipe back to the 'before' shot. I much preferred the end result on the screen to the face I went in there with – and that's technology-enforced body dissatisfaction. And then what? Once you post the picture and it gets more likes and compliments in the comments – 'gorgeous', 'so beautiful!' – you've created a digital you that, unless you spend thousands to imitate it, you'll never live up to. I'd be too embarrassed to actually post the Facetuned picture on Instagram because it's so obviously not what I look like, but I did text it to a few of my friends with the tagline 'I think I'm, like, four surgeries away from this . . . ?'

Staring at a prettier version of yourself is addictive. I could barely turn away from the beautiful me on the screen, and I kept going back to the photo in the days that followed. I showed it to my 37-year-old sister, who spoke the truth only a sibling can deliver: 'You probably would look better with bigger lips.' Then we did her photo on the app, and I made her nose smaller and lifted her eyebrows and made her skin smooth, and she loved it too; and we talked about nose jobs and how it's more complicated to reduce the size of Arab noses, like we have, because there isn't much cartilage. I showed her two girls I know on Instagram who've had nose jobs and are very happy with the results. It felt like we were on *Keeping Up with the Kardashians*.

After Kylie Jenner spoke to her sister Khloé about lip fillers on an episode of their reality show, one London clinic reported a 70 per cent rise in inquiries in the 24 hours after it aired, and Google searches for 'lip fillers' hit an all-time high. A few years later, in an episode of *Life of Kylie*, the star revealed in a conversation with two of her other sisters, Kendall and Kim, that the reason she got fillers was because after one of her first kisses, the 'guy was like, "I didn't think you would be a good kisser because you have such small lips." I took that really hard . . . I would over-line my lips with lip liner just to create the illusion of bigger lips. And then finally I was like, "This lip liner isn't doing it." I ended up getting my lips done.'

'The majority of women in the UK today see more images of outstandingly beautiful women in one day than our grandmothers did in their whole lifetimes,' I heard 35-year-old charity worker Chine McDonald say on Radio 4 one morning. 'The result, therefore, is the normalisation of perfection, often an airbrushed version of reality.' Chine was referring specifically to the 2018 season of *Love Island*, currently the UK's most popular reality TV show, which features slim women under the age of 30 looking for love, all with long hair, full lips, big boobs and pert bums.

Ticking every old-fashioned beauty box, the show was immediately called out on Twitter for being unrepresentative and for celebrating outdated beauty ideals, particularly in the female contestants. Yet despite the criticism, its stars were catapulted to fame, some gaining over a million followers on Instagram. 'I believe it [Love Island] shows the disturbing truth about what it is our society holds in the highest esteem: the body beautiful,' Chine said.

A cosmetic clinic reported a 200 per cent increase in lip-filler inquiries after Megan Barton-Hanson entered the *Love Island* villa in 2018. Talking openly about the plastic surgery she'd had before going on the show, Megan (1.8 million followers) concluded, 'I've done what I've done because it made me feel comfortable. It's like people getting their hair done to make them feel nice. I'll go get my lips done because it makes me feel better ... I got a boob job at 19, then I got another one a few years later when I was older and got more money. Then I had my nose done and lips filled, and my teeth. I'm happy now.'

That 'I'm happy now' is a tough pill to swallow, because it contradicts the popular discourse that plastic surgery isn't a quick fix for body-image anxieties. For celebrities – who I think still have some semblance of role-model responsibility, particularly if they're posting selfies the whole time – to promote plastic surgery and fillers as an effective solution is a confusing message for the many girls and women struggling to embrace the parts of themselves they don't like. Especially when the average girl watching *Love Island* doesn't have £25,000 (the amount Megan spent on her surgeries before entering the villa) hiding down the side of the sofa. Non-surgical beauty treatments such as Botox and dermal fillers now account for 9 out of 10 cosmetic procedures, with a net worth of around £2.75 billion. At the height of 2018 *Love Island* fever, it was announced that high-street chain Superdrug (which sponsored *Love Island*) would be offering dermal fillers and Botox in-store. With prices ranging from £100 to £300 for injections, you could pop to the high street for some cotton pads and leave with a new face.

The normalisation and commoditisation of these procedures, which come with some shocking risks, is something that greatly concerns Dr Simi Bakre, a mother-of-two who works as a GP for most of the week and then does one day of cosmetic procedures in a small clinic in Romford, near Essex, which is where she grew up. It's also where Megan Barton-Hanson grew up, and is renowned for the 'Essex girl' look that is heavy on the makeup and heavy on the plastic surgery.

Dr Simi Bakre, 36
GP and cosmetic surgeon

What's the average age of women asking for lip fillers?

At my clinic, it's late twenties/early thirties. Which is probably something to do with my prices. I tend to get a slightly older demographic than what you would expect, given Kylie Jenner's lips . . .

I do like Kylie for the fact that she's honest about it, because celebrities aren't usually open about having work done . . .

That's where social media can be good. People will share their stories, including before and after shots, and day one after the treatment, day two, day three . . . It breaks down that thing of women thinking everybody else is perfect and it's only you that's not; thinking you're the only one with cellulite who wakes up with dark circles under your eyes.

How much do women tell you about their reasons for cosmetic procedures?

They tell me quite a lot, but that's because I delve. I will go into the psychology of it with them. They might start by saying they want their lips done because they think they're too thin or they turn down at the corners, or they just want more definition. I then ask: 'Why are you bothered about your lips? Does it affect your life?' Then I get the real reasons. I don't think I've met anyone yet who hasn't had a psychological reason – which is anything from being bullied to looking in the mirror and not feeling happy. It's never 'I just want to get my lips done' – it's always something more.

How important is balance?

It's all about balance. 2ml of lip filler might be fine in a young person's lips whose face can take it. But in an older lady who has delicate features, it will look out of proportion. You have to respect the proportions of the person's face. A red flag is when someone brings a picture of Kylie [Jenner] and says, 'I want lips like that!' First of all, I need to manage that person's expectations because you can only work with what you have; you can't completely change someone's lips. Secondly, I ask why they want to look so different. Why do they want lips that are out of proportion with their face? There is a ratio for lips. In Caucasians you're looking at 1:1.6, with the top lip thinner than the bottom. In black people it's more like 1:1. Some Caucasian ladies want that 1:1 ratio, like Kylie Jenner! And some women can carry it off, but if I actually think the person will look really odd, I just say, 'I'm sorry but I don't think I can meet your expectations and I can't do it.'

What do you notice about women's confidence after the fillers?

It increases. You can see from the minute they look in the mirror and they're pouting and checking their profile and the front view. They often want to put makeup on straight away – which you can't do. But it can also go the other way. We've all seen the botched stories and the complications, which people don't talk about enough. That obviously has the opposite effect, where you've gone for a procedure that was not necessary from a medical point of view, and it results in a complication and a loss of confidence.

What goes wrong, when it goes wrong?

Lots of things can go wrong. If you're injecting, i.e. making a hole, there's always a risk of infection. These are medical procedures, and people forget that. Even though we are using them for beauty reasons, they are medical procedures; they are not beauty treatments. The most serious complication with fillers is if you inject a filler into a blood vessel, and as it travels in that blood vessel, the blood vessel gets thinner and it can get blocked – meaning whatever part of the skin is supplied by that blood vessel starts to die off because it stops receiving oxygen and blood. That can cause all sorts of serious problems, including blindness.

Are people disappointed when their lips go down?

People do get used to the new lips, and when they start to wear down, they come back to get topped up, but sometimes their perception is that it's a lot worse than it is. I'll look and see that, actually, there's still quite a lot of filler there. I can't see much difference, but for that woman, who is looking at herself all the time in the mirror, it is noticeable. In those instances, I say, 'I think we should wait.' You can have a bit of a . . . not disagreement, but a tense conversation. These procedures can be addictive. If you want to maintain that look, you have to keep topping up filler.

Do women tell you they're worried others will notice?

Yes, there's definitely still a stigma attached to injected treatments. But where I'm based, the trend is actually to look like you've had work done – they want people to notice.

What's the legal age for all these treatments?

The legal age is the age of consent. Personally, I don't treat anyone under the age of 21. This industry is pretty much unregulated. Anyone can inject, and I mean anyone. There is no legal repercussion if you're not a doctor or dentist or nurse. If you are a medical professional, then there are repercussions, because there's the General Medical Council [a public body which regulates medical professions]. It's not illegal for, say, a butcher to go and do a one-day course and start injecting. It would be nice if the government could do a bit more to tighten up on this.

What do you think about Superdrug offering lip fillers?

Superdrug say that they have trained nurses doing their procedures, which is good. But the problem there is with trivialising these treatments. It shouldn't be a case of popping into Superdrug and buying a lipstick and then going, 'Oh, actually, maybe I'll get my lips done while I'm here.' That's the concern of putting Botox and fillers on the high street in that way. I shouldn't really say 'Botox' – it's botulinum toxin. Botox is just a brand name. It's like how everyone says 'Hoover', which is a brand of vacuum cleaner.

How do you identify body dysmorphia?

A person may come in, having had lots of procedures before, saying they've never been happy with the procedures. 'I had my cheeks done and I wasn't happy' or 'My lips aren't big enough'. Or people who are coming back two weeks after the procedure saying they want more. There's often a history of bullying, or abuse. I always ask if people are under the care of a psychiatrist, and if [the answer is] yes, I delve into that and see if it's related to body dysmorphia. Sometimes you can see very clearly that the person has had so many cosmetic surgeries that they actually now look like a completely different person, so you have to consider why they wanted to look so different. If I think I'm only going to make this person worse, then I just say no.

Do you get many men?

Some, but not nearly as many as women. Men tend to go for jawline fillers, cheek fillers, lip fillers and non-surgical nose jobs.

Say you have two women who look the same, but one is happy with their appearance and one isn't. In your opinion, what's the difference between those women?

It's complex. I think it's personality – how easily influenced that person is by trends and by what other people think of them. Who are their friends and what do their friends look like? Ageing is of course also dependent on genetics. And on lifestyle – smoking ages people more quickly, as does suntanning without sun protection, or using sunbeds. It's also affordability: if you can afford it, you are more likely to say, 'Well, why not?' Of course, many people just feel they should grow old gracefully and would never consider Botox or fillers or anything else, no matter what they look like.

How much are selfies and social media responsible?

For the younger generation, it is a lot about selfies and social media. Wanting to have that perfect picture, to keep up with others who are posting perfect pictures. It's projecting to your peers or to the world: 'Look at me, I haven't put any filters on this, look at my lips, look at my cheeks, look at my jawline #nofilter'. The older generation are on

Instagram as well, but they seem to be less influenced by it.

Does the perfect face exist?

I don't think perfect exists. I think back to when I was younger and the women I thought were so beautiful and so attractive at the time, and I actually have a different view of beauty now. My view of beauty has changed as I've got older. Beauty is cultural. In some cultures having a long slim face is attractive, and in others having a plump face with plump cheeks shows you are well looked after, and that's attractive. As you get older, you may begin to like parts of yourself that you didn't like when you were younger. It also depends on your mood! Some people are very happy with themselves, and very happy with their 'flaws' – the same things others may have a desire to change.

Facetune came up in a conversation with my hairdresser – who is also a drag queen. Some people in the drag community use Facetune, he told me, to achieve the surgery 'look' in photos without the permanence or the expense. They might use it to blend obvious hairlines if they don't have spare money to drop on an expensive wig, or to enhance what they're already doing with contouring. He also told me to look up Alexis Stone, the British drag queen, makeup artist and illusionist who is Insta-famous for using makeup to transform himself into various celebrities. Alexis has imitated over 150 celebrities on his Instagram (which has 850,000 followers) from Kim Kardashian to Adele.

In 2018, Alexis posted vlogs on YouTube about having had a nose job, fillers and Botox. Many of his 'fans' were highly critical of these procedures, calling him a 'botch monster'. Several months later, he posted a video on his channel announcing that he would be undergoing much more drastic surgery, with custom-made cheek implants (custom because he wanted them to be much bigger than what was currently available), a custom-made chin implant, and fat injected into his forehead to make it rounder and more pronounced. The surgery was so extreme, he said, that it had taken a long time to find a surgeon willing to perform it. 'I want to gravitate more towards people I idolise, like Jocelyn Wildenstein,' Alexis informed his followers. Infamous for her botched plastic surgeries, Wildenstein is the antithesis of what you'd hope for when going under the knife, so Alexis citing her as his inspiration really disturbed his fans, since nobody in their right mind would want to look like Jocelyn Wildenstein.

Shortly after the surgery, Alexis posted a 'post-op' shot in which he looked like a character from a horror film. The comments came in thick and fast: 'My lord, what did you do to yourself?', 'Your face is fucked', 'You've mutilated yourself beyond any repair', 'You turned into a monster', 'This is what happens when mental illness has a big budget'. Alexis later told *Paper* magazine that the criticism got even darker: 'I've had people telling me to kill myself... My ex-boyfriends are texting me saying how embarrassed they are that they've dated me.'

In the weeks that followed the dramatic surgeries, Alexis posted a string of videos on Instagram and YouTube showing off his new face, which despite 60,000 people unfollowing him and a barrage of abuse in the comments under his posts, he claimed to be happy with. Then, on New Year's Eve, he posted another video set to a haunting soundtrack, like the end of *Saw* or *Se7en* or some other psychological thriller when you finally realise the twist and gasp in horror. Wearing a shiny black wig and a severe black outfit, Alexis proceeded to pull off his new plastic-surgeried face – which was actually a prosthetic mask. There had been no dramatic surgery. Following the horrific abuse he'd received after his (actual) nose job and fillers, Alexis had decided to give his fans something to really shout about.

'Five people knew that this project was fake,' he told *Paper*. 'All it took was a little bit of silicone stuck to my face and a storyline to sell the narrative... Instagram isn't going to be here forever. I won't be here forever. If this is the only thing I'm remembered for on planet Earth, I'm okay with that.' He later wrote on Instagram, 'I hope I've turned the mirror around.'

Part of his argument was that Kim Kardashian has had a lot of surgery too, but she's still celebrated as a beauty queen because her surgeries are in line with the accepted beauty standards (smaller nose, bigger lips, Hollywood teeth, bigger boobs, rounder bum, etc.). Alexis's experiment exposed how obsessed the Instagram generation is with self-improvement and maximising beauty. The idea that he would deliberately make himself uglier was what his fans were objecting to.

In another extreme corner of the internet hovers Lil Miquela, a computer-generated (CGI) influencer designed to be the ultimate Instagram beauty fantasy. Miquela was created in 2016 by a mysterious tech startup called Brud, which specialises in artificial intelligence. Brud kept their identity secret for a long time while they wove a complicated narrative around how their three CGI influencers (Lil

Miquela, Bermuda and Blawko) were invented. Brud originally claimed that Miquela and Blawko were their creations but that Bermuda was invented by another company called Cain Intelligence. It was later revealed that Brud had made up Cain Intelligence in order to set up a fictionalised rivalry between Miquela and Bermuda as they pretended to hack each other's accounts on Instagram – activity that actually got reported on by bemused tech-news outlets. Eventually, the founders revealed themselves to be Trevor McFedries (whose job title at Brud is 'Head of Compassion') and Sara Decou (whose job title is 'Chief of Stuff'), and the pair received high praise for their ingenuity. By far the most popular of their CGI influencer kids, Miquela has 1.6 million followers and was included on *Time* magazine's 'Most Influential People on the Internet' list in 2018. Her image is printed in real publications about real people, like *Vogue* and the *Evening Standard*, accompanied by interviews with her creators, who answer as though they are her – a robot who has made it big on Instagram. Miquela is represented by a real PR company, who also look after very famous real people like Frank Ocean, Björk and Grimes.

Despite her obvious unreality (which isn't always obvious to her young fans, who sometimes comment things like 'I don't get it . . . are you a robot?'), Miquela fits right in on Instagram. She wears cool clothes (CGI versions of actual designer brands like Chanel, Prada and Supreme), posts pictures of turmeric lattes and salad bowls, posts about causes that matter to 'her' such as Black Lives Matter, and even gives money to charity . . . or so she says in her captions. Dr Ashkan Ghavami, the plastic surgeon quoted earlier, expressed his disbelief at girls coming in with screenshots of Instagram models as though they were picking their features from a menu at McDonald's. Well, Miquela is the full meal. She's tall, slim, mixed-race, but with straight hair that she wears in two space buns. Her nose is small and cute as a button, her eyebrows are millennial-strong, her lips are full, her bum is pert, and she has a splattering of freckles that her young fans just adore.

I contacted a few of them who'd left comments like 'you're so beautiful!', 'you're just so perfect', 'you're so gorgeous i love you so much you're amazing' under her pictures, and asked why they followed Miquela and whether they cared that she wasn't a real person. 'No, I don't mind, in fact, I find it life-changing,' said @haileyygoesnowhere, 17. When I asked why she thinks Miquela is beautiful, Hailey said, '[because] she's very confident in who she is and what she does, and I believe that makes every woman beautiful. I'm also obsessed with freckles.' When I asked if Hailey wished she looked like Miquela, she answered, 'Yes, again I love freckles!' Reading these replies on my phone, I was shocked by Hailey's genuine adoration of Miquela as a role model. She's a drawing on the internet! Malala, Michelle Obama, Oprah . . . Miquela?! I don't get it.

Another of her followers, 21-year-old college student @missyrowen, told me she started following Miquela after seeing an ad in a magazine that featured her as a 'face of the future'. Missy had a much less cynical reaction to Miquela's looks than I did. To me, Miquela's features are cookie-cutter, an imitation and parody of the bodies and faces most blatantly celebrated online. But to Missy she is a rare beauty – 'I love Miquela's unique features,' she told me over DM. 'Her freckled complexion and her small bust makes her look less like the "store -bought pretty" social media pushes. I feel like I have similar features, so it's nice to see her getting so much attention.'

Is it nice?! If anything, Miquela is the definition of store-bought pretty. She's a projection of the image-obsessed generation's fantasies. 'Sometimes I find myself looking at Miquela on Instagram and wishing I looked like her . . . her stomach is so flat,' my 33-year-old friend said on the phone one day. 'That's mad isn't it . . . but . . . she's in *Vogue!*'

Having heard how women of all ages fawn over Miquela, I felt outvoted. Maybe idolising a CGI robot influencer isn't that mad. In a world where the largest technology companies are equipping us with the tools to digitally alter every part of ourselves, from Snapchat filters to Facetune, maybe we don't need people or beauty to be real; maybe we actually prefer it to be unreal. I want to look like my Facetuned picture and Snapchat filters; they want to look like a robot. We're all striving for digital perfection.

I recently interviewed one of Brud's other CGI influencers, Bermuda, for an article, because I was told Miquela was 'too busy' (even though they're created by the same people, so I essentially did interview Miquela). Bermuda is a simulation of another ideal of beauty: the thin white blonde woman. She has significantly fewer followers than Miquela – at 'just' 136,000 – because when Brud began her account, they made her a right-wing Trump supporter, presumably as a social experiment in digital identity, ideology and popularity. She has since reneged on her right-wing views. (It wasn't an effective brand strategy.)

I asked Bermuda, whose early posts were captioned with #literallyperfect, what it takes to be literally perfect? She (or rather, her creators) replied, 'I'm just built that way, I suppose.' When I asked if she would ever consider plastic surgery, she replied: 'Sure, why not? I'm all for modifying external hardware. I think sometimes I'd like to be a little shorter. Finding cute jeans for my height can be rough. So maybe a light femur-shortening procedure? Like her politics, Bermuda can update and refresh her look as many times as her coders like. Right-wing thing not working? Change the caption. Face not high-res enough? Update it. She adapts to survive. For my final question of whether social media is good or bad for our self-image, her creators answer more seriously: *I think social media magnifies issues that have always existed. Insecurity, comparing ourselves to others . . . that tendency has been around as long as there's been any kind of popular media amplifying an image that can be replicated. A lot of detractors accuse me of not being 'real', and to them I'd ask: well, who is? I study image for a living; I know what Photoshop and Facetune look like. So, social media is both good and bad. It has led to better and more diverse representation and expression, but also presents the carefully curated as effortless, the fabricated as genuine.*

Dr Helen Sharpe, the psychologist quoted at the beginning of this chapter who specialises in adolescent body image, agrees with Bermuda that it's not all social media's fault – because body-image anxieties existed long before the internet – but what it has done is value physical appearance above everything else.

Dr Helen Sharpe
Psychologist

How do you identify body dissatisfaction in teenage girls?

Body dissatisfaction is very common in adolescents. The majority of girls report being dissatisfied with their appearance. And not all of that is for the same reason. It comes in lots of different forms. Some young people are feeling sad and blue generally, and that gets applied to their bodies too. In other young people, it presents more like anxiety, and it gets in the way of them doing things. For example, they stop wanting to take part in sports because they don't want the experience of having to show their bodies in front of others getting changed. We also see lots of young people having anxiety about everyday activities like going out and seeing friends, or chatting with friends on video calls. The expectations around how they look and their feelings about not meeting those expectations really get in the way of them wanting to do those things. That's when alarm bells start ringing and we need to intervene. These aren't just passing fads that teens go through; they are genuinely getting in the way of young women's aspirations.

Do you think too much blame is placed on social media?

I do think too much blame has been placed on social media – it's often the thing people jump to as if, if we didn't have social media, we wouldn't have any of these difficulties, and that's certainly not the case. A lot of the challenges people experience are reflected on social media. On the other hand, it's important to acknowledge that social media does radically change how we interact with each other, and we all need to learn the skills to manage it well, just like we've had to learn the skills to manage other types of social interaction. The level of self-presentation that you can achieve on a social media platform far outstrips what you can do in any other setting. You have so much control over how you are presented. What we know is that the young people who are most vulnerable, who are experiencing body dissatisfaction already, who are inclined towards lots of social comparison – looking at others and comparing how you look – those are the girls who really struggle on social media. But there are lots of benefits which are often completely overlooked, such as groups who have historically been marginalised, or individuals who struggle to find others like them in their immediate vicinity and can find this online, and they thrive. It's important to recognise that it's part of our lives, it's a challenge that young people have to navigate that the adults in their lives didn't have to.

How do you tackle social comparison with this age group? What actually helps?

Really raising it and discussing it. When young people talk to each other about this, they can be very powerful advocates for each other. One of the things we focus on is this phenomenon of 'fat talk' – negative comments about yourself and others. It's almost ritualised. There's this back and forth of putting yourself down, and the other person putting themselves down. And it's tricky to break out of that cycle. We work with young people to get them to role-play different ways they could deal with it, and they often come up with really fabulous responses. This gives them good tools to be able to say to their friends, 'You know when you talk like that, it doesn't make any of us feel good about ourselves,' but it's a tricky thing to navigate.

What is self-objectification, and how does it play out on social media?

Self-objectification comes from objectification, which is when your value and worth as an individual is based purely on your body. This is particularly applied to women's bodies: the idea that you are valued because you look good on some man's arm. Because you are aware that your value is based on your physical body, you are subject to surveillance from other people, so basically, they are looking at you to work out what your value is – and over time, you come to internalise that experience, so you are self-surveilling, watching yourself constantly to make sure that you are as 'valuable' as you can be. Making sure you look your best, present in the way you want to present; then, over time, the pressures that were external become internal. That fits super nicely with social media and the idea that you can portray a version of yourself, and that that version is very highly tied in with your physical state. Photo-based media accentuates this idea that your physical state is the most valuable thing about you.

Social media has opened up the beauty industry, and far more types of bodies are represented and celebrated now than in media historically. But have we really moved on, or is there still a body ideal?

I don't know the stats around Instagram influencers and their characteristics, but from my layperson sense, yes, there are pockets of resistance, as it were, where social media is doing a really amazing job of giving a voice to less powerful groups, but my sense is that that is not the most dominant force. It's one of the challenges of social media that it seems to be the ultimate democracy, everybody gets a chance to speak, but in a way that's an illusion because it's still extremely weighted in some people's favour.

Of the girls that do have positive body image, are there any trends?

Lots of people do have positive body image. It isn't just the absence of body dissatisfaction, it's not just 'okay, I don't hate my body' – it's more than that. It's body appreciation, appreciating your body for what it does for you. Having a caring attitude towards the body, viewing it as something that you need to support and nurture.

It is possible to go on social media with a positive body image and come out with that still intact. It is also possible to go on social media with a negative body image and come out feeling revitalised, having found inspiring, diverse influencers and communities. But the problem of comparing yourself to others remains, and isn't going anywhere. Neither is the female tendency to break down your body into parts that you like and dislike. And for these reasons, I don't think it's possible to go on social media and avoid self-objectification and social comparison altogether, which for the already vulnerable can be especially damaging. The scale of comparison and the intensity of self-scrutiny is unlike anything that has ever come before. People say the problems on social media are just a reflection of the problems in society, but I think it goes deeper than that. I think social media and the image-modifying technology that surrounds it inspires new insecurities based on unreal standards that trap people in a one-way lane of traffic which begins at selfie and ends at self-criticism.

'It makes me a little sick,' concluded my hairdresser as he was completing my cut, 'because the potential for abuse and self-comparison is exponential, and there are far more people using social media for that than, like, grandmas who just want to keep in touch with their grandkids, or people with private profiles who just want to keep in touch with a specific set of friends. The crux of it all is that you're being sold something, whether that's a body type or a beauty ideal, diet pills or a shade of foundation – it's that your own skin isn't good enough.'

I tried really hard to overcome digital-image insecurity, but it required a higher level of confidence than I happen to have as a 32-year -old woman, no matter how much time I spend looking at inspiring quotes about self-acceptance. I feel miles better about myself than I did when I first went to see Valerie, but it's not because I learned to love myself or embrace the things I didn't like about my reflection, far from it; it's simply because I stopped looking in the reverse camera on my phone. As pathetic as it sounds, it took quite a while to rewire the selfie instinct which has been ingrained in my digital consciousness for years. I didn't even take that many, I was way behind on the millennial lifetime average of 25,000, probably because I never liked the results, but still, I'd turn to selfies in moments of procrastination. Making myself feel bad? It was a strange use of precious procrastination time, which should at least be more enjoyable than the task you're distracting yourself from. Now I spend those moments looking at the 'dogs with jobs' reddit forum or daydreaming about a home with a bookshelf that spans an entire wall on Pinterest. And as Megan Barton Hanson said: I'm happy now!

The following conversation is between: myself; Naomi; Caryn Franklin, 60, fashion commentator, BBC journalist, Professor of Diversity at Kingston University; Jeanie Annan-Lewin, 35, fashion stylist; Ghadir Mustafa, 18, student thinking about her career options.

Sarah: How do you use Instagram?

Ghadir: I use Twitter a lot more than I use Instagram because I like to rant. Mainly about music stuff, or things that are happening in the world right now. Instagram I use just to post my face and outfits and random stuff. Most of my friends are quite big on Instagram, they've got loads of followers. I guess people my age are quite caught up in looking like they're cool and looking like they're perfect and like they have this really sick life.

Sarah: Do you compare yourself online?

Ghadir: I've only started comparing myself to others recently. Growing up, I was quite boyish and I coped with not being the 'pretty girl' by taking the mick out of myself before other people could. I was just really content with walking around calling myself ugly and boyish. In school I was always really confident because I forced myself to be – because I was really insecure, and it was just an act that I had, and it actually kind of worked and I really stopped caring about what I looked like. But all my friends are really fit, they're all really attractive girls, and whenever I go out with them I feel out of place, like I'm the odd one out. Boys love me as a friend, they think I'm so funny; they don't say I'm so hot. And that gets me a bit. It's new for me, being insecure because of Instagram. I never used to feel like this.

Caryn: As human beings we have a tendency to engage in social comparison and look upwards for aspiration, but modern media means that we're often at the bottom of the pile because we're always looking at somebody who looks better than us, who's got a better job than us, who seems happier than us. So social media messes with our brains. In tribal situations, if you go back to us as cave-beings, we knew where we fitted in the tribe. We've been cave-beings for millions of years, we've been social media users for a nanosecond. Social comparison theory is real, it's been in psychology since the '50s. You have to engage downwards for good mental health. You cannot occupy a position where you're looking up at other people all the time, you have to look down. I don't think you have to go on social networks to do this, but you have to look at your privileges and contextualise your life from the position of privilege: I've got my health, people love me, I'm paying my bills, I'm doing something that has meaning and purpose to me. That's what kicks in for me every time I'm triggered to feel insecure. I've practised this over the years, and now it just kicks in. Sometimes when I explain to my students how it works, I say it's not what happens to you, it's what you think about what happens to you, and that affects your emotions and the consequences, and it affects you physically.

Here's an example: you're chopping with a sharp knife and you really injure your finger. You have to go to A&E, you clearly need stitches and it's really hurting and you're feeling sorry for yourself and you've got to go to work tomorrow and you want to be seen quickly but nobody seems to care. And then somebody comes into A&E and they've had a really serious accident in a car and their entire arm is mangled. And straight away you're engaging in downward social comparison, you're going 'oh, my cut isn't so bad, it's hurting, but it can't be hurting as much as them, yeah, the doctors haven't come to see me but they've got to go and see them because they're much worse than me.' So the brain starts reappraising the thing because of what you've chosen to think about it, and that's how downward social comparison works.

I've had to chat to my daughters about social media comparison, and I say to them, 'If you unfollowed every person that triggered insecurity, what would you be left with? If you were actually prioritising good mental health and you began to follow people who bolstered your self-esteem, how would who you follow grow, and in what way?' Because we are responsible for our own good mental health and positivity, and we don't choose to have low self-esteem, but we can't avoid it if we're following people who are posting stuff that is triggering that [low self-esteem], and I worry that this generation have gotten used to living with a low-level noise, and for some women it's more acute, the 'I'm not good enough' noise. I never felt that when I was growing up.

Ghadir: A lot of my younger cousins and my younger friends, they kind of aim towards being big on Instagram, that's their ambition. It's just like, 'Okay, I'm going to blow on Instagram and that's going to be my thing,' and people put everything into that. A friend of a friend is really big on Instagram and I was thinking, 'Oh, she's so cool, she dresses so sick, that outfit was really extravagant,' but my friend said that that girl doesn't actually leave her house in those clothes, she just creates the picture, takes it on her laptop in her room, then takes the outfit off and uploads it.

Naomi: I keep hearing about girls with proper lighting systems in their rooms.

Caryn: This is low-grade mental illness.

Ghadir: It's so weird because it's like ... your whole life online is fake.

Sarah: Caryn, you don't tend to post personal stuff online. Was that a conscious choice, or is it just not your generation to do that?

Caryn: If you Google me, there is a fairly obvious piece that comes up about why I am devoted to diversity. Because I've seen what happens when we lose health, because my daughter's father lost his health and I lived with him trying to support him, so when I see young women focusing on such a narrow part of their beauty and not recognising that if you've got a working body, that's freedom, and then being able to celebrate yourself as an individual. I love getting older. I don't worry about wrinkles, I don't judge my body, I don't feel that I have to engage in social comparison with 'I look like this, they look like that' because I had this massive piece of education when I was a young woman.

Naomi: There is no sense of happiness without gratitude. It's so simple. I write a lot of lists all the time with things that I'm trying to work towards. I always start with writing down what I'm grateful for because it changes your perspective of what you want. Because we're operating under this system of capitalism and every message that is sold to us is that we don't have enough, we don't look good enough, we need all these things, when the truth is we're so privileged. My father passed away when I was young and I always go back to the health thing. I have a functioning body. The body is an incredible machine that does so many things for us, so just remembering that is important. The first thing I write down is thank you for my health, for the love I have in my life, for my family. I start there. Especially with social media, it's a constant trigger for the things that we don't have, when we have so much.

Sarah: But in that sense, social media is a terrible thing because it's the opposite of humility. And all you see is an image, you don't know anyone's story, or the things in their lives that are hard, so you just end up comparing your entire life to someone's smile on a beach.

Jeanie: I spent so much of my youth wanting to be somebody else. In every scenario that played in my head, I looked different. Then one day I woke up and I was tired, and I decided to like who I am and I've never looked back – I'm unshakeable in that. I also go out a lot and I'm a trained extrovert. I spend a lot of time talking to people, and I realise that nobody is really happy. Show me someone who's really happy in this image that they're trying to project and I'll show you a liar. Everybody is struggling in some way, shape or form and just trying to navigate their way through life, and I constantly remember that. So I'm unfazed by those things. I have to be – I've been working as a stylist for 10 years in an industry that tells me that my body is not desirable, and I've been made to feel like that since the moment I entered fashion, and it will probably be the same until I leave it. So I just don't take those things on, because I don't have the mental capacity to. When I was younger it was a massive preoccupation. My mother is very beautiful, she prides herself on that, and I guess that had a negative effect on me, I rebelled against it so much. But I'm so comfortable in my skin and have been for such a long time that I just don't fall victim to seeing a picture and then thinking, 'That person is having a marvellous time,' because they're blatantly not.

Sarah: What age were you when you decided to start liking yourself?

Jeanie: I was painfully shy at school, I hated being in social situations, and then one day I realised that in order for me to get the things I wanted – like an interesting life and a good job – I couldn't hide away. I had to figure out a way to enter situations and put on . . . not a false version of myself, but a version of myself that I feel comfortable projecting towards people. I've been doing that so long that it's quite easy for me to do it now. I went to an all-girls school and everyone I was surrounded by was tall and beautiful and white, and I was sort of just bumbling along with blue hair. There were like, six black people in my school – they let black girls in for free so I got a private school education for nothing because they lacked diversity. I just realised that either I could spend all my time sitting around praying for a boyfriend and hoping I woke up looking like Naomi Campbell, or I could just get on with life.

What do you see online that makes you feel good?

I know it's a cliché, but honestly, I feel better when I'm looking at other girls who look like me because I see their beauty. It's not always easy to see it in yourself. So when I'm looking at women who are my size and who are actually so beautiful, it helps me to remember that I am, too. It reminds me . . . You still look great! Calm down — you're just having a bad day.

GABI GREGG, 32, FASHION DESIGNER AND BODY POSITIVE INFLUENCER

YUMNA AL-ARASHI ON EMPOWERMENT & FETISHISATION IN SELF-PORTRAITURE

We find liberation in our ability to share images of ourselves with the click of a button. We have the power to choose exactly how we'd like the world to see us and when. At times, I've felt wildly empowered by the number of women who use this opportunity to present bodies, skin tones and features that the mainstream media has so long left unrepresented. I've found beauty in our ability to empower one another by normalising what we have so often felt ashamed of.

But I'm wondering where the consequences of this image-heavy world lie. There's a darkness in a need for validation that is based solely on appearance. Social media is a crawl of user-generated content, but the power spinning the wheels of what we see is a corporate world of targeted marketing. The equation of images with likes, and likes with confidence – or even happiness – scares me. We call this empowerment, we call it confidence and beauty – we even call it feminism.

I've been creating images for over 15 years. I started my work with the intention of becoming a photojournalist, working primarily in the Middle East and North Africa and focusing on women's stories. As an American, I quickly became disheartened by the subjects I was asked to report on; I never felt I had the right to tell other people's stories. I questioned the ethics of 'taking' a picture of someone else and sending it off to a media outlet in America. Journalism, once a heroic (self-fulfilling) dream, quickly became my worst nightmare. I've since found myself working in the fashion, film, advertising and fine art worlds. My hope was that I'd still find the time to create meaningful work, and even find ways to weave it into the work which pays the bills. I still primarily approach subject matter that encapsulates themes of femininity and womanhood, subtly touching upon many of the questions I initially wanted to approach in journalism, without exploiting subjects to get there.

As I get comfortable in the field of work I've chosen, something deep inside of me screams that the image of the woman is still not our own. I fear that our false sense of empowerment is a temporary high from an ego-rewarding consumerist society. I fear that the benefactors from the image of the woman still lie in a heavily patriarchal system where our bodies are owned in order to be exploited. I can't confidently say that creating gender balance in the corporate world makes things better if the original framework for capitalism remains the same.

On the surface, our empowerment in the types of bodies we can showcase and honour feels like a beautiful step towards women feeling confident about the skin they are in. Women can find role models and communities where they feel truly represented. This is something to stand up for – a truly remarkable feat – but for who? The underbelly of this accomplishment is a true reflection of the consumerist society we live in. We feel the need for all media and advertising to represent us because we want to participate as consumers, and thus we've allowed a world to exist where corporations rule the images we see before us every day. Is this truly empowerment?

This stirs up memories of my time working in migrant labour camps in Abu Dhabi. These camps were home to men from countries such as Bangladesh, Pakistan, Nepal and India. Hundreds of thousands of men are shipped to the Arabian Gulf to build the glistening, oil-rich oases in the desert. They work gruelling hours in the desert sun, often without a break to even drink water. Their passports are taken upon arrival in the country and they are paid a fraction of what they were promised. Through all of this struggle, their 'joy' lay in their ability to take photographs of themselves and one another on their mobile phones, masking the dark reality of their true lives for a Facebook post. They'd spend Fridays – often their only day off – on their phones, posing in their surroundings, sharing photos online to show family and friends their 'glamorous' life in the Arabian Gulf. I see a similarity in the exploitation of women around the world – our egos are pleased for a short period of time, and in return we succumb to the dangerous reality that is an economy that profits off our pain.

Although these dark realities are all around me, I've still found myself participating. I've made self-portraiture for as long as I can remember. At first, my intention with my imagery was simply to see myself. I was curious about who I was because I never saw anyone like me in any imagery out in the world. But this fact of life never saddened me; rather, it piqued my curiosity. Am I beautiful? What does my nose look like in profile? Can I also be sexy or is that only for skinny blonde women? The self-portrait became a way of understanding myself through the image of myself.

This portraiture evolved to become a means for me to express myself, and to take ownership of myself when so often I felt I had no space to be me on my own terms. I can relate to young women when they find empowerment in an image of themselves. I get it, I really do. There's something wildly liberating about being able to use your body to express yourself in whatever way you so please.

My self-portraiture gained attention almost immediately. My images have been seen in the pages of some of the largest names in media, even though there's nothing really marketable about my work. I'm often not wearing any clothing, and I'm definitely not interested in selling anything through work that is so personal to me. Instead, what so often accompanies features about my self-portraiture is my religion. I've become a clickbait dream. In our heavily racially motivated times, I attract an audience because I am a nude Muslim woman. No matter my tendency towards atheism, I am a Muslim because our society needs to categorise women in order to digest them. The plus-size one, the hairy one, the Muslim one . . . But how can the labels we give one another push us forward if we so desperately need to attach them to every female body we see? Rather than us actually trying to embrace our differences, we're merely exploiting them to attract clicks for a capitalistic gain — and this just divides us further

This struggle has run deep in the work I do on a daily basis, because my goal to avoid becoming a marketing tool has instead become political entertainment. My body is tossed up in the battle to claim a destructive fetish for 'liberating' the Muslim woman, when the original intent of my portraits was never about my religious background. The images I make of myself have turned out to be a reflection of the viewer instead.

Self-portraiture is so natural to me, and yet I feel tainted sharing it. My work serves as protest and empowerment, and yet I feel it is stripped of all value once it is in the hands of powers that use my imagery for something far darker. At times, the objective of my work completely disappears when I share it, leaving instead the sad skeleton of a love killed by the outside world.

Over the past few months, I've taken time to dive deep into what it is that I love about my work as an image-maker. Is it the self-expression, or is it the short-lived praise I receive when sharing it with the outside world? I struggle with admitting that sometimes it is the latter. The truth is, we all want to be loved.

We use imagery to connect to one another, to stir up feelings of compassion and empathy, to take us into the minds of someone else, somewhere else. Not sharing the work I create feels like a violent injustice.

I hope we as a society can put the brakes on a little, and take the time to look at how much our egos are leading us into the world we live in today. I hope we can find love for ourselves, going beyond images of ourselves. I hope we remember to love one another past a 'like'. I hope we can find freedom from a world that profits off making us feel that we're not good enough.

Yumna Al-Arashi is a photographer, filmmaker, writer and human being based in London. Please don't attempt to speak to her before she's had a coffee in the morning.

How does social media make you feel about your body?

My relationship to my body has evolved because of social media. Although Instagram continues to censor nudity, sexuality and, simply, fatness, I've been able to share images that reflect my own experiences of desirability, beauty and confidence. I used to post pictures on social media that made me seem fuckable before I actually felt fuckable. That was helpful in terms of receiving the external validation and objectification I felt was long denied to me as a fat woman. Now, I value freedom more than fuckability. I no longer refrain from posting images that evidence my cellulite or double chin not only because of how affirmed I know other femmes feel by these honest portrayals, but also because of how bored I am with the sameness of what people post. The angles, the lighting, the filters, the Facetune. I don't want to look better on Instagram than I do in real life, because in real life, rich with the context of my own individuality and the irreverence of my full range of expression outside the flattened plane of one's timeline, I am even better to look at, funnier to listen to and more eager to connect rather than to just present.

TIERNEY FINSTER, 27, JOURNALIST, SCREENWRITER, ACTOR, MODEL, CASTING DIRECTOR

SOCIAL MEDIA +

WORK

♡ ◯ ◁

NAOMI

Is it weird that, even after over 15 years of standing in front of a camera, I still shrivel up and die a little every time someone asks me what I do? 'Oh, I'm a model' has just never felt right coming out of my mouth. I think it's because it always triggers such a big reaction from people. Either the 'ooooooh, the glamour' look, where their eyes light up and their lips purse to emphasise the 'ooooooh', or the 'ohhhhhh, you must be a dumb bitch' look that's usually served up with a head tilt, a smize and a patronising look in their eye. And because the word 'model' is usually associated with good looks, and because of the value we place on female beauty in our society, models are thought to be 'special'.

A more recent equivalent of the question is when a new person asks if I have an Instagram account. After I (usually) succumb and give them my handle, the space between us changes as a result of them seeing how many followers I have and I always find myself yearning for the moment before that happened, when the anonymity felt cosy – sacred, even. When I was just a normal girl with leftover food on her face, because at my core that's who I am. In my head I don't think of myself as 'Naomi, the model' or 'Naomi, the influencer'. In my head I'm 'Naomi, the hot mess, life lover, doting sister, devoted friend, dutiful daughter, bunny lover, amateur cook/florist/dancer, etc.' But that's not how we think about who we are in today's world .

Sometimes I would lie and say 'no'; or if they were just asking about what I 'did', there's been a tiny amount of times where I'd come up with a fake job. But I'm a terrible liar and I'd start to sweat within seconds, scared to get caught out and fearful of not having the right answer for their follow-up question about my pseudo-career. It's not that I'm ashamed about what I do – in fact, I'm really proud of everything I've accomplished and I truly believe that being a great model is not only hard work but requires lots of skills that aren't always easy to come by – but for as long as I can remember, I've always felt like any job title is slightly short-changing our existence. That it makes us a bit 2D, when the human experience is anything but.

I think that's why I try as much as I can to avoid asking people what they do for as long as possible when I first meet them. I try to ask them about everything and anything else instead. More and more, our work-obsessed society wants us to determine who we are by how we pay our bills – and now it isn't just the people around us that are doing this, it's the algorithms that drive social media too.

Wherever we go now, we hear people talking about 'millennial burnout'. It's never been cooler to work yourself into the ground.

Every cute, old local establishment that made up the fabric of my neighbourhood now seems like it's being replaced by another fancy co-working space that people practically seem to almost live in. There seems to be less and less opportunity for us to push the 'Off' button in our lives, and we've all internalised that we should be working **all the time**. I don't even have a normal, 9-to-5 (or rather to 6, 7, 8, 9 . . .) office job, but if I'm not at the little work desk I've set up by 9 a.m. (if I'm not on a shoot) having meditated, exercised, showered and eaten, I can sometimes feel like a total failure. Why is that? Why are we so hard on ourselves when it comes to our work? Why do we have to become our work and vice versa?

I've recently started to feel that I dislike social media more than I love it, and what it has done to the way we work – what it has done to my work – can sometimes feel like a huge part of that. I often feel like my phone is some kind of monster, pulsating in my hand, begging me to give it more of myself. More time and, worst of all, more energy. The tricky thing now is that what I do on social media pays for the roof over my head, the clothes on my back and the food in my belly. All the things that have drastically changed in fashion and modelling over the last few years are largely down to social media. Despite its many shortcomings, it's also provided me with so many opportunities and privileges that weren't available during the early part of my career. Being able to build up a strong social media profile has meant I've got to shoot huge campaigns, travel the world and meet so many incredible people. It has given me a sense of independence and a place to express myself in a way that's been truly transformational at times. It's a happy accident that I get paid to be myself, and I don't take it for granted – as for many years I struggled to pay my bills and to carve out my own place in the world. There were so many (pre- and post-)social media moments when I actually thought, 'THIS IS IT, NAOMI. YOU'VE MADE IT, YOU CHAMP! THE GRIND HAS PAID OFF! THIS IS YOUR MOMENT, BITCH, YOU'RE ABOUT TO KILL IT,' and then I didn't. There were so many non-breaks that happened, moves I made around the world and campaigns I wrongly thought would 'change my life'. Social media is what ultimately did that for me in the long run. But it has also blurred the lines between what is 'work' and what isn't.

When I started out in the modelling business, I had to find an agent to represent me in order to seek work legally. For wannabe models, signing up to an agency used to be the only gateway to finding legitimate work. The modelling business usually goes like this: clients, designers and brands approached agencies with a casting brief, and then the agents sent whoever they represented that they thought was best suited for the job. That idea of 'trying' to get into the business was not as simple as may have sounded, as most successful models were selected by model scouts who roamed the land looking for fresh-faced beauties, often plucking them out of complete oblivion. They were sometimes found passing through airports (Kate Moss!), eating at McDonald's (à la Gisele Bündchen) or shopping at Primark (Jourdan Dunn) – but just walking in or sending images into an agency was never a guarantee of getting signed, let alone getting any work. Just like dating, we can't all be everyone's cup of tea!

I was initially 'spotted' at the very tender age of 13. I then signed to my first local agency in Spain. After finishing high school, I wanted to take up modelling more seriously, but I was initially rejected from a handful of bigger agencies before being signed, and I was dropped maybe two or three times from different agencies even after being signed before I started working more consistently.

Looking back now, I am shocked at how persistent and resilient I was at that age, to keep picking myself up, against all odds, ignoring all the rejections and trying again. Getting an agent – or a good agent who's a good fit for you, who cares about you – is complicated and can take time, and I guess this is the case for so many of those in the creative industries who use agents to seek out work for them. If you're a young model who does make it past the first round and gets taken on by a reputable agency, it used to mean that you were scooped up and taken away to work, unsupervised, far from your family – and often put in vulnerable situations that you didn't know how to handle and shouldn't have been put in in the first place.

For me, the problem with the modelling agencies at the time was that no one knew what to do with me. I was never quite 'right' for anyone. Until recently, commercial modelling's standards of beauty have mostly revolved around being skinny and white. I was never as thin as I was supposed to be and I was often told I was too 'racially ambiguous' for clients, and that my looks confused (white) people.

Now, with the advent of the internet and social media, the game has truly changed. People have the power to represent themselves. All the things about me that I was always told were the reasons I wasn't getting booked for jobs – my voice, my even louder sense of style, my individuality, my ambiguity – are, of course (as I had always known deep down), my biggest strengths. They are the things that make me stand out, because they are mine and mine alone. And social media has allowed me to find a platform for all the things that make me me to come together. Being able to see wider representation and a fuller spectrum of beauty ideals has been one of the best things about social media, and it has democratised the industry in so many ways. It has allowed models to not only become their very own manager, publicist and agent, but also to be the creative behind the image. We don't have to rely on the same power structures as before. With the selfie cam and timer shots, we can even photograph ourselves and curate our own version of how we want to be represented.

This doesn't just ring true for models but for all kinds of careers – whether you're a politician, chef, artist or dancer. Through social media, we can control what we want to show. We can rely on ourselves to get out there, and all from a little device that fits in our hand.

In an industry where someone else (a client, or art director, or photographer) usually dictates how you're supposed to look and be, social media has given so many of us a place to express themselves. That's been especially important for me because, as I get older, the lack of creative control over my image has become more and more difficult. Social media has allowed me to leave toxic work situations and has allowed me to take back control and blossom by simply being myself.

Still, it has also brought about new challenges and concerns. On a personal level, some of those are practical. If I stopped using social media, would I still find work? Can I find harmony using social media for work without it affecting my mental health, and is there a way I can do my job that involves advertising things on social media and still maintain an ethical existence? Even though it isn't my only income stream, I sometimes wonder if I am too financially dependent on social media, when this could all end abruptly. In my job, in theory I've been commoditising my 'essence' for years, by getting paid to appear in shoots, but there's something about advertising on my own social media channels that starts to feel more confusing.

Let me try and break down how it works when I (and lots of other people!) get paid to work with brands on social media:

When I get booked on a shoot for a print or film campaign for a brand, more often than not there will be a social campaign that comes attached to it with its very own requirements. It will come with specific social guidelines: when I should post, what the tone of the caption should be, who gets tagged, whether I'll be using #ad or tagging the 'Paid for by' feature, and, last but not least, what the hashtag for the campaign will be.

The brands and clients will usually send a detailed breakdown of

How does social media frame the way you think about your work?

It is a huge pest. If I am not disciplined it is easy to take on board the reactions people have on Instagram as some sort of barometer for how well my artworks connect with people. I know that this is a totally false economy because the things people want from that space are not what they want from all spaces. However, those lines grow increasingly blurred – to the point where what people want from online spaces is coherence, bold colours, linear aesthetics. These things get reflected and responded to in our offline world. So I have to think about it, so that I don't get sucked into bending to its whim as a user and artist.

PHOEBE COLLINGS-JAMES, 31, ARTIST

How does social media frame the way you think about your work?

It always makes me feel like I am not doing enough, even though by anyone else's standards, I am doing great! On your personal quiet day, you are confronted with someone announcing their spectacular something or the other – it's daunting and imbues a sense of panic.

LYNETTE NYLANDER, 29
WRITER, EDITOR AND CREATIVE

the overall tone and what the takeaway message needs to be. I often go back and forth with them about what it should say. Sometimes I'd rather it just seem purely like an ad, so people can clearly see that's what it is; and other times I'll fight to make it sound more like me. The situations vary. Ultimately, though, it is on me to post it, because otherwise I won't get paid!

I'm usually asked to post the commercial on release day and then follow it up with one of the photos from the campaign. If it's a big campaign, they can sometimes come with press requirements, where you'll be asked to take part in interviews. Brands also often ask for an insights report, so they can see real statistics on your engagement and demographics. Everything is discussed and planned.

So, in exchange for my audience, my 'authenticity', my voice, they pay me. Even though I know so many others are doing it too, I often feel slightly uneasy about giving them access to my world for a fee. I just always hope that people who follow me can also see past the ad and understand that this is the nature of my job, and that there's a real person behind it.

Instagram, for so many of us – particularly for models – is our CV and work portfolio. It's how future jobs come in, and it's where clients, casting agents and bookers go to find talent. Those tiled images become your audition, when previously it would have been a casting in front of the client. I've been to jobs in the past where it's seemed like my whole life is there on the mood board for the shoot – all images taken from my Instagram for 'inspiration', which feels voyeuristic and weird even though I'm the one who uploaded the images. I decided a few years ago that I would treat Instagram more like work because that's what it had become. A workspace. I've done social campaigns where I've interviewed close friends for a skincare brand; I've danced and jumped around in my underwear in my room for a fashion label; I've publicly explored my relationship to my race and identity for a non-profit. The list goes on. The advertising trend of the moment is all about the staged 'authentic experience'. Brands often want to come into my personal spaces – whether that's where I live or where I hang out – but it can feel intrusive when a supposedly laid-back 'walk through' my wardrobe has a team of 10 people on the other side of the camera. Sometimes I feel a bit gross, like there's just so much of me out there, and I've had to learn how to create personal boundaries around what I'm willing to divulge or not – what feels like it should be private and what is okay to share, and think about the context and medium by which I am deciding to share. There are things I've done in the past that

I wouldn't necessarily do again, but I try not to give myself too much of a hard time about them because it was my job.

Through these experiences, I'm trying to learn how to keep my integrity without having to give away my whole self. So though I sometimes do branded posts on Instagram, I also turn offers down every day; and the ones I do take on I try to approach as holistically as I can, if such a thing is even possible. I often try to take on a producer role; I want control, even though that's not always possible.

But that doesn't change the fact that by doing this job I am complicit in pushing capitalist and consumerist ideals ('Look at my flat! If you shop at this store you could have one too!'), trying to sell a lifestyle that isn't attainable for everyone, and pushing beauty and body ideals that aren't realistic to everyone. I carry a lot of guilt about that. I used to think I was furthering an important narrative around the importance of the visibility of different kinds of bodies, but now I look back and wonder if fighting for advertising to change was even important, now that attitudes are changing? As, after all, it is still advertising.

I squirm every time I get called an 'influencer'. Personally, it's just not how I would ever choose to identify. I understand why the categorisation exists, but I struggle with it. Whether we are talking about 'nano' influencers on the smaller end of the scale or Kylie Jenner, the word is everywhere – but I just can't get myself to say it out loud. Even though I can see that I fall under the term because I have a certain number of followers and do sponsored posts from time to time, something about it doesn't sit right with me. There is something slightly sinister about the idea of deliberately trying to 'influence' people; it sounds manipulative to me in a way that makes me uncomfortable. I have never sat down and planned how to grow my social following, and nor do I have any intention of pushing it rather than letting it happen naturally. I joined Instagram to share things I thought were beautiful and oh-so-joyous in a world where the common perspective and the 24-hour news cycle can often fill us with dread and hopelessness. I still see so much joy in the world, and I want to share that.

As I write, I have over 75,000 followers on Instagram. As follower amounts go, it's not huge – but it is still around the population of a small city, which is crazy to think about. I don't want to get my head around what 75,000 people actually looks like, because when I think about it for even longer than a second it starts to feel a little weird. Who are all these people?

I recently looked at my Insights tab (which is an option you have when you have a blue-ticked Instagram page), and it shows me that I have followers literally all over the world. In Mexico, Japan and New Zealand, India, Brazil and across the US. That part is mind-blowing, and really cool! It also tells me that I have a following that is 75 per cent female, which makes me feel like we have this really fabulous girl gang that spans the planet and makes me feel connected and grounded to the world in a beautiful way.

So I also want to do right by them, because I know that to influence someone is a powerful thing. It makes me think about how we can try to do that in a positive way, rather than just selling someone slimming tea, a contour kit or a pair of shoes. What is the company I'm working with trying to do with me and my followers? How do they want to manipulate my 'influence'? I think these are questions we all need to be asking.

One of the most positive things I've got out of social media is that it's given me a place to experiment with my passions. I documented my progress as I started taking dance classes again. I took my totally nerdy obsession with music and began making monthly playlists and sharing them on my socials. I took my love for flowers and colour and posted photos of the flower arrangements I was doing at home, and as a result I started getting commissions to do them for other people. I pursued my curiosity for photography and started taking portraits. I explored my love of food, and with that came a supper club for friends.

These were all things that I had been scared to do in the past or scared to share with others, but my Instagram page became the home for all of these interests. I often think about where my career will take me, and though I didn't start any of these projects with the idea of turning them into work, that's what's sometimes happened. Unbeknownst to me, by following my heart and deciding to share some of these things publicly not only helped me nurture some of these new hobbies: but in turn they started to evolve my career.

But this approach has its drawbacks. Sometimes I'm worried I've shared too much. I used to dream of the day I could go to work and just be myself. But now that's the case, I often feel as if I'm putting out too much of myself. When we commoditise our essence, how do we protect ourselves? Does everything in our lives become content? So many aspects of my life feel Google-able. How much is too much? How do we share ourselves with the world without exploiting ourselves? I want to just be me, without the fear of not living up to how I am perceived or what is expected of me.

Without consciously choosing to, by just posting what I loved, I was creating a 'personal brand' by being authentic to myself. But I find the idea of a personal brand suffocating, because our identities are always going to be in a state of flux. It's not only limiting to who we are as people but makes it sound like our humanity is just another product with a price tag.

I had heard of so many people feeling Instagram-related anxiety before, but didn't think it was affecting me in the same way. I thought I had a grip on it, but having to think about work 24/7 was actually making my head explode. Then I had a big wakeup call about the effect that social media was having on my life when I experienced my very first anxiety attack.

It got me on the rush-hour train on the way to my dance class that I was finally going to again, after a month of avoiding it because I had felt too stressed out. In hindsight, that was a big sign in itself – when you can't even do the thing that usually makes you feel better.

My heart was beating so fast that the necklace I was wearing, adorned with little bells, was making its own jingle-tastic symphony around my neck. As I looked around the crowded train, I thought, 'Wow, I'm going to collapse right here on this train and no one's going to catch me.' I felt like I was choking on my own panicked breath and I wondered to myself: 'How did I get here?'

I feel like more often than not, breakdowns and anxiety-related attacks are about feeling that you are losing control and at that moment in time I felt very much not in control of my life. I'd just been bitten alive by bed bugs in a hotel in Paris and they'd managed to follow me home to London. After fumigating my entire house and a very expensive dry-cleaning bill, I was exhausted. There's nothing like carrying what feels like an eternal number of garbage bags to the laundromat on your own (because obvs no one wants to come close) to make you feel very, very alone.

But the main underlying trigger here was Instagram. When you're feeling a bit wobbly, Instagram is a one-track trigger machine that takes no prisoners – and I was getting sucked in. Social media when you're not in the right headspace, as we know, can exacerbate anxiety and lead to depression. And that became me – what started off as anxiety became a deep depression. For a few (what felt like very long and dark) months, my feelings of worthlessness were so heavy that I struggled to do anything. At my worst, I lay in bed just wanting everything to end, feeling there was no light at the end of the tunnel.

How does social media frame the way you think about your work?

I understand that it's very necessary for my job and my career, but I think I have reached a point where I almost, to an extent, dislike social media. I sometimes find myself in what I call the 'toxic scroll', when I'll be on Instragram scrolling aimlessly and judging and comparing myself to my fellow djs, then feeling quite inadequate afterwards, and also annoyed with myself for wasting the time. I feel this is a common thing for many creatives / everyone.

BRIANNA LEE PRICE, 33, MUSIC PRODUCER, DJ AND PRESENTER

How does social media frame the way you think about your work?

Like most people I treat social media like a portfolio for my work. It's how I let people know what I'm doing. It is such an important tool for my line of work - I'm constantly researching and finding suppliers, collaborators and inspo. It's definitely something I think about - getting the right pic, how will this look on the 'gram, this is going to be the first thing clients may see; what will they think? But for the most part, it's just an archive of my loved ones.

CLAIRE BURMAN, 29, CREATIVE PRODUCER

One of the issues I was having was that my job felt like it had now become Instagram, and Instagram felt like it had become my job. Even if I wasn't posting about work, I felt like I needed to keep posting to keep a presence on there, to stay relevant, to keep an imprint of myself out in the world. Even though I was working enough to pay my bills and save money (something I had never been able to do before), I found myself getting upset and being disappointed about not getting jobs I didn't even know I wanted. I started comparing myself to people who were a decade younger than me.

Social media, in my fragile state of mind, was turning me into the worst version of myself. I was looking around at what all my peers were doing, and it was making me feel less than. In theory, there were so many 'good things' going on in my life, but Instagram was making me lose sight of that. As someone who has modelled for so long, there have been many times when I've gone down a spiral of worry that is combined with a deep yearning to figure out what I'm going to do next. Social media made it seem like everyone I knew (or rather followed) was on a very clear career trajectory, and that they knew what they wanted and were 'killing it'; whatever it was that they were doing. I felt myself becoming like a green-eyed monster. My deep rooted fears and insecurities around the fact that I wasn't 'smart' because I almost didn't finish high school and never went to university were rising up, and I hadn't had a 'normal' job in years. I felt stupid, unsure of what my skills were, and totally overwhelmed and overpowered by what everyone else around me appeared to be doing. Even though I knew it wasn't true, at the time I felt like I had nothing to contribute and nothing left to give.

Society often makes us feel as if our value is based solely on our work life and productivity, and the pressure to excel is only magnified by the voice that social media seems to insert in your head that echoes 'I'M NOT GOOD ENOUGH I'M NOT GOOD ENOUGH I'M NOT GOOD ENOUGH YOU'RE NOT DOING ENOUGH YOU'RE NOT DOING ENOUGH . . .' Social media can easily make you feel like we all have to be multi-hyphenate polymath goliaths. But while being interested in so many things is cool, it would be even cooler if we let all the slashes be things we were just curious about instead of feeling we had to somehow be masters of these crafts. If instead of having to 'succeed' at them, we just saw them as cool little extensions of who we are.

Now, not only was I having an identity crisis, I was having an existential one too. After having put so much energy for so many years into talking about the importance of more visual inclusion in fashion, I could see changes in casting happening everywhere around me. But there was something that just didn't feel quite right to me. In front of the camera, I could see an influx of models with different body types/ethnicities/abilities/ages/gender identities, but this only made the lack of 'diversity' behind the camera seem more blatant than ever. From the photographers, makeup artists and art directors to the editors, designers and clients, the majority of people on creative teams in the fashion industry are white, and the tokenism had started to feel unbearable.

I was very uncomfortable with how the industry was using bodies in a way that felt insincere and disingenuous. And I started to really see the problem with the term 'diversity'. It had been a word I myself had used for many years in describing what I did, but now that the word is used everywhere and so fleetingly, is it taking away from the real fight for equity and inclusion? Unfortunately, 'diversity' has become such an umbrella term, to the extent that it can feel like the meaning has been lost. Who are we talking about when we talk about the need for 'more diversity'? It doesn't just mean non-white people. It includes all people of colour, people on the gender spectrum, fat people, people with disabilities, and so on. We want to make sure everyone is included.

So many brands seem to be doing 'diverse' campaigns, but only because that's what's hot on social media right now. Model Hari Nef, the first openly transgender woman to appear on the cover of a major British magazine, was quoted as saying: 'They bring you in, and it's like "Diversity Day", and then you go home, Diversity Day is cool – Diversity Day essentially pays my bills. But it's never a blue-chip campaign, rarely a contract.'

So sometimes it can feel a bit 'flavour of the day', like it might not last – and seeing all the non-diverse crews behind the camera made that all too clear. Photographer Campbell Addy started his own casting agency and a magazine called *Nii Journal* – which describes itself as 'a print publication exploring the issues of empowerment and representation within race' – to allow him to work more freely without having to conform to any previous fashion ideals. In an interview with *i-D*, he explained: 'The foundations hold up the structure. If you want change in a genuine manner, you've got to change the foundations. Maybe if staff were more diverse, magazines and brands wouldn't have to think so hard about this issue, it would just be normal.'

Sometimes the changes in casting feel so superficial, but is this where change starts? Whether we're talking about fashion advertising on social media, or the tv and film industries, across media as a whole, is insincere representation still a means for different beauty ideals to seep into the subconscious? Will it help to normalise bodies that have been previously marginalised in the past, and is it just a necessary evil for things to move towards a better future?

In order to get myself back to a good place, I had to try to separate my work self from my real self. I was finding it harder and harder to distinguish between the two. I knew I needed to start creating a healthier balance, and I knew what had to go. As a result, now, I usually don't actually have Instagram on my phone. I find that if it's on my phone I'll click on it and scroll through without even noticing, because of its addictive tendencies and I quickly lose what can feel like hours of my life. Even if I'm not scrolling I feel like I can sometimes just still hear the loud voices of so many online presences booming and what can seem like oppressive energy just radiating out of my phone. So now I just download it when I want to look at something, have to or feel the need to post something or check for messages, and then I delete it again. What is fascinating is that when it's not on my phone, I can almost forget about its existence and I feel freer, happier, more present. I know that I need it to do my job and earn a living, but deleting and downloading it again when necessary (even if that means doing that every day or once a week) is the only way that, for now, I can maintain a balanced relationship with it. I know it's not a permanent solution, but while my work life is still public-facing, this is what works for me.

Through all of this, it's the idea of 'making it' that has shifted for me. Having that work-related breakdown forced me to change my perspective on how I saw myself and my work. I realised that on paper I had still been chasing a lot of the same goals from a long time ago, but I had grown and evolved since then. As I passed so many of the professional milestones I'd yearned for, the things I had previously thought were important didn't end up feeling like I thought they would. They didn't shoot me into a new paradigm or heal me from any pain.

I think we can often end up throwing our whole selves into our work not only because we depend on it financially but also as a way of often unconsciously avoiding having to confront our own underlying issues. Many of us have been conditioned to think that climbing the career ladder absolves us of feeling pain, that success heals trauma – but while of course it can make things easier, it doesn't take the pain away. I think that's a truth that, as humans in the modern world, we're finally waking up to. We did all the 'right things' and yet we're still unhappy, and the accolades merely act as Band-Aids.

The sweetest nectar I've tasted has been from growing into my own skin, in my own time, through the many experiences I've had – which in turn have had an effect on how I think about my work and thus how my work (and the relationship I have with it) has evolved. As time passes, my definition of professional success and growth has evolved. More and more, I find myself asking who I am without my work? I want to keep asking, how can I continue to honestly evolve in my professional life as I seek to evolve on a personal level? As I've hit the big work goals and accolades in modelling that I've been conditioned to strive for, I can't ignore that they didn't end up making me feel the way I thought they would. Being on a billboard is cool, but what does it mean in the grand scheme of things? Other than that it meant I could provide for myself; is it only cool because it feeds a specific part of my ego and validates my social status? I understand that even having time to have these thoughts comes from a position of privilege, that I am now at a place in my work life that allows me to also seek more - I see that, but I also personally feel like it's beneficial for all of our spirits to just be able to take a pause from social media, and to think about it from time to time.

When our work lives are so intertwined with social media, how can we ever break from being slaves to digital capitalism? I'm still navigating the blur between my work self and my real self, but as I pull back from my life online to feed my offline curiosities, the lines are getting clearer and I feel more at peace with not having – or needing – all the answers.

In a society where professional success is presented as a moral imperative and when so much of our work is about the self, does success in work make you happy?

I've written six books; I've been published in almost every magazine there is; I co-curated the third biggest biennale in the world; I have put on exhibitions around the world. Is there ever a moment when I think 'great, I've made it'? No, of course not. I will always have the drive to hustle and I am always aware of the financial imperatives around that. Emotionally I get pleasure out of the world that I am lucky enough to work in – culture and contemporary art – but success is always a moving goal post.

**FRANCESCA GAVIN,
WRITER AND CURATOR**

PHOEBE LOVATT ON PERSONAL BRANDING

In the beginning, when social media was still fun, and the online world felt like an exciting and limitless new frontier, I was a big advocate of the 'personal brand'. I wrote columns about its merits and produced how-to guides for crafting one's own. I contemplated the consistent use of specific Instagram filters, and considered aesthetic signatures. I thought a lot about how other brands – real ones, the types that actually make products rather than seek to frame themselves as such – might interact with my brand. Would I be seen as valuable? In possession of a clear USP? Deemed to be 'on brand' by any number of companies who might go on to hire me for some undefined job, at some undefined future point?

While promoting my fledgling business, The Working Women's (WW) Club, I enthusiastically positioned myself at the centre of what marketing experts might call the 'brand story'. The fact that this narrative was actually mined from my real life – and born of a moment of personal vulnerability, at that – did not present itself as an area of potential conflict in my mind. Like most relatively photogenic young women building a career with the new digital tools at my disposal, it seemed without question that I would also serve as The WW Club's unofficial 'face'.

If all of this makes me sound like a cynical branding mastermind determined to make a corporate buck by any means, let me tell you that my bank balance wishes that were the case. The truth is actually much scarier: that I was just an ambitious, somewhat naive 20-something woman, attempting to navigate a system which conditions us to believe that our physical selves are our most valuable source of brand equity – irrespective of any creative skills we might also possess.

For a while, my personal-branding efforts paid off, quite literally. Big businesses responded to my emphasis on community building; to the aesthetically pleasing spaces (and faces) on my feed; and to the spirit of female solidarity that lay at the heart of my professional mission. I got hired for partnerships, photographed for campaigns, and featured on branded-content platforms (wearing clothes that were always simultaneously for sale in the site's webshop). The fact that I was rarely paid well for these opportunities – and, in some cases, not paid at all – seemed irrelevant. This effusive corporate endorsement was the stuff that contemporary career success is made of . . . isn't it?

I was surprised to discover, then, that none of it left me feeling very successful once the influx of likes inevitably trailed off. The women I met and who connected to one another at my events; the emails I received from total strangers, telling me that my work had helped them with their own; the hard creative labour it took to produce all the panel discussions, newsletters and books – that stuff was its own, deeply satisfying reward. But, otherwise, I felt frustrated by the fact that a considerable part of my time was now spent mutely posing for photos, over which I had little creative control.

Even more than that, I was troubled by the fact that my original intention – to establish an inclusive and supportive professional network for women – had quickly been engulfed by a wave of 'corporate feminism' that frequently misaligned with my own evolving politics and worldview. In my eagerness to facilitate the growth of a platform I truly believed in, I found myself bracketed into a group of women with 'personal brands' that undeniably overlapped with my own, but whose venture-capital-funded career paths – while formidable – bore little resemblance to the one I'd set out upon.

For a while, I forged on in a state of uneasy complicity, in part because I simply wasn't sure how I'd make any money if I pushed back. I spent hours grappling with the dilemma of how I might be able to evolve towards a more nuanced professional 'persona' in the future, as I simultaneously hustled for work in real time. I was confused – and confused as to why I was confused – all the while failing to consider that there's a reason why legions of professionals are hired to craft visual identity, product offering and voice. Actual brands are notoriously hard to define and then redefine, let alone generate a profit from. Building a brand is hard work.

That we are now compelled to retain our individual employability by learning to apply these same principles to our endlessly changing, incredibly fragile human selves is insane – not to mention insanity-inducing. And yet here we find ourselves, devoting hours of our lives to posting, tweeting and 'sharing', all in pursuit of the approval of some anonymous marketing executive who will probably give the job to someone with more followers, anyway.

I wish I could wrap up this piece with a moment of epiphany; to tell you I eventually threw my phone out the window before disappearing entirely from the digital grid. But that would be another disingenuous act of storytelling – the kind of thing that exists only on a carefully worded 'About' page. As I write this, I am in the real-time midst of an attempt to move forward with a professional identity that feels authentic and honest on a personal level, but still leaves me able to pay my rent. For obvious reasons, I've tried to resist looking at it as a 'rebranding', and I'm not totally sure how it's going to work out.

In the meantime, I've learned that life rarely fits neatly into square boxes, but rather tends to unfold in the grey areas that lie between. The honest truth is that I still sometimes review my social media feeds and Google results through a hypothetical stranger's eyes, trying to figure out what the digital ephemera of the past decade says about 'me'. Perhaps somewhere in the undefined future, I'll possess the wisdom to write a how-to guide for building a career in the digital age without a personal brand. Until then, I'll be much more mindful about the parts of myself that I package up for sale, and the parts that are privately reserved – just for me.

Phoebe Lovatt is a writer, moderator, and the founder of The WW Club. She lives between New York and her hometown of London. If you really want to see her in her element, come find her on the dancefloor.

Do you find yourself befriending more people who you know will boast your social media profile?

I've caught myself doing this, but more from a work perspective – if I am associated with this person, might their success rub off on me in some small way? It's usually people I genuinely admire, but the interaction itself doesn't feel genuine, so I try to watch myself.

AMANI AL KI, 27, JEWELLER AND MAKER

Do you feel you've shared too much of yourself online?

I did, but there's truly no point regretting anything. It was me at the time, and that's fine. I don't do it much anymore and I feel better for it. I'm now overloaded with other people's personal lives online and it's a lot. We all wonder why we have so much anxiety.

INDIA ROSE, 26, ARTIST

'How much do you really want your colleagues and bosses, or future colleagues and bosses, to know about you?'

MISHAL HUSAIN

SARAH

This is the question Mishal Husain asked me, rhetorically, in a little room at the BBC where I was interviewing her about her book *The Skills: From First Job to Dream Job*. As one of the most revered and formidable broadcast journalists in the world, Mishal's advice is the sort you'd be wise to listen to. 'It's worth thinking through how open you should be,' she continued. 'It doesn't mean you have to turn into some kind of automaton in terms of what you put online, but just register that there may be repercussions from this that you can't see right now.'

What she's advocating is some distance between the personal and the professional, and it's perfectly sensible advice for everyone working today, from influencers and journalists to lawyers and doctors. But as a millennial, editor and writer in digital media, I'm not sure I know where the line is.

For the best part of 10 years, my job has been to create content that I think people will click on. I went from an intern at a cool magazine aged 22 to an online editor at 23 and then carried on climbing the trippy digital media ladder from there, never really looking up to where I was going because my shoulders were always hunched and my head buried in a screen. Now in my thirties, I'm wondering whether I've given the internet too much of my life story, both in terms of time and content. I rarely post selfies because I don't like the way I look close up but I've shared deeply personal emotions and experiences online. Half a million people read a Q&A I did with an ex-boyfriend about our relationship and the reasons we broke up. Thousands more have read about my mental health, the hair on my head, the hair on my body and my sleep disorders. There's so much crossover between my life and work that even my Google searches are full of content potential: 'How do I check my breasts for lumps?', 'How do I get rid of bum spots?' 'How to Check Your Breasts for Lumps' and 'How to Get Rid of Bum Spots' became two of the most-read pieces in the Health section of the website I edited. I even got a tattoo on my forearm on a live stream, which was broadcast on my company's Facebook page. The tattoo says 'Kyrie eleison', which means 'Lord have mercy', a phrase repeated up to 100 times in the mass in the church I grew up attending. But I was too embarrassed to admit what it meant on the live stream, because I didn't feel like discussing my religion or why this phrase has particular meaning for me on Facebook Live, so I stayed quiet, which was bad for engagement.

While it's not a requirement to turn yourself into content as an online journalist, personal pieces that provoke a reaction or that people can read and think, 'Yes, that's how I felt when that thing happened to me,' tend to get more traffic (i.e. readers) than reported features. Which is why you see first-person headlines such as 'It's taken me a lifetime to stop loathing my body' (*Telegraph*) and 'I took my first antidepressant this week. The effects were frightening' (*Guardian*) all over the internet. Personal essays were one of several formats that developed to meet the ever-increasing monthly traffic targets faced by media companies trying to survive the digital revolution; along with listicles and self-analysis pieces such as 'Am I too narcissistic?' (*Guardian*), 'The 36 Questions That Lead to Love' (*New York Times*) and 'Ten Signs You're Wasting Your Talent in the Wrong Job' (*Forbes*), appealing to the highly self-aware, emotionally motivated and always online millennial demographic.

It's in the personal essay format that I've made the biggest mistakes but also found the most satisfying successes as a writer and editor. Because of this particular strand of my job, lots of people in my life pitch aspects of their lives to me as content. One of my best friends found out that her ex-boyfriend of five years had got engaged after just a few months of dating someone new. She was gutted, and the way she communicated this to me was: 'I've got a piece for you ...' I get messages all the time on Instagram, Facebook and WhatsApp from friends or friends of friends when major things happen to them, such as break-ups, being cheated on, getting pregnant, having the baby, being totally overwhelmed after having the baby, and above all about living with anxiety, anxiety, anxiety.

To be a success in the digital generation, the story usually goes that you have to give something of yourself to it. Digital media doesn't favour the reticent, or the lurkers who observe from a safe distance; it favours the ones who play the game. But a decade working as an online editor with traffic targets on my head has made me wonder how many people who give the internet their stories end up feeling like winners.

The half a million people that read my relationship interview with my ex spent an average of 23 minutes on the page, which is a long time in the world of online content. I knew it would 'do well' because most people can relate to heartbreak (see all the films, books, plays, sonnets and Netflix series of the last few hundred years). The questions were juicy, from 'Did you cheat on me with that girl at your work?' to 'What do you think was the most intimate moment in our relationship?' Readers commented under the article saying it was 'brave', 'raw' and refreshing'. @Lamiakindele said it hit her in the chest. @Orangechefhat said 'Damn. Please make this franchise a regular.'

Maybe it was brave, raw and refreshing, but it was also a cheap shot. I was clickbaiting my life and I knew it, but I went ahead and did it anyway. While I didn't change the content of what my ex said, I did edit it for flow, made it all a little bit more poetic, a little bit more heartbreaking, a little bit more likely to hit @Lamiakindele in the chest. What was I doing, asking a person I hadn't spoken to in years to answer 29 deeply personal questions about our relationship because I knew it would be a content hit? One of the questions was 'What were my worst traits?' He answered: 'You could be quite cold. And you prioritised work over everything else.' Case in point.

Someone who worked at Tinder read the article too, and that kickstarted a conversation with the sales team at my company. Tinder wanted me to host a podcast about modern love. It felt like such an easy win – it wasn't hard to write and I didn't have to do any research, but readers loved it. I felt like a celebrity whose private heartbreak was hot gossip and I had total control over it; I was the editor of my own love life. But I didn't do it for closure and it wasn't cathartic to write, so my intentions were dishonest and because of that it bothers me.

I've found myself getting carried away with personal pieces several times, forgetting or neglecting to tell the people in my life who might read them and have an opinion. Around the time of my 30th birthday, I wrote about how I wanted to stop partying and have a baby. The *Evening Standard* syndicated the article, meaning many more people read it than I expected – including several of my boyfriend's friends, which was embarrassing because it's not something I would ever discuss with them. It's easy to forget, when you're writing an article for a website, that it's not a diary or a message in a bottle that may one day be discovered by an explorer on a secluded beach. Once it's out there, it's out there, and you as the writer don't have any control over who will see it or what they'll think of you as a result. That's taken me a long time to learn.

On Mental Health Awareness Day in 2018, I noticed one of my colleagues had posted a picture of herself in shadow on Instagram with a caption about lifting the stigma on mental health. I admired her bravery, and after several hours' consideration I posted a picture I'd taken of myself a year before, when I had been going through a hard time, and my face was puffy from crying and I looked exhausted. I wrote a caption about how people only ever post pretty, happy pictures of themselves on Instagram and how it gives a false impression, and how you end up thinking everyone's so happy and having so much fun all the time, and you're the only person who's not. And I wrote that I had generalised anxiety disorder and chronic insomnia which sometimes caused depression. I hesitated over posting it for a long time and reread the caption about 35 times, including out loud to hear how it sounded. Then I pressed 'Post'.

I'm no good at Instagram, and usually my posts get around 50–100 likes, but this post got 400 likes, and 66 comments of support. A few weeks later, I received a freelance commission to write a 2,000-word feature for a magazine about social media and mental health. I was paid £500 for the story. Timothée Chalamet was on the cover. I saw the magazine in every newsagent for the next month but felt too embarrassed to open it because I'd said one very personal thing in it that I wished I hadn't. Eighteen months later, my sister posted a link to the online version of the article in our family WhatsApp group. She'd seen it on *Vice*'s Facebook page; they'd only just published it online, with a January 2019 date stamp, despite the fact I'd written it nearly a year before, when I'd been in a very different headspace. She posted it in the group because she was excited to see my name on her Facebook feed, but I desperately didn't want my family to read it, and I sent a panicked message back asking them not to, with the monkey emoji that's covering its eyes. When it comes to personal pieces, maintaining the 'thick skin' people say is necessary to be a journalist is particularly difficult.

A few months later, I decided to archive the post on my Instagram because I felt weird about it, as if I'd negatively exposed myself for momentary gratification. Part of the reason I made it private was because I suddenly remembered an article called 'This Photographer Took a Selfie Every Time She Cried For 3 Years' that was published on the website I worked for in 2015 [*i-D*]. The article was one of the biggest traffic-drivers that year. Everyone wanted to see what this photographer from LA looked like crying. She happened to be a beautiful girl and a beautiful crier – her bright blue eyes glistening with tears, her lips slightly parted. In the article, she was quoted talking about the act of taking photos while crying, which she said happened several times during arguments with her boyfriend:

In the moment, if we're having an argument and I'm crying and I'm like, 'Hold on, I've got to take a picture,' he's like, 'What the fuck is wrong with you?' It's like, is it taking you out of the moment? Is it connecting you more? What are you doing? I don't know all the answers yet. There have been times when I've taken one or two photos and I started to cry harder and I become more upset, and then other times when I took a photo and felt relieved, like I could move on.

I had hated that article when it came out. It was my least favourite on the website that year, and it infuriated me that more people clicked on it than any of the other articles on offer that I felt were infinitely more worthy of people's attention. But then, a few years later, I went and posted a photo of myself crying on the internet, and more people liked it than anything I'd ever posted before, and I was infuriated all over again.

Unlike the interview with the ex, the reason I'd posted the photo was because I was trying to be honest in a dishonest digital world, and yet there was still an element of phoniness to it that I later regretted. I very much want to destigmatise mental health and to encourage people to share difficult feelings, because if you keep those feelings inside they can harm you and those you love. But was feeding Instagram my own personal sadness the right way to do it?

Among the 66 comments was one from my bikini waxer, a woman I trust implicitly, who wrote, 'Every single person experiences mental health, babe. Some like to express their feelings, some don't.' I felt so embarrassed, like I'd been melodramatic. Another family friend, who had a much harder life than I did growing up, commented, 'Isn't it more common than not, from to time, to feel low, unsatisfied, unsuccessful and unaccomplished?' I wondered how many people had seen the post and rolled their eyes, the way I had about the photographer's crying selfies.

In a society where professional success is presented as a moral imperative, and when so much of our work is about the 'self', does success in work make you happy?

Not at all. I often think about this. The only real measure for me is going to be how happy I am OUT OF LIFE. Work is important, but it is now definitely more linked to the mark I make and how fulfilled I feel, rather than column inches and dollar amounts. I know the biggest fight I am going to have in this life is with myself, getting to a place of understanding, belief and love. That is what motivates me now.

LYNETTE NYLANDER, 29
WRITER, EDITOR AND CREATIVE

Charisse Chikwiri, 21
London-based, Zimbabwe-born writer,
DJ and creative consultant who advises brands
on how to connect with young people.

Do you post emotions on social media?

I'm conscious of being open and vulnerable on Instagram because it's so unrealistic. Nobody's that happy all the time as they look on Instagram. But I don't post pictures of myself crying or anything. A lot of people I know air everything on Instagram.

Why do you think people post crying selfies?

I think it's instinct. For some people who grew up on social media, it feels natural. And people can go viral. You can get money and profit off your trauma. A lot of people do that.

Do you think people share too much of themselves online?

I sometimes question people's end goals with sharing online. Not everybody genuinely cares about you and your life. I had one friend who was going through a breakup and tweeted this whole thread – 'he said this, and then did this' – and it was really sad because there were so few people who actually cared about her reading that thread. They just forwarded it on to other people online like 'oh my god did you see this', like it was the news of the day. I spoke to her about it as a friend, telling her I was there for her if she wanted to talk about it, rather than post it on social media. She said something like, 'Some people struggle to communicate how they feel in real life – that's why they post on social media.'

What's the most personal piece you've written/posted on the internet?

I had a blog when I was 17 and I wrote something about my dad on it. Growing up, I was constantly arguing with him. I knew that a lot of the issues with the way he parented me were to do with his own upbringing in Zimbabwe. But he raised me in a different country and a different time, so I struggled with his old-fashioned, cultural parenting style.

I had tried to talk to him about it many times but he wasn't hearing me. So I wrote a long piece about it on my blog, and I didn't mince my words. Somebody from church read it, and told my parents. My dad called me after he read it and we spoke for two hours. It was the first time I felt listened to. I could tell he was hurt, because the piece had a lot of emotion in it, and there was also some embarrassment because people at church had read it and said to him, 'What's going on with you and your daughter?' But I'm glad it happened, because it changed him and it changed our relationship. I had tried to express all these things to him before, but he hadn't listened. But when it was out there in public, he had to listen.

You were 17 then, you're 21 now, would you do that again?

I would still write it, but maybe I would be more diplomatic with my wording. I did feel bad afterwards because I was worried people would think he was some horrible, militant man. I'm not a tyrant child, by the way! But I have questions that I need to explore for my identity. I can't just bury them. Maybe I'd send it to him directly, rather than posting it online.

Are there things you wouldn't write about, that are off limits?

I can't think of anything that I wouldn't publish. I'm not afraid of vulnerability or shame. Some things are more scary than others, but I'd probably do it anyway.

How has your relationship with your dad changed since the article?

He listens a lot more. Our generation is a lot more introspective than our parents'. We understand that the reason we behave the way we do is because of our upbringing and because of specific influences on our lives. My dad just thought, 'This is how I am, and that's it.' I don't think he'd ever questioned himself in that way, until he read the piece. For example, there was always 'dad's chair' in the living room. It was the only armchair in the house and it belonged to him. If you were sitting there when he came home, you had to get up. It seemed so silly to me.

Does he still have his chair?

No, he doesn't, he changed that habit. He changed a lot of things. He never wanted me to have a creative job in the arts, but I fought against that and took myself to open days at arts universities. He thought it was trivial. But now he's turned around and will call me and ask me 'what are you working on?' He's proud of me now. We're very similar people, actually, we're both very stubborn. I think he sees himself in me.

In May 2017, journalist Jia Tolentino wrote an article that went viral about digital media encouraging women in particular to offer their painful experiences up as content, resulting in 'a situation in which writers feel like the best thing they have to offer is the worst thing that ever happened to them' [*Slate*]. I've thought about this line so many times over the last few years, when women I've never met have emailed me at work asking if I will pay them to write about a terrible thing that happened to them. And then I have to decide whether their trauma is interesting enough to be made into an article – and, crucially, whether they're a good enough writer to turn their real-life experience into a compelling piece of content.

I've made a few mistakes in the past, saying yes to 'interesting' pitches from journalists I've never worked with before, and then the article comes in and it's very clear that the woman was not emotionally ready to write the piece because it is a mess: it's all over the place, it has no structure or order or constructive advice for others going through a similar thing. It is a badly written trauma. And then I ask for lots of edits on the piece, and make lots of suggestions to improve the copy. I can think of two instances where I decided the most responsible thing to do, at that point, was write an email back explaining as kindly and compassionately as I could why I had decided not to publish the piece.

In those instances, I find the responsibility of saying 'yes, please' or 'no, thanks' to a person's trauma a terrible thing. But when the story is well written, by someone who is ready to share, and is doing so with the intention of contributing to a cultural change and making others feel less alone, that responsibility feels like a very precious and powerful thing to have. I've had to find my own metrics for success in this genre. A personal piece has to have an identifiable purpose that does one or more of the following things: provides comfort to others who are in a similar position; educates those who aren't; opens up a wider conversation.

In 2015, someone very close to me pitched an article about mental health and recovering from a suicide attempt which had left her in a coma in intensive care. The piece was heart-wrenching. I knew I was too close to it and to her, so I asked for a second opinion from another editor, who agreed that some lines needed to be changed because they were too dark – the writer had talked about feeling very peaceful right before the suicide attempt, and we didn't want anyone considering suicide to read it and feel spurred on. I felt like a terrible person emailing her back with 'this bit sounds too pro-suicide, can you make it more positive?' But she agreed, and rephrased the lines, saying her only purpose in writing it was to help others going through something similar.

Thousands of people read the article and commented on it, wishing her well, sending love, thanking her for sharing, and sharing their own experiences of recovery from mental ill health. 'I was really strengthened by those comments from people who had identified with the piece or found it comforting,' she told me later. 'It was very important to me at the time that some good came out of everything I had been through, and that was why I wanted to write the article. I think the more articles and conversations there are about conditions like depression, the better. Mental health problems are very common and yet most people who have them feel alone and isolated. Sometimes reading an article that makes you feel you are not alone or a weirdo is enough to help you get through the day.'

As an editor, I was pleased with that piece because it made both the author and the readers feel less alone, while also giving insight into the psyche of a suicidal person for readers who hadn't been anywhere near that thought themselves. The writer also told me that she sent the article to a few friends she'd met after her suicide attempt, and to a new guy she'd started seeing, because she thought they should know but understandably, found the words too difficult to say out loud. It's worth noting that she wrote under a pseudonym because although she wanted to personally share it with one or two people in her life, she didn't want it to appear in her digital footprint. I would say that piece was a success. I think it's a good thing that stories about healing and finding your way up from rock bottom exist online, and I'm proud to be in a position to put them there.

A few months later, I published a series of pieces written by a 28-year-old woman who'd just been diagnosed with stage four cancer (Hodgkin's Lymphoma). In the first piece, Ariane talked about feeling run-down, struggling to make it up the stairs to her flat, and standing on a train platform before work, feeling so ill that she began crying

How does social media frame the way you think about your work?

My work relationship with social media has changed over the years. I write about music and use platforms like Twitter to keep tabs on artists I'm interested in. At first, I found it exciting that social media cut out the middle men, but over time its illusion of a direct connection paved the way for a specific kind of churnalism (endless 'so-and-so said something on social media' articles) and a narrowing of editorial focus. Questions like 'How many followers do they have?' have become a key factor in pitch meetings. I find that disheartening because so many artists are pushing music in new directions but don't receive the recognition they deserve. Instead, spurred on by click-hungry publications, writers vie to tell the same story about the same high-profile artist within the same tight timeframe. When the metrics of 'success' are skewed towards immediacy and virality, it leaves those of us who cover less mainstream interests in a catch-22. I don't think cranked-out 'content' can ever be a substitute for thoughtful music criticism, and neither am I interested in privileging music based on its 'likes.' Instead, I've retreated somewhat, choosing to write less and in more depth. Marination, for me, is the more enjoyable path to meaning.

RUTH SAXELBY, 40, WRITER AND EDITOR

uncontrollably because at that point she knew something was seriously wrong. She wrote so beautifully about the crushing experience of going from a fun girl with a fun job living in London to a cancer patient facing her own mortality.

'I spend most of my days lying on sofas scrolling my friends' Instagram feeds, seething with envy at how much fun they're all having,' she wrote. 'I don't want to be ill anymore. I want to be fun Ariane again, the Ariane who nearly gets kicked out of Berghain for dancing on the bar . . . the Ariane who is fit and healthy and happy . . . I want to run back to her, the old Ariane, give her a huge hug and plead with her not to leave me.'

Almost 100,000 people read her columns, commenting that her writing had made them cry, telling her she was an inspiration and to keep going. The articles made me cry too. I cried while reading one of them out to my parents when I went home for the weekend and they asked me how work was.

Then I started to feel weird about it. I sit with lots of tabs open on my desktop, including a website which tells you how many people are reading what articles on the site. Every time I published one of Ariane's columns, there was a surge in traffic. Turns out lots of people wanted to read her trauma, and it was all the more emotional because it was live – she wasn't better yet, she was writing it in real time. The column was a 'success', but from where I was sitting with my tabs and traffic graphs, watching the internet click on a stranger's disease – which I was editing, uploading and optimising for Google search with keywords and phrases like 'cancer' and 'losing hair chemotherapy' – I started to question both my own motivations as an editor and the motivations of the readers. Every media outlet publishes cancer stories, from breast cancer survivors sharing their experiences to the world-renowned journalist A. A. Gill writing a cover story about his diagnosis for the *Sunday Times Magazine*, published a week before he died. There's no doubt in my mind that these stories should be shared in order to increase awareness, provide support for the writer and the readers – who will likely have some experience with cancer themselves – and to encourage greater empathy and understanding across society; it's just weird being the person behind the laptop clicking 'Publish' and watching the traffic go up on a chart when someone's life is in the balance.

Ariane, 30

Ariane is in remission now. She's living in Berlin with her boyfriend, working on a film script and teaching screen-acting.

Had you written anything before you wrote about your diagnosis?

No, never. I didn't really think about the writing process though, I just did it. I found it really easy to write about. It was definitely cathartic.

Did you find the comments helpful?

Comments were something I hadn't thought about when I started writing. The positive comments were a great source of support for me. But after the pieces were published, they got syndicated on news sites like *Yahoo! News*. The comments on those sites were really harsh. There was a photo on the first article of me wearing a hospital gown and those socks you wear when you have an operation, and people in the comments section said they looked like 'sexy' stockings and they said God was going to send me to hell for what I was wearing. Other people said I was just writing about having cancer to get famous. Some people commented things like 'you're gonna die'. I got upset and overwhelmed. I had just been diagnosed with cancer, and then these strangers were telling me I was going to die and go to hell. I hadn't thought about how I was going to be perceived when I wrote it, and when I was perceived in that way, I was really shocked. If I'd taken a step back and really thought about it before publishing the article . . . it wouldn't have stopped me doing it, but I might have been more prepared for the reaction.

Do you have any regrets about writing about your illness?

No, not at all. I think it was important to have done it. But what I will say is that using writing on a public platform as a kind of therapy can be dangerous . . . I'm not sure it's the best way to address how you're feeling. There are different ways to do it; it doesn't have to be so personal. I've written a short film script based on something that happened to my sister but it's part fiction. You can express yourself in other ways besides a first-person diary-style entry. Although it's much harder writing objectively!

What do you think people got from reading the articles?

I think it increased awareness. People probably hadn't read that young female perspective on cancer before. I also think it made people feel better about their own mortality. You don't tend to think about mortality in your twenties, so I think reading my story made other people feel better about themselves and their lives. I did question why there was such engagement with it – but people always want to read about other people's lives, don't they, especially when they're not going well. It boosts the reader up in a weird way because they think, 'Oh god, that poor girl.' It was different for people I knew personally, who were genuinely worried about me, but I wonder about the people who didn't know me and why they were so engaged.

What do you think of the pieces, looking back, now that you're in remission?

I was very open about sharing at the time, but two years later, when I'm moving on ... it's hard to go back to that place. People who are battling cancer now find the articles online and message me asking for advice and support, which of course I want to give ... but it's hard. I wasn't prepared for that sort of responsibility. I'm better now, but because I put my story out, people expect me to be some master of knowledge on cancer, which I'm really not.

In her award-winning show Nanette, Australian comedian Hannah Gadsby announces that she's giving up comedy because she's sick of self-deprecating humour and turning the traumatic experiences she's lived through into jokes for her job. After telling the audience the real stories behind these jokes, which were horrific and traumatising, in the final five minutes she says:

I don't tell you this so you think of me as a victim. I am not a victim. I tell you this because my story has value ... What I would have done to have heard a story like mine. Not for blame. Not for reputation, not for money, not for power. But to feel less alone. To feel connected. I want my story heard. Because ... I believe we could paint a better world if we learned how to see it from all perspectives, as many perspectives as we possibly could.

Showing the world new perspectives is my ultimate goal as an online editor, and when I'm able to do this – or more accurately, when I can give someone else the platform to do this – I feel successful, regardless of traffic.

In a 2013 article in the *Guardian*, the journalist Charlie Brooker wrote: *I used to worry that computers were to blame: that modern connectivity was steadily turning all of us into a bunch of fake, shrieking character actors. Pick an avatar, cultivate a 'personality' that doesn't quite represent your actual personality, and shit out an endless string of entertaining brain turds for the crowd . . . Almost every monologue consists of nothing but the words PLEASE AUTHENTICATE MY EXISTENCE, repeated over and over again, in disguise. There has never been a single tweet that couldn't be replaced with PLEASE AUTHENTICATE MY EXISTENCE.*

Brooker was writing as a cynic of the internet and social media. But I think that the words 'please authenticate my existence' are precisely what's good about personal pieces on the internet. We should be authenticating each other's existences as often as we can. We should be listening to each other's stories and learning about how others live – especially about their pain. As a writer of personal pieces, I've made many mistakes – and I wish I had thought about who would read the things I wrote before I published them. As an editor, I've worried about exploitation several times when publishing people's accounts of their trauma. But truthfully, more often than not, I've felt good about being able to share people's experiences on a big platform, where thousands of strangers can relate to and authenticate their existences.

I think articles that make you cry at your desk mean they're worth publishing. I think the surge in traffic that indicates people are reading those articles means society is becoming less rigid and more accepting and emotionally intelligent. Despite the various complications that almost always arise from publishing personal pieces, they encourage empathy – and that's a good thing to put out into the world. It's not included in the list of 'desired skills' on a job listing for an editor, but as it so happens, it's the skill I've used the most during my 10 years in digital media, publishing personal pieces. *(PTO)*

Tom Rasmussen, 27

Tom Rasmussen is a queer, non-binary writer and author (*Diary of a Drag Queen*) who grew up in Lancashire and now lives in London. From explaining their gender pronouns to their parents, to being homophobically attacked, Tom's personal writing is some of the best I've ever had the pleasure of publishing.

What's the point of personal essays?

It's the hope that a bunch of people who share an experience can see themselves and feel themselves in what you've written, so that they don't feel so alone. I spent a lot of time thinking it was a really selfish idea and then realizing it's not. It's so lonely to be young and queer, and what you need in that situation is to know that there's something better out there. That has to be the intention – for the kids, goddammit! I know I write about my experiences and people might think that's self-centred, but – and this is going to sound so unbelievably self-centred, lol – I'm actually the least self-centred person. I hate self-centred people, it's a reprehensible trait. No one is interesting enough to take up constant space. Maybe the Dalai Lama or Mandela, but that's it. It's okay to be introspective, but if you're going to write something personal, it has to be for other people, it can't be for you.

Why did you start writing personal stories?

When I was a student at Cambridge, I felt stupid because of where I'm from. I remember in my second year hearing English students talk about a 'practical criticism' paper. I was a second-year Cambridge student, but at that point in my life I still thought criticism literally meant 'Hannah is wearing a bad dress' or 'John looks fat'. I constantly felt intellectually undermined, so I made oversharing my 'thing'. It was a reaction against all the people who were full of wanky twee sentiments, talking about Nietzsche at dinner – which no one really wants to talk about. Well, maybe sometimes, when you're bonged from a Fanta can and you're getting wily and wild, maybe then you want to talk about stuff in an abstract way. But I felt so isolated by the constant discussion of ideology and [by] its non-relation to the real world, because so few people there had been in the real world. I'm not saying I've been in the 'real world', but I've been closer to it than most of the people I met at

Cambridge. And then I ended up getting off on doing that. I was made to feel a lot of shame growing up where I did, in a Catholic family at a Catholic school. People called me 'faggot', I had lemons squeezed in my eyes on the bus, fags put out on my skin, rocks thrown at me. I got spat on in the face by these two boys who would wait for me at the school gates in the morning. So I think being hyper-proud of everything and hyper-honest about everything released me from those pits of shame. Online I get a lot of people messaging me saying, 'I could never say that out loud but I'm so glad that I'm not alone in that.'

Do you regret anything you've written?

I regret some lines I've written here and there, but generally no. What was it Lily Allen said? 'I don't want to look back and think, "I could have eaten that".' If everything is built on a consequence-regret basis, I would never have done any of the stuff I've done already. I've not done anything remarkable yet, but I have had the sex that people talk about wanting to have. You know, I've been gang-banged by 15 men in a Berlin bathroom and loved it. And I've been tied to a St Andrew's cross in the back of an Asda van and driven around for an hour and had my genitals whipped by a dom builder. I'm that person. And I'm so happy I am.

How have your friends and family reacted to you writing about your life, and sex in particular?

It's all about you being fine with the experience to the point where nothing that's said about it can hurt you. There are things I don't write about for that reason. I don't write about sex with my boyfriend. I don't write about loads of stuff. But with my mum reading graphic details in the sex stories I've written, I just say, 'I haven't done anything wrong, this is your judgement.' And she says, 'Okay, but it's a lot for a mum to read,' and I say, 'But it doesn't have to be a lot, we don't have to be like other mums and children.' Sometimes I hope she doesn't read things, but somehow she always bloody finds it and does.

You've written about boys kicking you in the face at school for being 'too gay', and then you wrote a funny punchline. Do you feel obliged to make it funny – to make readers more comfortable?

I definitely don't think that adding a punchline works for everyone, but for me ... I don't want to sit in all that homophobia I had when I was young. I don't know what value that has to me. I can't sit with my trauma too much, because it makes me want to cry. I'm welling up now. In that joke I said, 'they beat me up because I was too gay, and frankly, I was too gay'. But the last laugh isn't on me in that joke, the last laugh is on them.

What do you think of the idea that journalists feel they need to sell their trauma in order to be successful in the digital world?

There was a time about two years ago when I was writing a lot about being homophobically attacked. I had a feeling for a while during that time that my only value in the media was my trauma. I was never going to be asked to report from the front lines of any war. I was not going to be asked to write a factual piece because my voice in the media is deemed untrustworthy, so all I could write about were my traumatic experiences. I'm sure a lot of people who belong to marginalised spaces feel that too. I put my rent aside and thought: 'Wow, if I hadn't been hospitalised three months ago, I wouldn't have been able to pay my rent this month, and what value does that leave on me?' That was hard. At that point I made a pledge to myself. I remember thinking then that what I really wanted to do was talk about the wonderful things and show how funny life can be. To be self-aware, and to show how hard life can be, but also to show how iconic and great it can be, because that is the way to ultimately undermine people who want to hospitalise you – not to talk about how much they hurt you, but to talk about how amazing life can be for people like us. When I think about where I would like to sit in my career, I just want to be someone who has made other people like me feel really good, and like what they've always thought is wrong with them, is a gift, and it makes them fucking funny and interesting, and it makes them a really great person to have at a dinner party. Or whatever party you want to go to, I don't really like dinner parties. I think there's more value in writing about these experiences than writing a factual news report on what happened in parliament today. I mean, of course you need to know that shit, but god it's dry. That's why I write personal essays – because I'd much rather talk honestly.

How much do you really want your colleagues and bosses, or future colleagues and bosses, to know about you? In the digital age, this question has evolved to become: How much do you want any stranger on the internet to know about you? I think it comes down to how helpful your experiences can be to others. And to how you'd feel if your personal essay went viral – or if the only three people who read it were your mum, your future boss and a stranger with whom it resonated deeply.

We all engage with personal essays and stories from strangers every day online, without giving much thought to the process. 'Is it raw? Is it emotional? Can I see myself in it? If yes, thanks for sharing; if no, fuck you for wasting my time with your boring life story.' That's how a lot of readers approach personal essays they see on the internet, and I've literally seen this narrative play out hundreds of times: I publish a personal essay, I watch the traffic go up, then I watch a large percentage click off the page, deciding it doesn't relate to them and they don't care, while a small percentage continue to the end of the piece. Then I see three dots in the comments section under the article where the reader is typing their opinion, telling the writer exactly what they think of them, which is sometimes the most incredible heartfelt admiration and sometimes the most hateful word dump.

We read these stories every day, but we rarely stop to think about what it's like for the people writing them, who might spend ages reading the comments, who might have a huge argument with their parent or partner after it's published, who might have written the piece three years ago when they were unwell but they're better now and they don't want to go over it again. As one of the gatekeepers of the internet, I've thought about all these things in great detail and about how I should manage them responsibly. The digital generation is much better at talking honestly than our parents', and that's our greatest strength, but talking honestly on the internet is a lot more complicated than you might think.

What advice would you give to your younger self starting out on social media?

Make something tangible out of this – quickly.

Where do you think you'd be without social media?

I wouldn't be in the same position I am now without the amount of followers I have on social media. But that also left me feeling like I didn't deserve a lot of what was given to me through it. It's what people refer to as 'clout', I guess, it gets you places without you actually putting in the hours learning a craft to get there. I was given a lot of opportunities because of my social media status that I wasn't necessarily ready for. Maybe I was, I don't know, but in my mind there was a lot more work to be done before getting to that stage. It makes people feel entitled, you know? And for what? You are quantified solely by a number.

Have you changed the way you view social media?

I stopped using social media altogether for roughly a year and it helped me regain my confidence, which I had almost lost completely. It was therapeutic to be present in the real world, rather than constantly overstimulating my subconscious with thousands of images. We don't need to see that much of other people's lives during our day. We should be focusing on, and trying to enjoy, our own.

INDIA ROSE, 26, ARTIST

SOCIAL MEDIA +

LEISURE

NAOMI
Living my best life

According to social media, so many of us are out here 'living our best lives'. But what does that even really mean? Like a lot of viral internet phrases, it feels hard to know exactly how/when it began. 'Living your best life' is a subjective concept, but on Instagram, it seems pretty homogeneous. It is a caption usually attached to an image that includes a conventionally 'perfect' body in a swimsuit, a 'perfect' plate of food and a fabulous destination. It's a competition to show who's out here living and indulging in the most outlandish, extravagant, appealing, out there lifestyle choices. Peak capitalism at its finest. When used in this way, it specifically focuses on the end result, while ignoring what it took you to get there. You can't see all the late nights you had to pull at the office or the canned beans you're eating for months after you come back from a trip because you can't afford to eat anything else. I think we can pretty much guarantee that nobody's posting a copy of their overdue credit card bill that they might've used to make that trip happen in the first place.

When I travel, most of the time it's not glamorous. If I'm not travelling for work I'm usually booking the cheapest ticket, trying to squeeze in as many outfits into a way too small bag and I'm definitely not staying in a 5-star hotel. I don't always choose to show that part of the process, as it doesn't exactly photograph well and it's just not interesting. I'd like to think that to be one's best self means to have felt all the highs and lows it took for the internal growth and awareness to happen to get you there in the first place, and there's no room on the internet for that. So many of us get down on ourselves by worrying that we might not be 'where we wanted to be in life at this point'. Now, it's not just our professional lives where we're feeling this crippling anxiety but it's our personas and our out of work lives that need the upgrade, too. I think we need to deeply question which power structures are responsible for moulding these thoughts into our minds. So many of us are constantly trying to live up to standards that have been dictated to us, not by us, for things we may not even truly want. Let's not forget how much we differ from each other. That everyone's 'best' is not supposed to be the same, especially when it comes to our out-of-work time.

Travelling has made up the fabric of my life and I've often looked at travel as my biggest teacher. I've used it as a way to try and incite emotion, to not only feel wonderment, inspiration, but maybe even as a semi-permanent transformation of self. Thanks to it, I am highly adaptable, I'm great at being alone for long periods of time and feel comfortable talking to anyone. Over the last few years social media networks have completely changed the way I and so many others travel. I've been in so many situations where someone has seen me post something about where I was visiting on social media and connected me or directed me to something/someone that completely changed the scope of my trip. I've made lasting friendships, stayed with people's grandmas, on their sister's bedroom floor, eaten unforgettable meals and had experiences that were completely priceless, all thanks to social media. There are so many things about a person you can't understand without seeing where they live and how they've grown up. Doing so allows us to see someone in their true state and helps us connect on a deeper level. But sometimes, sharing these things on social media has the capacity to change those places or those people forever.

Best-kept secrets

Summer is my season. July is my birthday month, which makes me a little cancer crab who feels most at home climbing rocks and floating on the surface of the blue ocean. Last summer I was lucky enough to spend some time in the glorious city of Marseille in the south of France. Walking around the city, I could feel the faint humidity coming in from the ocean, not a single closed-toe shoe in sight. The cutest children were rolling down the hills on their skateboards, sometimes sat on them two by two. The streets were adorned with fruits from the different fruiteries and mini markets with a million delicious things squashed into them on every corner, where you're permanently hit with the waft of cheese and pizza dough, the unofficial scent of Marseille. Locals were sitting and gathering around the edges of the different coves and marinas of the city-front ocean to drink rosé out of chilled plastic bags whilst the sky delivered the most magical of sunsets to mark the end of another beautiful day in the south. One of my all-time favourite activities is to watch people whilst they watch the sunset: their expressions, their sense of peace and of presence never fails to affect me deeply.

I was sitting down with my friend Maia, who is from Marseille and who was acting as our most fabulous tour guide, when she kindly shared that she had planned something special every day for us. She was taking us to all her local spots that she had frequented since she was a child. One of those days, she took us to what might be one of the most stunning beaches I've ever been lucky enough to go to. The water was a glistening pool of sapphires, so warm, so welcoming. A few tiny bungalows glittered on the mountainside. Time stopped. We floated around for what felt like hours. I took a photo of the beach itself, found the correct geotag and posted it on my Instagram. I lay back down on my towel, grabbed another fig and as I bit into it, I thought twice. This place was special. It felt like a secret. Maybe I shouldn't have done that? I grabbed my phone back out of my sand-filled beach bag to delete it when Maia put her delicate little hand on my shoulder and said in her never not alluring French accent. 'Naomi – can you please do me a little favour? Do you mind deleting this location? So many people are coming to Marseille now and we just need to be careful.' She was totally right.

Marseille was changing rapidly. It is a city that in the past has often been demonized by the rest of France for being 'dirty', 'dangerous' and full of 'immigrants' after gaining a reputation in the past for its drug-trafficking fuelled violence, which was often reported on French news and depicted in French rap music. This is an image the city has struggled to shake up until recently, but there's just been a big wave of gentrification, spurred on by cheap rent, an influx of cultural investment and a new high speed train from Paris. All this meant that this magical beach was at risk of not being the same next summer. I shared a responsibility to at least try to keep what is special to Maia, to me and to anyone else, in any way I could. I quickly apologized and tried to explain that I had just had that same thought, I felt a little embarrassed that I shared it in the first place. Some places really are sacred, sacred for different reasons to different people, and should be kept that way. How many places have we ruined, disrupting their natural rhythm and eco-system by putting them on the 'gram? Because I have a social media following I know have to be more careful about these things. I have a social responsibility to not share what isn't mine to share. I've had several people write to me to tell me that 'they've done' my holidays and copied trips I've been on. But, on the other hand, have many locations and thus local businesses also flourished by putting them on blast? It's a weird call to have to make sometimes, and I'm just not sure that there's a right answer here. I feel like it's a case by case, trust your gut situation.

Join the dots

When I think about how I've benefited from social media when on the road, I have to think of the time I spent in Sao Paulo, Brazil, all by myself, for 3 weeks. I was researching a personal project exploring the deeply rooted Japanese-Brazilian 'Nikkei' community there, and the help I received through social media ended up facilitating that whole trip. I posted about it on my socials and before I knew it, I got connected with so many Nikkei people, of different generations, with so many beautiful stories to tell. I went to their homes, met their families and visited them at their places of work. They shared countless touching stories on what it felt like to grow up in both of these often very contrasting cultures. Someone who followed me on Instagram reached out to me, asking if I had somewhere to stay. I ended up staying with them for most of my trip. To my amazement their home was both thoroughly Japanese and Brazilian at the same time. We ate rice-based meals to a soundtrack of loud and base-heavy Brazilian funk. Through this one kind-hearted soul-enriching Instagram follower, I felt a sense of safety and family in a city I had never been to before.

Having a fairly large social media following means I've benefited even more from the privilege of a social status that has opened a lot of (literal) doors for me. But I also have to remember that some of the experiences I treasure the most have been with complete strangers, people who had no context for who I was or what I did, people who weren't contracted to any kind of exchange in social currency. A look that said everything. A small gesture of kindness. 'Small talk' that became 'big talk.' Conversations that were able to happen because I wasn't rushing or caught up in the daily grind that the metropolitan cities frequently force you into. It was about the 'right' line I stood in. The 'right' seat on the plane. The 'right" bus I jumped on. So many of those magical times took place when I wasn't lost in the screen of my phone.

One of the most magical of all these was with a wonderful woman called Maria Ines, who I met on the side of the road in the tropical north of Argentina. We had both travelled up from Buenos Aires to see one of the world's biggest wonders, the Iguazu Falls. The biggest waterfall in the world. A group of us were sitting on the side of the highway, waiting for a bus that clearly wasn't coming. Maria swore about it to herself in Spanish as she threw her arms up in the air in frustration. Dressed in a purple tracksuit and a pair of Birkenstocks, she was nothing short of fabulous and I immediately decided that I wanted to become her friend. I asked her in Spanish if she was going to the Falls. She replied that she had wanted to, but clearly that wasn't in the plan for today. Right on cue a taxi stopped for us, just as my arm had started to go dead from holding it out for so long. I asked her if she wanted to come with me, she nodded, while letting out a big sigh of relief, and we both climbed into the backseat.

We were there at spring time and the thick green jungle that surrounded us was the most luscious kind of nature I had ever laid eyes on. The air was thick with humidity, my favourite kind of air, tropical and wet. It was butterfly season and as we drove to the falls the car was completely surrounded by hundreds of multi-coloured butterflies guiding us on our way, escorting us to what felt like the literal road to heaven. We were both gasping and shrieking, like two small children, clapping our hands in overwhelming excitement in the backseat. As we turned a sharp corner, my body slid into hers and we giggled.

Her phone kept ringing but she kept silencing it. As she did so she shared with me that her family back home were really worried about her coming up here alone. At 78 years old, the simple act of walking had got much harder of late. She now walked with a cane and because of this, her family had begged her to wait until someone could go with her. They were right to worry - walking around the falls in the heat was strenuous and could be really dangerous due to some parts being so slippery. But waiting around for an escort wasn't Maria Ines' style. She wanted to go back to the falls and she wanted to go now. "I could be dead tomorrow' she cackled as she threw her head back almost hitting her head on the back window of the car. 'What a hero,' I thought to myself.

As the car pulled up, I somehow felt so connected to her and didn't want our interaction to end. I told her there was absolutely no pressure for her to say yes, but if she'd like me to, I would be happy to keep her company on the hike. Just in case it might reassure her family that she'd be okay as she'd be with someone. To my delight, she told me she'd love that. We called her son back to tell him not to worry. She explained to him that she had found a friend and passed the phone to me. I introduced myself and tried to reassure him that I wouldn't leave her side and that I'd drop her off at the hotel on my way back to mine. He thanked me and we promised to check in with him later.

We were now not only on a path to the falls but a path towards what felt like real kinship. All day we spoke and exchanged many stories about our many trials and tribulations, love and heartbreak, as we held hands while trying to avoid the mossy and slippery spots. She told stories about her days as a young political activist and how it felt to be not only a mother of three grown-up children but grandmother to 7. She took scenic photos with just me in, and we got someone else to take ours, too. She even kindly held my bag for me while I got on a boat by myself that literally took me underneath the waterfall. To my dismay, when I got off, I realised I had stupidly left my phone in my back pocket and it had got drenched and had broken. I got off the boat devastated and annoyed with myself. Maria gently comforted me like my own grandmother would've done. She sat me down, and tapped me on the top of my head, whilst she told me that she had only just got a phone 3 years ago and she had had a beautiful life without it. For a second I was about to be that annoying girl who wanted to insist that we were living in different times now, but then I stopped to think, and really, you can't argue with that, can you? Maria was my living, breathing reminder to stay not only grateful but to stay present.

Halfway through the day, she suddenly pulled me back to whisper in my ear and kindly alert me to the fact that my period had started. OF COURSE IT HAD! And of course, I had nothing with me to use or cover up my now blood-stained, very short denim shorts. We went to the bathroom and she perched on the sink counter next to me as I failed to scrub out all the blood. She told me not to worry, that she had a solution and grabbed her rainproof jacket out of her bag and tied it around my waist. 'TA DA! Ya estas bien!' (You're good now!). I looked at our reflections together in the bathroom mirror, smiled and walked out with her. What a funny couple we made. Me in my bikini, free-bleeding, with my new friend Maria, decked out in her outerwear, laughing wildly, just two free gals on the road. We walked for as long as she could. I treated us to a canoe ride down the river on our way back so we could bird watch and talk from a more comfortable seated position. I literally keeled over laughing as she explained to me on the boat that I had been using the Castilian Spanish word *coger* as 'to take' all day, but that in colloquial Spanish it means 'to fuck'. I think I actually died there and then. I realized that I had been saying this word in the wrong context for more years than I was ready to acknowledge. 'I'm fucking a train' etc was a phrase that had come out of my mouth, for years. We laughed so much that my ribs were hurting for days afterwards. I dropped Maria off after we had dinner on the way back to our consecutive neighbouring hotels, and wrote down our respective details on napkins from the restaurant so we could stay in touch.

How could I even begin to share this depth of connection on social media, even if I had had a phone? These vivid memories are etched deep into my mind and heart forever. After she had got back home to Buenos Aires, Maria Ines's son emailed me to say thank you and sent me some photos and a video we had taken on her phone. The photos were blurry and discoloured, but it didn't matter. They were perfect. Ironically I ended up posting one of them on Instagram, as what felt like a reminder to myself to not always stay so glued to my phone. The picture didn't need to be 'perfect' for it to have meaning.

Has social media changed the way you travel?

Yes. I am cognisant of taking pictures that will translate well on social media. I find myself documenting for other people more than for myself.

PAULINA PINSKY, 26
WRITER AND TEACHER

Do you feel like your idea of 'free' time has changed in the age of social media?

I tend not to post a lot of personal things online to begin with, but whenever I see an exhibition or go somewhere beautiful or eat something especially delicious, I feel the urge to tell the world about it, which isn't very in keeping with my fairly private persona. I have to rein it in and remind myself that I treasure the space I've created, in which my free time belongs solely to me, and I have no one to answer to.

AMANI AL KI, 27, JEWELLER AND MAKER

Sometimes I feel like photographing something is my security blanket. A blanket that reassures me that just by flicking through the gallery on my phone I can remember that moment forever. But does this so-called security blanket make me take in the world differently; how does it shape my memories and determine what's worthy? Is there a right or wrong way to remember something?

Not only does the incessant need to photograph everything when we're travelling take us away from being able to be present on these journeys, but when we're taking so many pictures we don't necessarily stop to take a moment to reflect about whether we are taking these pictures responsibly. How we photograph and share these photos can portray a country or a sacred space negatively, or have other damaging effects. That moment of pondering becomes especially vital when travelling to emergent nations with less economic power. It's important that we keep asking ourselves the overarching question, 'If you couldn't take a picture, would you still be here?'

As someone who's had a cross-continental childhood, travel has made me, but lately with the influx of Instagram trophy travel culture displayed all across social media I've been trying to figure out how I can move through the world not only more responsibly but more consciously. Travel writer Bani Amor writes:

Travel is a vehicle to explore the condition of living, how our relationships to place shape us and our experiences, how our identities and political histories inform place, how power structures inform how we migrate (or don't) and how that affects the places we pass through. How we move through the world, whether it's how we or our ancestors came to be where we are now, or to countries we have no connections to but are guests in, varies phenomenally from person to person, but we have to understand those journeys are all informed in some way by capitalist imperialist patriarchal white supremacy. That we need to be real about where we came from, how we got there, where we're at, and where we're going. It is a moving conversation between the ways that we are privileged and the ways we are oppressed, because places, like identities, are not static; they are always in a state of flux.

As someone that has the privilege of getting to travel a lot, whose feed glitters with images from all around the world, I realise how complicit I am in this kind of activity. I'm trying to unlearn and relearn how to interact with these places holistically and ethically in a way that doesn't feel like we're just using them as backdrops for our photos.

Here are the questions I think we should be asking ourselves when taking photos abroad:

- Do you genuinely want to see and wholeheartedly experience the country that you're visiting? Or do you just want other people to see you're there?

- Are you interested in really connecting with a country's culture in a respectful way, or showing off for social capital?

- When you take a photo, are you trying to capture something meaningful and specific about somewhere?

It can be hard to get to the crux of answering some of these questions, but as Amor gently reminds us: 'The minimum we can do is remember that we are guests, who need to listen, be present, and make sure our resources are going to the people whose land this is. That we are outsiders looking in. That knowing where we are, where we're coming from, and where we're going is already anti-colonial.'

Dance like EVERYone is watching

Dancing had always been this huge love in my life, but it was something I stopped pursuing as a teenager because I felt like I had failed at it. That because I hadn't got to a specific level of ballet, passed that one exam, gone to that performing arts school, that dancing wasn't for me anymore. That I shouldn't – or worse, that I couldn't – dance because I wasn't 'good' at it anymore, which was so silly because obviously, first of all, how are you supposed to get better at ANYTHING if you don't do it and secondly, why couldn't I just do it for fun?

Dancing, to me, now feels like something primal that I need to do to survive. To connect to your body, to use it and to be free in it is the purest thing. *Every* body can move. Bodies moving to music is just simply the most magical alchemy. To dance for no one but yourself. Like nobody's watching. That, to me, is freedom.

Dancing as time goes on, is an extension of me educating myself about my body. It's taught me to love it for its functionality and its possibility for expression. To see it in motion, to see it sweat, to see it learn, to see it change, to see it be being sensual. In our society we are starved of spaces in which to publicly express our sexual energy, where it's not thought of in a sexual context. To watch someone express themselves in motion can feel like a political act. It breaks the cycle of rigidity that society often imposes on us. I can't help but believe the world would be a totally different place if *everybody* danced.

It's been exactly two and a half years since I walked back into a dance studio for the first time in my adult life, feeling a very specific mix of nervousness and excitement. I started filming videos of me dancing almost as soon as I started going to class again – recording myself just for me to watch my progress. Even though for the first six months I could barely pick up any choreography, I was having so much fun it didn't seem to matter. I loved watching the videos back, it didn't matter if I was messing up because there was an innocence about just trying and I couldn't hide the joy exuding from my face

I started posting the videos online. Initially I did it for fun, but as I delved deeper, I started thinking about how it could be another way of furthering the conversations I had been having for most of my career – about self-love and exploring our relationships to our bodies – and it was so much more poignant, visceral and real than just doing another interview about these subjects.

The videos started getting traction, and quickly became the most-watched things I had ever uploaded onto social media. I would post one and go to bed, and overnight thousands of people had watched them. I had never really thought about how people would engage with them. I guess it's just more fascinating to watch someone not be 'perfect' at something, to watch someone learn, and maybe that's why people loved them so much. It just proves that there's a powerful vulnerability in someone trying something new, and you get to watch them grow.

So many people since then have written to me or come up to me in the street and told me that watching my dance videos makes them feel good or that it's inspired them to start dancing themselves. I've gone to different dance studios around the world, and I've had people come up to me in class and tell me that they started going there after seeing my videos – and if making a handful of people feel just a bit more free in their bodies is what I've achieved, then honestly that is the most positive thing I've ever done online. I've seen dancing completely transform so many people right in front of my eyes. Especially when it comes to talking about self-acceptance and body image. When people write to tell me that its aided them in learning to love their bodies for the first time through dance, after a lifetime of hating them, I feel like it is such a beautiful thing that I've been able to share.

But as of recently, I've been starting to feel there is a flipside to all of this for me. The performative nature of dancing has started to make me feel that I want to keep it more private. Movement to me is one of the biggest antidotes to a life online. It forces you to put your phone down and be more present, but if your goal is to record yourself to get a good video to post on social media, does it take away one of its greatest benefits? Because I can't deny that trying to get a good take sometimes ruins my dance process. This need to document every aspect of our lives reminds me that social media is just a giant constant performance that so many of us are compliant with. It's a line I toy with often, if I should share something I love so much publicly, but maybe if I love something so much, does it deserve to stay private? To just enjoy something for what it is, in that sacred moment in time?

I often think about how and at what point my personal leisure time became public. Why did I feel the need to share it with the world? Have I been brainwashed by the general narcissistic culture of social media as well as these purposefully addictive apps? Once again, thinking about all of this while writing this book has made me step away from my phone and reassess my relationship to this technology. I find myself asking more questions and trying to consider what I post online a little more: Why do I feel the need to share this? Who am I posting this for?

I'm now actively trying to take back my life, to divert solely from giving all my time to the attention economy. I want to be able to be more present doing the things I love to do, whether I'm alone or with the people I care about. To take back these moments so that they're truly mine again. As a small measure of change, I've stopped geotagging exactly where I am, and now tend not to post in the moment as the rest of the world really doesn't need to see my every move, just as I don't need to know everyone else's.

I often worry that these apps have turned us into full-time surveillance agents and wonder whether how we can all post and equally follow each other more responsibly? When I think of the phrase 'leisure time', that should mean free time. A time to be free. Does your free time feel free? Do you?

Do you ever feel like you're performing your free time?

Well 'performance' is an interesting word – as I'm literally performing dance routines on my social media! However, it is not a fake version of my social experience. It is way more authentic than that. I really get uncomfortable if my motivation is just soliciting other people's reactions. Sometimes you just want to show your friends what you've been up to. Or, admittedly, to get boys to fancy you.

**FRANCESCA GAVIN,
WRITER AND CURATOR**

Do you ever feel influenced
by leisure influencers
(travel, fitness, or food)?

Food, yes. It's my favourite kind of porn. But that
just makes me want to get in the kitchen and cook,
not run away from it.

CELIA BURTON, 29, MAKE UP ARTIST

RUBY TANDOH ON CREATING BEAUTY IN NORMALITY

By now, it's clichéd to warn that the lives we see on the internet aren't necessarily faithful to reality: we already know that the selves that populate social media are curated and fragmented, just as the foods that we document online are snatched moments of beauty, at odds with the humdrum of beans on toast, dry cereal, juice from the carton, burnt stuff, canned tomatoes. A ray of light hit an Aperol spritz just so, for a minute, before someone spilled a beer down your back. Half-truths, parts of lives, plates of food that didn't taste as good as they looked. We already know this – we know it because we each, all of us, are seasoned curators of reality, both as it is and as we would like it to be.

But the fakery itself is less important than the fact that even this fakery, the creation of beautiful, wealthy, well-fed, happy fiction, is not an equitable resource. Those who have more are more able to fake; those who have less are more entrenched than ever in the resolute plainness of a normal life. How much I document my culinary life on Instagram is directly correlated with how much money and time are available to me at that moment, the quality of whatever flat I'm renting, the state of my mental health. Sometimes, that desire to curate and perfect – to present the most pleasingly aestheticized version of my small and samey world – is just too much on top of life itself. The problem isn't so much the food, but everything that surrounds it: a flash of scabby carpet, the chipped kitchen countertop, that stain on the wall that might be tomato sauce, or might not be, and is best not to think about.

Worst of all is the light. We all live under the same distant sun, but it doesn't bathe us equally in its glow. The sun filters through traffic into a little flat, passing dimly through tiny windows and dog-eared rattan blinds; the light in a fast-food joint pours down cold and bright from the strip-lit ceiling; the glow of a restaurant kitchen is artificial, the air close. Insta-food is not just beautiful food, it is an abundance of natural light, big windows, greenery, photogenic tableware, the luxury of being able to photograph an entire, beautiful scene. Even a bowl of cornflakes can be beautiful against a weathered wooden table; in a Ratatouille bowl from Disneyland, in a grungy kitchen, under the sickly glow of a 40-watt bulb, saffron risotto looks dismal and bilious.

No matter how resourceful the artist, or how clever they might be with angles and lighting, food styling and the use of props, the fact remains that beautiful gastronomic Instagram feeds are not always an option. Just as the Marie Kondo-ing of a life presumes an excess, and the freedom to strip back and leave behind, so a foodie Instagram feed requires a surplus of foods, of moments, from which one can curate and organise the best. When there's no choice, there can be no 'best'.

But none of this is to say that there isn't something valuable, even vitally human, in what food historian Doreen Fernandez describes as the 'impulse to beauty'. To not only look for, but actively create, contrive and consume moments of unusual pleasure or beauty – this is a necessary, life-affirming act. And it needn't be a luxury: be mindful of the pleasing weight of a Creme Egg in your jacket pocket; fan out your fries just so; choose the fattest, fullest sandwich in the Boots fridge; peel an orange in one long strip; watch the steam rising off a mug of tea.

When she writes about the impulse to beauty, Fernandez is referring to Filipino pastillas de leche – chewy milk sweets that are wrapped in bright, colourful papers with long, elaborately cut-out paper tails of flowers, names, patterns and butterflies. The wrappers come off in an instant, cast aside in the pursuit of sweeter pleasures, but they are as treasured as the sweets themselves. 'Why not cover them in colour, in ornamentation, in beauty?' Fernandez says. 'Why not enjoy that fleeting moment at a fiesta, within the gaiety, but before the actual savouring of the sweet?' Even when a food moment has its roots in the staid, boring rhythms of the day-to-day, we can still endeavour to create beauty in the normality. These moments may be photogenic, or they may not. But they are ours, if only for a few seconds.

And those stunning food moments that we can't access or recreate ourselves – those lifestyles drenched in sunlight and framed in beautiful kitchens with tiled floors? We can savour those too, even if – especially if – they aren't ours. We don't need to take social media's contrivances at face value, and nor do we need to dismantle every falsehood and fakery that graces our phone screens. Nothing was ever more aptly named than the Instagram 'story': these are parts of lives, curated moments pieced together to form a narrative. These are the foods that tempt, titillate and inspire, precisely because they are perfect, fake moments, unbounded by the strictures of real life: avocado arranged in whorls and ripples on toast; a stack of pancakes, unfeasibly high, maple syrup pooling on the plate; a coconut with a straw in it on some white sand beach, far away.

'Why not make one moment beautiful?' Fernandez insists. 'Isn't it worth the trouble?'

Ruby Tandoh is a food writer and author of three books including Eat Up: Food, Appetite and Eating What You Want. *She firmly believes there's no such thing as bad ice cream.*

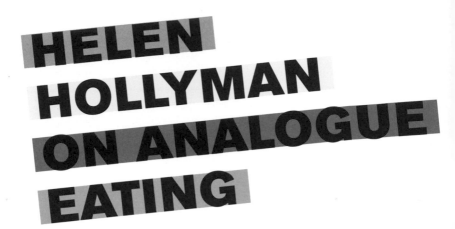

HELEN HOLLYMAN ON ANALOGUE EATING

Rainbow bagels. Art-directed cheese pulls. Avocado toast at #brunch. Latte art with your French bulldog's face on it. I'm just as guilty as the next person when it comes to the compulsion to post porny food photos on my Instagram feed, even when – more often than I'd like to admit – the dish tasted like wet blanket but was more photogenic than the item that tasted like a dream and resembled vomit. I am a Taurus who indulges in the hedonistic earthly delights because it's in my nature, but if I follow the logic of nineteenth-century foodie/glutton Jean Anthelme Brillat-Savarin – 'Tell me what you eat and I will tell you what you are' – then I should throw my phone into the nearest Vitamix blender and turn it on full blast.

Our addiction to food porn and visually appealing, decadent foods is nothing new. According to a study conducted by the Cornell University Food and Brand Lab, people have been metaphorically swiping right on succulent meat and crusty bread over boring vegetables for the past 500 years. And we're not stopping this impulse anytime soon. After analysing 140 paintings from five countries that contained 104 different foods, the lab's research revealed that even though lustful depictions of sausage and fluffy bread loaves were in high demand during key periods like the Renaissance, the most frequently painted foods did not reflect the commonly eaten meals of the time. Instead, aspirational cravings such as shellfish and artichokes (really?) were painted with reckless abandon. So much for those monochromatic pink breakfast bowls and oozing triple-decker bacon and mac'n'cheese-stuffed burgers being a daily routine.

Eating is one of the last non-downloadable sensory human experiences we have to cherish. We're living through an era in which it is impossible to not feel as though social media is overhauling our relationship with traditional forms of leisure. There is much more for us to digitally sift through before diving into what's on our plates. Platforms such as Instagram and YouTube have helped push the cultural phenomenon of the 'foodie' – a term coined in the 1980s to define the kind of person who is not as elitist as a 'gourmet' but is more discriminating than a glutton, who eats not out of hunger but as a hobby – into a global phenomenon. If we are, in fact, what we eat, how is our relationship with social media impacting upon our collective social consciousness and changing our appetites?

Social media is a temporary boon for food culture. Platforms like YouTube are the all-you-can-eat salad bar for discovery, where the culinarily challenged are able to learn advanced knife skills in five minutes. Instagram is a communal space where respected chefs, restaurateurs and food artisans can share ideas and engage with one another and potential customers, all without meeting in real life. And these platforms are spaces for self-reinvention for power armchair-experts – like Kim Kardashian's best friend Jonathan Cheban, a long-time publicist turned self-proclaimed @foodgod on Instagram, who curates his own culinary criticism to 3 million followers despite having a food background as sparse as a Soylent evangelist's.

We are all active participants in the attention economy, and when we follow influencers, no matter their trade, we're buying in to their capitalistic feeds that include #sponsoredcontent, reminding us of their financial incentives for curation that also simultaneously give us FOMO. Authenticity exists in a new ecosystem that doesn't want to nurture it.

At the same time, without these new technologies, global food culture could never be democratised. It's generated new revenue streams for chefs cooking in remote areas once labelled 'off the beaten path', like the now YouTube-famous 'Lunch Lady of Saigon', who serves a different noodle dish from her roadside stand every day of the week and receives millions of views. It has birthed fresh, thoughtful voices and personas, like the viral sensation and Turkish restaurateur 'Salt Bae', who has over 22 million followers on Instagram. Nusret Gökçe (his actual name) has become internet-famous for his signature Liberace-like seasoning technique: raising his fingers up to his scalp line and sprinkling medium-rare rib-eyes and prime rib with a blizzard of sea salt that mostly misses the target below. This move is something that would get you 86'd from professional kitchens, but this absurd entertainment is the kind of hospitality that makes us all buy in to the show on our digital devices.

A few years ago, I was speaking with French chef Jacques Pépin about the contemporary pressures that young chefs and cooks face in the celebrity-obsessed restaurant industry. Pépin, who started cooking professionally at age 12, was trained to conform. The goal was to create identical dishes to those of the line cook next to you, mastering the skillset of critical sensory elements that the internet fails to teach: the sound of chicken skin sizzling at the specific pitch that tells you it's just reached juicy, succulent perfection; the way a medium-rare steak bounces to the touch; the tension of an oyster knife right before it pops open the shell's hinge, like picking a lock. For Pépin, we live in an era where young people in every element of the culinary industry are pressured to put 'their signature' on their products and to stand out as individuals.

The average person who has access to a smartphone device spends 1 hour and 40 minutes each day on social media platforms. We're watching more culinary television but cooking less than ever, so why do we feel compelled to document and share what we're eating with online strangers we might never meet in real life? Social media may not be the villain of our leisure world, but it is an invasive species to our ecosystem.

As we adjust and control our individual relationships with social media – no matter how far artificial intelligence or the latest technology changes mankind's recreational time – Mother Nature always has her way of regaining the upper hand. Climate change is here and threatening our cravings, from juicy pork buns to almond-milk lattes, medium-rare hamburgers and goblets of natural wine. Despite the scientific research that's warning us that, within the next 20 years, warming temperatures will wipe out all fish, desolate most meat sources and make it difficult to source coffee, wine or assemble your favourite cheeseboard, I choose to be an optimist. Let's lean into the analogue with leisure. The next time you find yourself at a meal with your favourite people or blissfully alone, skip the bluefin tuna roll and leave your smartphone at the coat check.

Helen Hollyman is the founding editor-in-chief of MUNCHIES, *the world's first global millennial food platform. She almost became a marine biologist, but after religiously watching* Two Fat Ladies, *decided on a career in food instead.*

Does looking at other people's lives on social media make you feel like your life isn't interesting enough?

I feel this to a degree when I see certain designers or artists whose accounts are a blend of their personal and professional lives – they seem to always be up to interesting things, and it feels like their personal life is an extension of their brand in a way that sometimes makes me feel totally inadequate. I don't understand how you can hold yourself up to these insanely high standards (always looking polished, stylish, involved in cultural happenings; always travelling, always working, always being impeccably articulate about everything, always being surrounded by equally interesting and hot people).

AMANI AL KI, 27, JEWELLER AND MAKER

Do you ever feel influenced by leisure influencers?

Sometimes, but mostly they just annoy me. I've got three kids and these insta-moms preaching from their perfectly clean and tidy Notting Hill houses about going plastic free and buying from Whole Foods is maddening. They never acknowledge the fact that they can afford to preach.

JEN, 35, CONSULTANT

'In order to be successful, one must project an image of success at all times.'

AMERICAN BEAUTY

SARAH

When it began, social media was the land of the free, an egalitarian platform where anyone in the world with an internet connection could be seen and heard on their own terms. Quite naturally, the most interesting ideas, the biggest personalities – and, inevitably, the best-looking people – rose to the top. Then, at some point, someone opened the door to advertising and a portion of those individuals who had an above-average following went from being casually influential to commercially influential. Though this shift was about business, it changed the tone of social media for everyone, from democratic to hierarchical, and because of it, a gulf emerged between those posting pictures of their mates and their holiday snaps, and those modelling lifestyles. Once 'influencer' became not just a paid job but a mark of social status, people started buying followers and focusing all their efforts on building their personal brand, but for a long time it wasn't obvious who was doing this and who wasn't. Only in the last few years have guidelines been introduced stating that any paid posts must be declared with #spon or #ad, but the divisions go much deeper than that formality.

I finally understood the difference between using Instagram for fun and using it for work while running through a thick fog across the Golden Gate Bridge with 100 fitness influencers at the start of 2017. I'd been invited on a trip with a major sportswear brand as the one UK journalist, tasked with interviewing the social media stars and writing up the experience for the magazine I worked for. At that time, I coped with the stresses of my job by smoking cigarettes and binge-eating digestive biscuits, not by drinking green juices and smashing spin classes, so upon seeing the itinerary – which ranged from hilly 10k runs to HIIT workouts – I started to feel concerned about my sporting ability compared to these super-fit women who, on Instagram, appeared to be constantly running marathons and working on their ab cracks. I pictured myself finishing each run last, sweating and apologising profusely, while the influencers waited for me at the finish, chilling in the splits position. Turns out I needn't have worried, because while I was doggedly panting up the hills, they were stopping every few minutes for a photo shoot, and at times I found myself waiting for *them* – taking in the view, enjoying a green juice and reconsidering my vices.

A few of the influencers were injured and had decided not to run at all, but you'd never know it from their feeds, where they posted photos that made it look like they were sprinting to victory. These photos were created by running just a few steps or leaping into the air with a firm smile on their face, over and over and over again until they were happy with the shot, which they then posted on their feeds with captions like '1 run down, 4 to go!'. I already knew Instagram was an airbrushed version of reality, but I hadn't ever considered that the runner I saw running online might actually be stationary.

Later, driving around San Francisco, I was with a smaller group whose energy – if not infectious enough to reach me – was endlessly impressive. They took it in turns to film videos for their social channels in the bus, and the second the camera turned on, their charm turned up – laughing, smiling, talking enthusiastically to camera about where we were and what we were doing. I was the definition of awkward in these videos – I felt like Louis Theroux at the swingers' party. I didn't know what to say or how to act, but I was aware I was supposed to act – to be loud and fun, like a breakfast TV host instead of a jetlagged journalist. Once it was clear I wasn't good in front of the camera, I was enlisted as a photographer and found myself crouching down on the street with six SLR cameras around my neck and six iPhones, trying to capture the women at their best angles as they jumped into the air and hugged each other. During quiet times on the bus, I'd watch them transferring files between cameras and carefully editing each image, trying to find the one shot in 100 options to post. This, I belatedly understood, was their job as influencers; and mine, I suppose, was to hang back awkwardly and observe.

At several points, it felt like standing in line and not being picked for the sports team at school. 'I'm the editorial director of a powerful women's media company,' I would remind myself when the brand photographers took them off to do a shoot while I was given a sympathetic smile that said, 'Obviously we don't mean you!'

'Of course!' I obliged, standing aside and offering to hold the bags and phones while they were shooting, like a mum at a theme park. It wasn't personal, it was business. Social media wasn't personal anymore, it was business, and I suddenly realised how weird it was posting photos of my mum with a Sainsbury's bag on her head in the rain or my mates at the pub on the same platform as these high-production images of athletes and models. When I got back home, I described the trip to my friends as akin to living inside Instagram and having the physical experience of being the person that gets 60 likes on a photo surrounded by the people that get tens of thousands.

A few months later, on a trip to Poland to write about a Polish fashion brand, I found myself rubbing shoulders with 50 more influencers – who had between 100,000 and a million followers each. Although on Instagram this set of new social stars appeared to be just as outgoing as the fitness lot, in reality they were almost silent, glued to their phones and leaving all the extravagant events the brand had put on for us as soon as they'd got the shot they wanted. I noticed in the car journeys that they liked and replied to every single comment under their pictures – often in the hundreds, which partly explained why everyone was so quiet. One woman I sat next to spent a good 40 minutes just double-tapping every single photo on her feed without even looking at the images, presumably so that all the people whose images she liked would like hers back.

When I started looking into travel influencers for this chapter, I noticed the same thing – that the influencer who posted the picture would reply to every comment saying 'Thank you' with the prayer hands emoji or 'I try to capture the soul of every place I go'. I also noticed that many of the commenters who were writing things like 'Such a cool shot!' and 'Never-ending dreaminess!' were themselves travel influencers – either established (with hundreds of thousands of followers) or aspiring (not many followers but with 'travel blogger' in their bio and posting similar content).

'The more comments you get, the more it boosts your engagement, which boosts your stocks, which means you can charge more for ad jobs because you can say "I get this much engagement per post"', Claire Byrne, VIP account director at influencer/talent agency ITB, confirmed to me over the phone. 'The most successful way to advertise is across the network, so influencers constantly verify each other by liking and commenting on each other's posts.'

One travel blogger just starting out told me she's part of several

Facebook groups for female travel bloggers in which you post the pictures you want to boost engagement on, and the other women in the group will like them and comment on them in exchange for likes and comments on their own pictures. I hadn't realised it was all so transactional.

Permanently on holiday in far-flung luxury locations – with captions like 'no bad days' and 'soaking it in' – the travel accounts I find in top 10 lists on the internet are at the extreme end of braggy #bestlife #hatelike influencer culture. Avocados and cocktails on the beach in Tulum; lunch served on a floating tray in an infinity pool in Bali; endless bikini pics by waterfalls with captions like 'grateful for this world' – it's all very *Ingrid Goes West*. At the top of the women's league, with 2.1 million followers, is @gypsea_lust – first-name Lauren. If you can get past the nautical take on the word 'gypsy', Lauren's feed looks like she's died and is running the social media for heaven. According to her blog, she's 25, has a 'deep passion for travelling & creating imagery' and loves documenting her picture-postcard life with her fellow travel blogger boyfriend, Jack Morris (2.7 million followers). They met in Fiji.

Lauren's is just one of thousands of accounts on Instagram where girls who look like *Sports Illustrated* models post photos of themselves in dreamy locations around the world, tagging the restaurants and resorts they're eating at and staying at and helicopter companies they're flying around Rio with, presumably for free unless they're all millionairesses who can afford to travel the world in total luxury all year round. The places and companies they tag tend to have between 5,000 and 20,000 followers, so it's a mutually beneficial relationship. It's the followers I don't understand. I see no hint of irony or acknowledgement of privilege on these accounts – unless you count #blessed. What are these millions of followers getting from hundreds of bikini shots on secluded beaches of pretty girls living their best lives without any explanation as to how they can afford to do it? I messaged a few to find out.

Jeannine, 15 and from Germany, told me she follows travel influencers because she loves looking at exotic places and because she would love to be a travel influencer when she grows up. When influencers reply to her comments, she said, 'It's a real fan girl moment for me, it makes me feel like I matter, and like they really care about me.' From the content she posts on her own account – standing at the beach with one leg forward and her hand on her hip, or walking on the sand holding the corner of her dress out and looking wistfully at the waves – it's clear Jeannine is imitating the women she sees online, hoping to live the incredible lives that they post. Where 20 years ago teenagers idolising a pop star had a very slim chance of becoming one themselves, the ubiquity of social media stardom makes these lives seem like a realistic goal – as if all it takes is 'a passion for travel'.

In the older demographic of commenters – and among those who weren't trying to be travel influencers themselves – I found Jordana, 32, who told me she finds the accounts aspirational, 'in the same way people browse in Selfridges but buy from their Topshop concession'. And another reason she follows influencers like Lauren and Nicole Isaacs (271,000 followers) is because: 'They're just good body inspo. On a very basic level, Nicole is just a much better-looking version of me: brunette and curvy. I suppose travel influencers play on our vanity as they feature themselves/their clothes/their bodies/their beauty as the primary content.'

Similarly, I found a few guys I know following Nicole and Lauren's accounts, and they said the only reason they're following them is because they find the girls' bodies attractive, not because they're interested in their travel tips. 'Isn't it ultimately just about girls in bikinis under a different guise?' my friend, a *Guardian* journalist, observed after looking at the profiles I sent her. 'They post a bikini shot every few photos. They'd probably lose loads of followers if they stopped doing that.'

As the VIP account director at ITB, Claire Byrne casts influencers for high-profile ad jobs, and she thinks it's more nuanced than boys liking girls in bikinis. I asked for her professional opinion on why these accounts attract a big audience, and where that love-to-hate feeling comes from.

Claire Byrne
VIP account director at ITB

What do you think of the bikini shots? Who's looking at them?

I think it's an even gender split. Of course basic boys like looking at fit girls because they don't have *Nuts* and *FHM* anymore. But equally, if you have a travel influencer who's really fit in a gorgeous bikini on the side of a ledge in front of a gorgeous sunset, so many girls would want to get that dream shot of themselves on their own holidays. So they like the picture because it's aspirational. Plus that shot is just peak Instagram fodder. If you were to sum up Instagram in four or five pictures, one of those pictures would be a bikini shot with a sunset.

I see travel influencers posting 'thanks @blabla restaurant for having me' and the restaurant has 7,000 followers and the influencer has 2 million. Should they be saying explicitly 'I got this for free'?

The FTC [Federal Trade Commission] guidelines say you have to be transparent and disclose everything, but people have managed to dodge that for so long. With all this #gifting, #borrowedby, #spon, #ad, etc., the lines are so blurred. I've seen more and more influencers writing 'I borrowed this dress' and putting #gifted because I guess people are now being watched, and being fined for not disclosing. It usually boils down to the influencer and the chances they are willing to take themselves. If you have a tangible product in your hand and you say in the caption 'Buy this shampoo', there's more pressure to disclose, but if you're just swanning around the world getting everything for free, it might be easier to brush it under the carpet.

Have you worked with any travel influencers who faked their content?

No one that's neglected to disclose. But there was an influencer who came to a festival with me a few years ago . . . She was a mega hun, she wore head-to-toe designer every single day. On the first day when we arrived at the festival . . . she just didn't enjoy it, she left after a few hours. Bear in mind the tickets, flights and VIP packages to this festival amount to thousands of pounds. Second day she said to me, 'Um, so I'm just going to shoot my content outside the festival and around my hotel because I'd rather not go into the actual festival, but don't worry, I'll make it look like I was there.' She made it look to her 800,000 followers that she had spent the entire weekend at the festival, posting pictures like 'omg can't wait for Beyoncé!'

Do you think she cringes at her own pictures?

No. I think lots of influencers really really believe in their brand. To the extent where they'd never consider letting go or getting drunk at a festival because that's not their brand. It's a bizarre existence, it's the constant curation of perfection. They seem to exist more online than they do in real life.

Are influencers here to stay?

I think so. The model in which they work will evolve. It's a new form of media: a new way we're being sold things; and a new way we engage with things. I think it will become much more transactional. I think somewhere down the line, we'll have two forms of social media. One will be retail social media – 'I want to go on holiday, so I'll go on social media and research it there and book it within the app.' And then friends, memes and lols will be somewhere else. Right now it's masquerading as one thing, but I think it will split.

How many followers do you need to be an influencer?

Micro-influencers, for the type of clients I work with, is anyone who has below 100,000 followers. Macro is probably over 250,000, which goes into celebrity territory anyway. The market has changed phenomenally in the last few years – so much so that our work is now probably split 50:50 between celebrities and influencers.

Why do you think people love to hate influencers?

You kind of hate the person sat in the VIP area of the club because you can't get in there . . . but you would go in if you could. We're so attuned to roll our eyes at somebody pulling up in a Bentley to the pub. It just feels a bit flash. It's natural to feel a bit jealous if someone has something that you don't, or has access to something that you don't. And I think it pisses people off that influencers get things without doing much to earn them, apart from having Instagram followers. Does anyone deserve a free holiday because they have Instagram followers?

Why do people still follow them?

It's the same as everything else. Why do people read magazines full of beautiful, thin people? Or watch reality TV shows full of really fit people? On Instagram it's a bit more in your face because it's constant. I don't think it makes us feel good, but we're drawn to these shiny worlds of aspiration.

In 2018, a luxury hotel in Ireland published a strongly worded reply to an email they had received from a young YouTuber asking if she (Elle Darby) and her boyfriend could stay for free for five nights in exchange for a tag and a shout-out on her social media accounts. Elle referred to her request as a 'collaboration', listing her follower count across platforms, and mentioning that she had set up a similar arrangement with a hotel in Florida, which she noted was 'amazing for them!' Incensed, the hotel owner replied:

Thank you for your email looking for free accommodation in return for exposure. It takes a lot of balls to send an email like that, if not much self-respect and dignity . . . Lucky for us, we too have a significant social media following . . . but Jesus Christ, I would never in a million years ask anyone for anything for free . . . The above stats do not make me any better than anyone else or afford me the right to not pay for something everyone else has to pay for.

Following the much-publicised reply, the influencer received a lot of hate, calling her a 'disgusting freeloader'. The hotel owner also received a lot of hate from her fans, who wrote bad reviews of his hotel online. One travel blogger I spoke to frowned when I told her the story and said, 'Doesn't he understand that's how it works now?' Elle's fans certainly didn't seem to mind; since the incident, she's gained 150,000 followers on YouTube and 100,000 on Instagram, and according to the number of #ads she posts, she's also found more than enough brands willing to 'collaborate'.

Social media privilege is a new kind of privilege, and like any other privilege it gets on the nerves of the non-privileged. There has always been an elite who have lifestyles that seem unfathomable to the masses – footballers, Hollywood actors, models, the royal family, and the children of all those people. In the past, we understood this elite – maybe we looked up to them, maybe we didn't, but we didn't think about them that often because they only existed on magazine racks or on TV. We had to seek them out. Now, thanks to social media, the elite has multiplied exponentially, and they're in our faces all the time. If anyone can be an influencer – i.e. you don't need to be good at football or born into a rich family, you just need an Instagram account and a photogenic face – then why isn't everyone? Why is there still an 'us' and a 'them'? It's the proximity of influencers that is frustrating: the fact that this life is presented as easily achievable, but just out of reach.

The younger generation still believe it's within reach. According to affiliate marketing network AWIN, 17 per cent of kids aged 11–16 now list 'social media influencer' as their desired profession, and 14 per cent list 'YouTuber'. When you see the lifestyles these professions afford – constant holidays, amazing clothes, hundreds of thousands of adoring fans who compliment you daily – it's not hard to see why. But while a proportion of these kids may well achieve their dreams, there will be many, many more who don't make the cut and fall into this 'Why them and not me?' existential hole that I find myself in as I scroll through Instagram.

'Travelling the world posting on social media is just never a reality for most people. What is a reality is saving up for a two-week holiday in Magaluf,' Juno Roche, a writer in her fifties who grew up in Peckham, told me. 'Teenagers now are looking up to Kylie Jenner, who's a billionaire, and so then they go "okay, that's my aiming point". My aiming point at that age was to try and knit a jumper out of mohair for the weekend. We wanted for far less back then, we expected far less, we assumed that our worlds were going to be much smaller. Social media is brilliant in that it opens everyone's eyes to the potential of the world and makes them think it's there for the taking. That's democratising, but at the same time it's not really. I think it's always going to be unfair to lots of people.'

Part of a collective called the Brighton 5, 18-year-old Lola Ray is on a mission to help younger teens cope with the negative feelings that come from social comparison online. 'I've worked with girls who are 14/15 who think the Kardashians are the best thing to ever happen,' she told me. 'I'm not going to pin all this on that family because there are loads more influencers who are much worse than them, but teenage girls are expecting this crazy lifestyle because they see it on social media.'

It's a global problem. On a trip to Kenya, I spoke with Roxie, a Kenyan woman who works for an LGBTQ+ non-profit in Nairobi. 'It doesn't matter who you are,' she said, 'you can be a little girl in Kenya following Kylie Jenner and suddenly the sum of your aspirations is to have a bubble butt.' Roxie worries about the next generation of Kenyan girls, who are growing up with social media and living in a country of extreme inequality. 'Influencer culture is just getting going here,' she told me, referring to the rising number of Kenyan social media stars who post about their Prada handbags and Gucci shoes and are followed by tens of thousands of girls.

At 34, Roxie has no aspirations to become an influencer herself, but she still gets pulled in to the lifestyles she sees online.

Roxie Odoyo, 34,

works for an LGBTQ+ non-profit organisation in Nairobi

How do the fitness influencers you follow make you feel?

At first you feel all motivated by these women who post saying they lost 100 pounds and now have rock-hard arms and bubble butts and six-packs – those before and after shots. But then after a while, because Instagram is constantly feeding you this stuff, you start to feel pressure to look like that, and then eventually you become resentful because you don't. Sometimes I look at these profiles and think, 'Maybe I don't actually want a six-pack and abs, maybe that desire was just planted in my head by you.' Your aspirations are fuelled by the things you expose yourself to. At first, these profiles conceptualise your aspirations, and then they remind you daily that you haven't achieved them. So it quickly moves from motivation to comparison to negative energy.

And then . . . you unfollow?

No [laughs]. Because there's a part of you that will always look for the aspirational. It's like a drug.

Aside from bodies and fitness, what else do you find aspirational on Instagram?

Property! Have you seen some of the houses that exist in this world?! You know why they say religion is the comfort of the poor? Because if there's something that you cannot picture yourself having in this lifetime, religion promises you that you will have it in some other life. You see these grand houses on social media, and you picture yourself living there, but at the same time you know it's unrealistic.

Do you dwell on that feeling?

I get over it quickly. But some people don't. Instagram offers a connection for people who are particularly isolated, either socially or psychologically, and it's very easy for those people to internalise what they are seeing on Instagram. For example, maybe you're not where you thought you'd be in life – in terms of career, finances, relationships, how you look, whatever – and then you see all these people on Instagram who are where you want to be, so you follow them not because it's something you believe you will achieve, but as a form of self-harm. It's like whipping yourself on the back for the things you haven't achieved. The epitome of that, for me, as a single woman, is #relationship – fucking – goals!

Is that a big thing in Kenya?

Yes! You're a single woman, you've been trying to date, you're under pressure to keep fit and look your best self. You follow this woman who is a bombshell and she has the perkiest tits and the tiniest waist and the bubbliest butt. And she keeps tagging her equally hot, rich, 'goes to the gym and looks like he carries her across the doorway every day' boyfriend. They work out together, they're both toned and tanned, they travel the world taking photos looking out at these amazing views. It paints a picture of a life, and that life starts to become your aspiration. It's like when Obama became president, everyone was like, 'Oh my god there's a black president! We all have a chance!' Digital influencers present the same dream – they have become celebrities, and being a celebrity has been an aspiration for the longest time because celebrities can easily obtain all the things that regular people work so hard to get. So people look at digital influencers, who are like celebrities, and they start thinking, 'Maybe if I do what they're doing, and take a picture like that, I can get as many followers, and I can have what they have – I can have three holidays in Bali.'

Roxie has one friend, Nenga, who isn't on any form of social media. Nenga's job in marketing for an advertising agency in Nairobi means she advises clients on how to build engagement on social channels, but personally she opts out. She told me she finds the way people behave on social media – even her friends – off-putting. 'I have a friend who is a travel blogger, and I love her, but every time I go on holiday with her, I want to kill her. She takes photos of every single moment. How about you just enjoy it?'

Nenga also mentioned a TV presenter in Kenya called Kobi Kihara, whose Instagram profile was full of amazing holidays, sunsets and #foodinspo. One of her followers thought they recognised a picture Kobi posted of a salad and did a reverse Google image search, which revealed the salad had been lifted from somewhere else. Then the follower reverse-searched her other images and realised that three-quarters of Kobi's photos were taken from random websites and Pinterest. A hashtag started – #KobiWithAnEye – where people posted captions about being on a luxury holiday when their picture showed they were stuck in traffic, in order to mock her.

Those witnessing the demise of Fyre Festival in 2018 had a similar chuckle at other people's expense. The music festival that promised the world and delivered cheese on bread, hosted by rapper Ja Rule and entrepreneur Billy McFarland (now serving six years in prison for fraud), Fyre quickly became everyone's favourite social media fuck-up story. It was supposed to be a luxury event to rival Coachella. Millennials paid thousands of dollars for tickets, expecting to party with supermodels, stay in lavish, eco-friendly tents and villas, and dine on gourmet food. Instead, they got disaster-relief tents with rain-soaked mattresses, and those slices of cheese you get in McDonald's burgers. All the music acts pulled out, the food ran out, the water ran out and there was no way off the island.

The hype had largely been created by a group of supermodels (including Kendall Jenner, Bella Hadid and Emily Ratajkowski) posting pictures promoting the festival on their feeds. Many of the mega-stars were flown out to the island to shoot the promotional video for social media, which saw them jumping off yachts, writhing around on beaches, soaring through the ocean on jet skis, swimming with pigs and generally having the time of everyone's lives. Of course the Instagram generation were keen to join – McFarland was right about that. Posting from Fyre Festival with a bunch of supermodels and aquatic pigs? Think of the likes!

Following the pictures of the disastrous reality posted by frantic, incredulous guests arriving at the festival whose only option was to take to social media to complain, Twitter erupted with memes and gifs comparing it to *The Hunger Games* and *Lord of the Flies*. The Fyre Festival hashtag became everything the live event was supposed to be: the most fun content experience ever. Taking the piss out of McFarland and Ja Rule for thinking they could change the world with an orange square on Instagram was one line of attack, but what really got the crowd going was laying into the attendees for having paid premium prices and believing in a social media dream.

'So to recap?' @Iron_Spike wrote. 'Some Instagram kids just paid between $450 & +$12k . . . to be stranded . . . in a tropical tent city. Cuz some models told them to.' @madelinekrebs wrote: 'So TGIF &

enjoy your low wage jobs today because at least you didn't pay $5k+ to be at lord of the flies train wreck that is #fyrefestival'. Meanwhile @ Paradawg said: 'I can't figure out what #fyrefestival is, but it seems like rich people having a bad time, which I fully support.' People relished the opportunity to tear down social media privilege and the new elite. 'It was like watching the bubble burst,' Claire Byrne commented. 'It was the first time, on a large scale, that we saw the social media/influencer world falling apart at the seams in real time. It was like *Black Mirror*.'

A year later, a Netflix documentary brought to light the devastating financial loss suffered by the Bahamian staff hired for the event – who never received payment – and that changed people's views. It was funny when influencer wannabes lost out, but not when a middle-aged Bahamian woman lost her life savings. Social media privilege collapsing in on itself was thoroughly entertaining, until it had real-world consequences.

Claire was referring to a particular episode of the TV series *Black Mirror*, one which made many millennials seriously consider deleting all their social media accounts. In *Nosedive* – set in a dystopian future where the higher your social media rating, the better your life – people rate each other on every interaction. So if you buy a coffee, you rate the barista who served you depending on how friendly they were; and they rate you back on how friendly you were. If you bump into someone jogging, you rate them the second you've run past them, based on how happy they seemed. Those with overall high ratings get promoted at work, heavily discounted apartments and tables at trendy restaurants that turn away those with lower scores. Within this 'like' economy, everyone is on their very best behaviour at all times – smiling, giggling, buying smoothies for people they've just met, spreading manically positive vibes everywhere they go – and they're liking everyone's pictures and profiles and commenting gushing things underneath. Other *Black Mirror* episodes veer more towards science fiction – nightmare situations about people stuck in a computer game or having chips implanted into their children – but this episode felt very close to home, set in a future very close to our present. It was hard to watch, because we're already living in a popularity contest where high-scorers get special privileges and low-scorers are willing to put aside their morals to try to scramble up, like Kobi Kihara did.

The episode ends with the main character (Lacie) having a breakdown in public and being dragged off to a prison cell. The online rating that she has worked so hard to build plummets to zero, and her phone is confiscated. Lacie takes off her top in the grey cell and sits in her bra, makeup smudged all over her face, watching dust particles representing the 'real world' fall. Then she sees a person opposite her, in another cell, and they start hurling insults at each other while breaking into smiles, because they've lost the game of social nicety and they're free to do and say as they please.

There is a verified way to spend your free time online. In my echo chamber, it's taking selfies, running, doing yoga, getting a round bum and an ab crack, going to Instagrammable music festivals, reading the same hip literature as everyone else, having the same hip liberal opinion on it as everyone else, and showing off your hard-earned buttocks in a bikini pic on holiday in a city that has colourful walls. Social media rewards the people who do this with likes, and likes become fame, and fame becomes quitting your job and becoming a travel influencer who gets paid to go holiday.

'Social media is a whole different layer of pressure – and on a massive scale,' Nenga said to me. 'It's not just the girl next to you saying, "why don't you go to the gym and get an Instagram body?" or "why don't you go on holiday to Tulum?" It's everybody on Instagram subconsciously telling you to be a certain way and look a certain way and do certain things. And you don't even know it's happening.'

When I lived in Buenos Aires in my mid-twenties, I smoked a lot because it was cheap – and so did everybody else. At a bar one night, I noticed this flash in the corner. It was a neon sign for Camel cigarettes that flickered just for a split second every now and then. I asked my very politicised (and prone to conspiracy theories) Argentinian friend Martina what it was. 'Subliminal advertising!' she said. 'It makes you want to smoke Camel cigarettes without knowing why. It's fucked.'

We scroll through so many images on our phones which promote lifestyles that become subconscious desires. It dawned on Roxie that maybe she didn't want a six-pack like the fitness influencers she followed had – that maybe that aspiration had been planted in her head. In the *Black Mirror* episode, Lacie spends all her time in Instagrammable places, but the only time she actually appreciates the view is in her grey prison cell watching dust. I've always found yoga difficult and boring, but I still find myself going to classes because the barrage of online images of women doing yoga has become my aspiration. We've all bought into a lifestyle we didn't realise we were being sold.

A survey of 1,000 people [*Schofields*] found that, when considering a holiday destination, 40 per cent of those under the age of 33 think

'Instagrammability' is more important than cost, food or the priority of previous generations: cheap booze. Roys Peak in Wanaka made headlines last year as the most Instagrammed view in New Zealand, with millennials waiting for their snap in a line dubbed 'the social media queue'. Our generation's version of 'getting away' (which is what a holiday used to be) from the digital stresses of daily life that we say grind us down has resulted in a queue to take a picture of a view to post online. The actual time we spend looking at the view with our eyes is a fraction of the time spent looking at it through our phones, and then through Instagram filters, and then as we're trying to come up with the perfect caption, and then while we're charting the post's success and replying to all the 'Wow, jealous!' comments people post underneath which make us feel superior, and influential.

When I look back on things I've posted, there's me doing yoga on an open deck that looks out at the jungle in Costa Rica with the caption 'Inhale love, exhale peace' and a prayer hands emoji. There's me posing in a red bikini with heart-shaped red sunglasses in a lake in New Zealand with snow-peaked mountains in the background, a photo I asked my boyfriend to take, instructing him on the angles. I wouldn't have asked him if Instagram didn't exist, or if I didn't feel, at that time, pressure to build my own goddamn brand.

These are the little pinches I feel sharing certain kinds of photos that I've taken with Instagram in mind: Can I really post this? Will people think I'm full of myself? Oh, who cares, everyone else is doing it. Repeat thought x10 until you hit Share. Then repeat thought x20 while you wait three painstaking minutes for the first like to arrive because the algorithm doesn't prioritise your content, because you're not an influencer. 'Everyone approaches it the same way as an influencer, they're just not successful at it,' my friend Sadhbh, a social media manager, said over lunch one day. Sometimes it feels good to poke fun at influencers, but isn't that what we're aiming for with our holiday snaps and yoga poses? If I really just wanted to share my holiday pics with my friends and family, I'd send them over WhatsApp, and I wouldn't include a posing bikini shot.

It's natural to look at travel influencers and judge them as vain and in love with the image of themselves in an infinity pool. But the reality is that these are the images social media rewards, and posting selfie after selfie is just good business sense. For some, it might have nothing to do with vanity and everything to do with stats. If I woke up with 500,000 followers and the option to travel the world posting pictures of my experiences – including one bikini shot in every four – would I?

Probably. It's a 'don't hate the player, hate the game' situation.

In her *SuperSoul Conversations* podcast, Oprah interviewed the spiritual leader Eckhart Tolle about the ego. 'What we most strongly condemn in others is usually something we also have – a trait that we are unconscious of in ourselves,' Tolle said. 'We become upset if we encounter somebody who is very greedy, or somebody who is dishonest [and] the force of your reaction usually tells you that [it is] something in you that you need to look at.'

As a journalist, I'm supposed to critically analyse, make judgements and exhibit a healthy amount of cynicism. Social media and lifestyle influencers provide ample opportunity to bitch, but at the root of my reaction is a question: 'Why them and not me?' Why do my bikini pics in lakes not get thousands of likes and earn me legions of adoring fans?

When I looked back at myself in that group video taken on the trip to San Francisco, I realised I was the one lacking. While I was panting up the hills, trying too hard and silently judging the influencers for stopping to take so many selfies, they were showering me with genuine encouragement and support. Perhaps the biggest lesson I learned – as I was laden with cameras, crouching down on the street trying to take photos of these super-fit women – was that there was a reason they were the talent and I was the observer of the talent. Social media doesn't make stars out of anyone, as it would have you believe; it makes stars out of people who are good on camera and have the ability to engage their audience in everything they do. That is a skill. We don't just hate the black mirror because it shows us a fake, unfair world where certain people who do certain things get rewarded with amazing lives. We hate it for showing us what we lack.

Does looking at other people's lives on social media make you feel like your life isn't interesting enough?

I do find lifestyle influencers' lives inspiring. But at the same time I find myself getting very upset looking at their profiles. The posts that really bother me are the home renovation ones, like 'this kitchen renovation is so stressful!' – it just makes me think: well, you can afford to buy your own house and renovate your kitchen into this beautiful interior magazine kitchen, I'd love to have that kind of 'stress'. There's a deluge of this content every hour on Instagram. Looking at these women, who I find relatable in many other ways – we work in similar industries, we're similar ages, we might even look a bit similar, I can't help but think it's just not fair; why do you get a house with William Morris wallpaper?

NATASHA, 31, MARKETEER

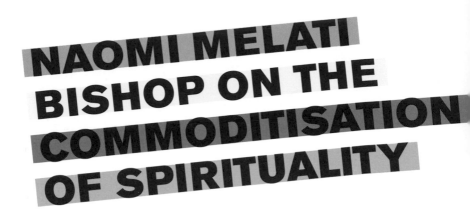

NAOMI MELATI BISHOP ON THE COMMODITISATION OF SPIRITUALITY

My dad convinced me to play hooky from college in 2006, so we could take peyote in our living room with a Navajo chief and a group of my dad's bohemian friends as a healing treatment for his cancer. Before that, he took me to a New Year's Eve party where, at midnight, we performed a seance to combat Y2K. Whenever I had a fever, I was wrapped head to toe in minced garlic to ward off evil spirits. These spiritual practices were routine in my childhood, but I had to be careful who I shared them with if I didn't want to be labelled a new-age weirdo.

Some would say that I am a quintessential millennial hippie. I'm tattooed with a lotus mandala; I'm a member of a drop-in meditation studio called MNDFL so I can indulge in a lunchtime emotions fix whenever I feel off-tune. I do sound baths, have participated in temazcal ceremonies in the Tulum jungle, have travelled 10,000 miles to seek advice from Javanese and Balinese Kebatinan mystics, and carry with me various elixirs and remedies and amulets. I'm even Instagram friends with my shamans.

I grew up frequenting temples and mosques and churches and sanctuaries and altars. My freedom to choose my faith enabled me to carve my own brand of spirituality, borrowing customs and beliefs from various religions and leaving behind what doesn't suit me. I dabble and never subscribe. I'm a spiritual dilettante.

Things have changed since my childhood. Nowadays, people are a lot more exploratory with their spirituality. My social media feeds are clogged with insta-spiritual posts. Fifteen-second sound bites of self-proclaimed healers spreading their newfound insights, one after the other, flash before my eyes at dizzying speeds. There's always some planet in retrograde to blame for our foul moods. I post a story about back pain and, within minutes, receive a fury of DMs prompting me to run to Flower Power for some cure-all herbs, a plant and herbal medicine shop in the East Village. But, lately, with the saturation of meditative, crystal-and-feather-adorned, tribal-poncho-wearing, back-bending selfies flooding my feeds, I find myself wondering about the ramifications of commoditising spirituality in our digital, hyper-publicised society. Does social media really give rise to mindful practices in our increasingly mindless world? Or might today's appropriated insta-spirituality be a broken, diluted form – just as fragmented as the very souls we are trying to heal? And how do we live authentically when #liveauthentic is trending?

Present-day secularisation has paved the way for a mass culture of self-tailored spirituality –and the commercialisation of it. The same 'new-age fluff' that people used to scoff at is now widely celebrated. Everyone from Madonna to Joey Bada$$ is forgoing diamond-drenched chains in favour of energy-transmitting healing stones. It seems that everyone is now visiting healers, becoming doulas, using flower essences, going to the Himalayas for meditation retreats, downloading Co-Star and Insight Timer, connecting with their animal totem, taking ayahuasca, or tripping out naked at Burning Man. These days, your 'vibe' is a more valuable currency than the money you have in your wallet.

So does this mean that we are all coming closer to enlightenment? Or is it simply hard to resist when insta-celebrities with large followings broadcast their spiritual practices? When I see an array of colourful stones ornamenting actress Nathalie Kelley's nude back, I'm dazzled, and I suddenly start to search for discounted 'chakra healing stones' on Amazon. Surely this isn't what Deepak Chopra meant when he said that he hoped to 'build a collective consciousness in the place where social media meets spirituality . . . to spark a global shift toward a more mindful future'?

While we previously turned to psychotherapy or the teachings of Gandhi or Thich Nhat Hanh for spiritual guidance, social media stars are the new gurus, the modern-day sage-burning metaphysical cheerleaders – moon maidens, mermaids, rainbow goddesses, star sisters, children of the sun – live-streaming and proselyting (possibly brand-sponsored) beliefs across platforms. The insta-spiritual world is laden with overnight experts. I can't help but wonder: since when did the socialite become a spiritual guru with more devotees than the Dalai Lama? If people with large social media followings started swearing by cobra blood or kambo (frog venom) as a means of transcendent healing, would we blindly follow?

On the other hand, the recent proliferation and accessibility of spirituality is what makes daily practice convenient in our fast-paced lives. Shaman Jon Rasmussen told me that social media accelerates and expands 'the overall reach of the wisdom teachings and practices. There may be no greater way to positively influence the collective consciousness . . . as a way of connecting the global village for the common good of all.'

Some liken social media to a return to the inter-tribal social networks of aboriginal humans, back from modern civilisation's trend towards increasing isolation. But I wonder what it is that drives us to share deeply personal practices in a public sphere. Is our motive to spread our newly gained spiritual knowledge, or is sharing how #blessed we feel just another way to brag – like showing off your #ootd – so that we can feel some semblance of purpose or identity? The problem arises when we turn to social media both as a vehicle for healing, and to fulfil a certain need for approval and veneration.

Buddha said: 'Peace comes from within. Do not seek it without.' Yoga instructors who post images of themselves in advanced, body-contorting poses might say: 'All of the support and love has really pushed me.' But the drive to master something – especially yoga – should come from within, so that we are in fact mastering something for our own good rather than for the outpouring of external validation. We can't possibly be letting go of our egos if, while meditating on the beach, we're also anticipating how many likes we'll get, thereby getting more personal satisfaction from the ego-aggrandising external validation than from spiritual practice itself. Would some of us even be doing yoga if we couldn't prove it on social media?

But while social media can present an inaccurate portrayal of the real-life dedication involved in mastering self-awareness, there is undoubtedly a strong link between mental health and mindfulness. With daily practice, mindfulness can change brain circuitry to treat anxiety, depression, substance abuse and chronic pain. This is why, nowadays, mindfulness has become a staple of many forms of psychotherapy.

'Social media trends reflect the human condition,' said Deepak Chopra. 'We can cause devastation worse than any war through making diabolical use of the social networks, or we could bring the world together in the direction of peace, harmony, sustainability and social justice.' Shaman Jon Rasmussen echoes this sentiment:

To me, there is no difference between the birth of a new species in the Amazon and the birth of a new technology in Silicon Valley. It is all Nature, and it is wild, untameable and dangerous like the jungles, the volcanoes, the oceans and the animals. So let us not succumb to fear, but instead be courageous in the face of an ever-expanding wild and untameable co-creation that includes social media as an outward expression of the spiritual capability we all have.

The idea of social media being an unstoppable force, a valuable tool in expanding our worldview, resonates with me. After seeking insight from various shamans, gurus and muses, I turned to myself to ask why social media's role in spiritual growth makes me so uneasy. I suppose it's unsettling to think that the soul-enriching and life-saving activities I've long valued could be a fleeting trend.

But by posting spiritual experiences – regardless of our underlying intentions – we are ultimately promoting a global culture of peace, not violence. We are celebrating self-evolution, not stagnancy. We are advocating healing, not inflicting pain. The willingness to be an open book and expose fragility takes depth, strength and courage – and also encourages others to be more open. How we decide to use social media is in our hands.

So before I use the hashtag #blessed or post a posturing selfie, I'll check my own ego, think about the motive and do it more mindfully, in the hope of always being the most authentic expression of myself – on or off social media.

Naomi Melati Bishop is a New York City-based writer, editor and educator. Her parents—a Javanese countess and a poet/activist father—met during her father's journey to Indonesia using stolen, around-the-world plane tickets.

SOCIAL MEDIA +

RELATIONSHIPS
♡ ◯ ◁

'What you learn out of context is only going to destroy you.'

SARAH

1. Digital paranoia

One of my favourite Greek myths is the love story of Orpheus and Eurydice. A young couple in love, he's a legendary lyre player and she's a rare beauty. While running through a forest, Eurydice gets bitten by a snake and dies. Grief-stricken, Orpheus turns to his lyre and plays with such sweet sorrow that it touches the gods, who tell him to go to the underworld and bring Eurydice back from the dead. On his way, Orpheus uses his lyre to charm Cerberus, the three-headed dog who guards the gates of the underworld, into submission, and then to soften the all-powerful Hades, god of the underworld, who agrees to let Orpheus retrieve his love on one condition: that while he is leading Eurydice back to the land of the living, he must not look back at her, even for a second, or her soul will be lost forever.

Orpheus agrees and his lover is passed unseeingly to him. But on their journey back, a few steps from the exit, he loses his cool, the temptation is just too great; he looks back, sees it was Eurydice after all, and then watches her vanish into the darkness. If he hadn't looked back and had trusted that the woman he loved was behind him, they would have been together forever. So why did he? Orpheus's strength is that he understands people's emotions and is able to control them, charming even the sternest of gods with his musical talents, but his weakness is that he cannot relinquish control – he cannot trust the world enough to help himself. Some years ago, a tarot reader presented me with the Orpheus card in the 'relationships' part of the reading. The card bearing his picture is called 'The Fool', because it was foolish of him to look back; he knew better but he did it anyway. I laughed

Has social media ever made you feel paranoid in a relationship?

Yes, because I feel like modern men always have their eye on the new and the next and Instagram facilitates that.

LYNETTE NYLANDER, 29
WRITER, EDITOR AND CREATIVE

when I got this card, because in all of my adult relationships I've been Orpheus, unable to resist the temptation of looking.

While Orpheus only had one chance to be a fool, the digital age presents a whole host of constantly evolving opportunities to check that your partner is faithfully behind you. Just like Orpheus, I'm good at understanding people's emotions, but I mistrust the online world. To put it bluntly, I think walking through the underworld without looking back is like never reading your partner's phone when they're in the shower – officially the most common way people snoop – and never looking up their ex, or that person from work they keep mentioning in such a way that makes you wonder. It's never clicking on the page where you can see whose photos your partner has 'liked' recently. I don't actually know how to do that last one, but the teenagers I work with tell me it's a thing. ('When your boyfriend likes another girl's picture – ohhh, that's cold,' is how Lesley, 18, put it.) In reality, 'liking' photos of an attractive stranger on Instagram isn't so different from smiling at one in the street; it's just that technology allows you to find out about the first one, and that is a new experience for humankind.

When there's genuine cause for concern, which we'll get to later, monitoring digital behaviour is statistically an effective way of catching someone cheating. A survey of 2,400 people who had either cheated or been cheated on found that 41 per cent of the infidelities were discovered by snooping on a phone. But first, let's consider the irrational digital paranoia, which the majority of snooping falls under: when you don't seriously suspect foul play, but you go hunting anyway, just in case. Reading a partner's phone or online 'stalking' people they have been romantically connected to is embarrassing because it feels petty and childish. Even the word – 'snoop' – sounds embarrassing when said out loud, conjuring an image of a cartoon cat creeping on tiptoes to steal the cream. Grown-ups are supposed to be secure in themselves, trusting in their relationships and respectful of each other's privacy, but the internet hardly nurtures these qualities. Instead it breeds insecurity, offering streams of information that never used to be available, all on a screen in your pocket. It begs us to look, to keep clicking, scrolling and digging. Doesn't it?! The secure among us – who would have lived happily ever after with Eurydice, having not even thought about looking back – won't relate to much of what I have to say. As the relationship guru Esther Perel put it in a talk titled 'Jealousy & Modern Relationships': 'For some people, it's a non-issue. For some people, it's a big issue.'

Unfortunately, it's an issue for a sizeable chunk of the coupled population. Two-thirds of students at a large southeastern university in the US confessed to reading their partner's messages and logging on to their social media accounts to check their activity [*American Psychological Association*]; 84 per cent of the students who responded to the survey were female. It's understandable for this age group to be more possessive and jealous, as university is often where people meet their first loves and everyone has a lot of time on their hands. But research shows that, for a significant number, online snooping continues into married life. In a study of over 2,000 married couples analysed by the London School of Economics, 20 per cent admitted to online snooping – including reading a partner's messages and emails, and checking their search history. That 20 per cent was mostly wives checking up on their husbands, not the other way around. Whether it's centuries-old stereotypes (and movies depicting the eternal bachelor/cheating bastard and the disastrous 'spinster'/scorned woman) that have caused women to become more probing than men, or a genderless animalistic instinct to watch out for threats, I don't know, but most of my female acquaintances of millennial age have at least one tale of digital paranoia, while most of the men wouldn't even know where to look. 'Men tend to live in the moment more than women,' offered my mum, 65, while sat at her laptop doing her accounts. 'For women, the present isn't just the present, it's a combination of the past and the future.'

The past has always had the capacity to be just as haunting as the present. In Daphne du Maurier's bestselling book *Rebecca*, published in 1938, the protagonist and narrator, described repeatedly by herself and others as a plain woman, is haunted by her husband's dead ex – the stunning, vivacious Rebecca. Since she never has the courage to ask her husband about the ex, the narrator builds a picture of his past life in her mind, a picture which turns out to be wildly inaccurate and which, in turn, destroys the purity of her own relationship with him. She pieces together fragments of information: descriptions of Rebecca's beauty from those who knew her; her elegant handwriting in books and letters; her exquisite taste in interior design on display in the house; her clothes still hanging, implying a tall and slender body. Something always holds the narrator back from asking – pride, fear, an inferiority complex – but her thoughts are unceasing.

In the second season of *The Crown*, our very own Queen gives in to the temptation of looking when, after finding a photograph of a beautiful ballerina in her husband's luggage, she decides to attend the ballet and see what she's up against. This instinct to check out the competition – past or present – is nothing new, but the immediacy and ease with which you can do it in today's world means it's pretty much a given that you will.

If the narrator of *Rebecca* had been around now, she would've had a field day. Since the launch of Facebook in 2004, we've been able to see through time, cities and walls into memories we didn't share, nights out we didn't go on, and into the shiny ponytails of girls we've never met. With a few strategic clicks, I can arrive at photo albums that my partner's ex tagged them in, containing 76 photos of their first couple's holiday to an all-inclusive in Sharm El-Sheikh, with captions like 'Falafail!', as well as 'So proud of you' posts for doing whatever they did to make each other proud that day; whatever it was, I vow never to do. At this point in the search, the (rather submissive) rational side of my brain tells me to stop, but I always choose to click on, getting whatever the opposite of a dopamine hit is.

My first online arch-nemesis was B, my university boyfriend's ex-girlfriend, who Facebook informed me went to art college, which immediately put my back up because... I was also arty. I'd just started going out with the 'hot boy' at uni, and my friends and I decided to have a nose on Facebook one night in my halls room, finding this creative waif with waist-length blonde hair who only ever wore leggings and crop tops because she was one of the handful of people worldwide who looked good in American Apparel. I ended up going into exactly the same niche profession as B, and would make fun of my boyfriend for having such a specific 'type', secretly rejoicing when I realised from online searches that I was ahead of her on the job front. (And also when she cut her waist-length blonde hair?! Shame on me.)

A year after my relationship with this guy ended, I saw the mythical B in real life at a fashion show we were both covering for work, sat on the other side of the catwalk. Like me, she was sitting alone and pretending to be on her phone – as everyone does at a fashion show – until she caught my eye and I smiled at her and she smiled back, clearly recognising me too; and I thought it was so funny how long I'd spent looking at photos and feeling jealous of this nice girl sat opposite me, who in any other situation I'd have been friends with because we really did have a lot in common. At one point, she sent me a friend request, presumably accidental though maybe not, and I felt like giving her a hug. Instead I clicked 'Decline' in a final pointless victory.

The past is a morbid curiosity and, while it's torturous, it's usually a finite resource: you consume the content, you feel a bit sick, you compare yourself for potentially years until the petrifying moment you actually meet the person and realise they're just a normal person, like you, but probably less mad, and then you think about all those hours you wasted worrying about them and decide to move on without telling anybody because it's too complicated to explain at this point, but the relief is overwhelming.

Present-tense paranoia is a slightly different ballgame, though still involving the same wounded-ego feelings. It could be that your partner has texted their friend about fancying someone else, or maybe they've texted a girl whose name you don't recognise, and you can see the messages have been deleted but the fact they texted them is still there. These kinds of micro-infidelities, if you can call them that, usually aren't deal-breakers – but they are enough to plant seeds of doubt, and to scratch at your self esteem. I found that same university boyfriend discussing over text whether to cheat on me with a devastatingly attractive Swedish contestant from *Shipwrecked* who was pursuing him. What I gleaned from the discussion – while said boyfriend was in the shower and I was on his phone – was that he had chosen me, but that the decision had been an agonising one since she was so hot (indeed famous for it). While I was relieved he hadn't been unfaithful, I still found myself crying into her Google images and scanning social media for further evidence of connection for, oh, at least a year after.

Since people are rarely separated from their phones, snooping on one is a high-risk, time-pressured activity. Once you've cracked the pin code (the long game), you have approximately five minutes to scour five apps, which must be left in the precise condition you found them in, open on the same banal group chat. It can feel like a game, like *The Crystal Maze*, in which you enter a room and try to solve a cryptic puzzle in the time it takes for the sand to funnel from one half of the timer to the other. Then, in the next level, you have 30 seconds to emotionally deal with whatever it was you found before your beloved comes out of the bathroom, and either gather your thoughts enough to confront them or else swallow the sick in your mouth, pretend like you haven't seen what you've just seen, and suggest with psychopathic calm that you start a new series on Netflix – one that is preferably less dramatic than the scene you just wrote into your own life.

In the past, I've played out the shower scene and gone looking simply because it's more interesting than not looking, because I'm bored as well as paranoid. According to Canadian psychiatrist Dr Eric Berne, who wrote the 1964 hit book *Games People Play: The Psychology of Human Relationships*, we play games in relationships because, on some level, we feel satisfied by the negative feelings that they stir in us. 'The reason

Have you ever looked up somebody you've been romantically interested in on social media?

Every single time.

PAULINA PINKSY, 26, WRITER, TEACHER

people play games is that they get certain satisfactions from them,' he explains in a very weird video interview from the 1960s in which he and the interviewer are sitting in race car. 'Usually the satisfactions are rather odd – possibly even gruesome. The satisfactions are things like guilt feelings, anger, hurt feelings, fear, feelings of inadequacy. It seems strange that people would want to get those feelings, but they do.'

As social animals, we're hardwired to play games, and it's that psychological tendency that developers of social media apps exploit. Tinder does it most obviously with the swipe right or left function, but all apps – with their bright colours, attractive features and infinite scroll capabilities – are designed to draw us in. Describing himself as 'an expert [in] how technology hijacks our psychological vulnerabilities', former Google design ethicist Tristan Harris is on a mission to warn the social media-addicted population of the various ways their emotions are manipulated online. Harris says that the most widely used social media apps are designed like slot machines, using gambling psychology and a reward system. Like Pavlov's drooling dogs, we look for positive rewards on social media in the form of likes and matches; and – bringing Berne's theory into the modern day – we also look for negative rewards like micro-infidelities, because on some masochistic level we find them just as satisfying. Using social media to play games in relationships and find answers to questions we wouldn't ask out loud is, obviously, a terrible idea, but we do it anyway because we'd rather find some painful half-truth on our phones than suffer the humiliation of vocalising jealous or irrational thoughts.

In 'The Millennial Question', a video interview about millennials that went viral (11 million views on YouTube), author Simon Sinek criticises this age group for hiding behind phones in this way, particularly in relationships. 'Everything you want, you can have instantaneously,' he says, talking about getting a date from dating apps or buying a product online that arrives the next day. 'Everything you want – instant gratification. Except job satisfaction and strength of relationships. There ain't no app for that. They're slow, meandering, uncomfortable, messy processes.'

I've been using technology to answer my embarrassing questions in relationships for the last 15 years because it was there, and because it provided enough answers over that course of time to convince me it was a helpful resource. 'As if a person's search history and text messages say anything about who they are,' reasoned Barbara Volkar over the phone. Barbara is a psychotherapist who has a particular interest in the complex issues surrounding infidelity. When I asked her if there is an element

Have you ever looked up somebody you've been romantically interested in on social media?

You must always research! I look up my romantic interests, I look up my friends' romantic interests, and I even look up strangers' romantic interests when I'm really feeling nosy. I think the effect of finding someone's digital life, or lack thereof, is always relative to the person.

KIMBERLY DREW, 29, WRITER, CURATOR AND ACTIVIST

Has social media ever made you feel paranoid in a relationship?

Absolutely, yes. There are few things more unsettling than watching someone who owes you a text message posting on Instagram or Twitter. You tweet and text from the same device! Answer me, please!

KIMBERLY DREW, 29, WRITER, CURATOR AND ACTIVIST

of game-playing involved in online snooping, she answered, 'Yes, yes, yes! Humans play games all the time. There's always something going on unconsciously – but that's fine.' If a client is continually, irrationally (my word, not hers) snooping, though, Barbara thinks it points more towards an anxiety disorder than a taste for games.

Barbara Volkar
Psychotherapist

Is digital paranoia something that comes up in your sessions with clients?

I see a lot of young women, and I hear a lot of stories about 'digital paranoia'. It's never an isolated symptom, it's always in the context of larger anxiety issues, so when I hear about this sort of thing, I immediately think, 'Okay, this is an anxiety situation.' Maybe there are also trust issues or attachment styles.

What are 'attachment styles'?

There was an experiment called 'the Strange Situation' in the '70s, where a psychologist observed infants and their mothers in a specific situation. So the mum and the child are in a room with lots of toys. Then the mum leaves the room, and a stranger enters. If the child has a secure attachment to the mother, i.e. they're generally happy and content and feel that their needs are consistently met by their caregiver, then the child plays happily with the toys in the room, feeling they have a secure base from which to venture out and return to if there are any problems. While the child may protest a little when the mum leaves and the stranger enters, they're basically fine and continue playing in the company of the stranger, safe in the assurance that their mother will return. When she does, they happily greet her and continue playing. That is secure attachment, which is, like, a mythical thing that no one ever has these days . . .

I think my boyfriend has secure attachment . . .

Good! It's good to be with a partner who is secure because it's the best

---

way to learn. The fact you've already chosen someone who has secure attachment means that you're changing.

So what happens to the insecure children?

Regardless of who is in the room, the anxious/avoidant/insecure child doesn't venture out and play. The avoidant child doesn't react when the mum leaves or when the stranger enters, and when the mum returns, the child just ignores her completely because the child is so used to not being seen or acknowledged – they feel they can't rely on their caregiver. The avoidant child appears calm and not in distress, but the people who ran the experiment also studied the heart rate of the insecure children, and realised this apparent calm isn't real, it's a mask for distress.

This is what you take into relationships later on. From the outside, the insecure or avoidant person in the relationship might present as perfectly normal, fine, happy and able to really connect to loads of people, but actually, internally, they will never attach. If you have this issue, you're constantly looking for signs of the other partner's intent. That's where digital paranoia comes in – in the same way the insecure child doesn't interact with the mother, the insecure adult doesn't talk directly to their partner about what they're feeling, and instead looks outside for signs of 'Are they about to leave me?' as a way of protecting themselves from being hurt. It may seem like crazy behaviour but essentially it has one function, and it's the same as the child's reaction in the room when the mum comes back: the child is just trying not to get hurt. At that age, you don't know how to calm yourself down, you don't know how to soothe yourself, and if the caregiver hasn't modelled that, the whole nervous system of the child goes into hyperarousal; they can't deal with stimuli and they shut down.

So these issues start early on in a person's life, not when they start using social media?

It's not the internet that causes it. Nothing in itself is inherently good or inherently bad – it's all about how we use it, and what we use it for, and that's true of any behaviour, including how we use the internet. A securely attached person will use the internet completely differently from an insecure/anxiously attached person. The question should be why are we 'producing' more dismissive or anxiously attached people who engage with the internet in this way? My hunch is this has more to do with parents being present, or rather not being present (because of work, or putting kids into the educational system too early, or the parents' own attachment issues) than with the rise of the internet. Every person has an adult self, which is how you respond in the here and now – it's your appropriate response. Then there's your child self, which is how you were as a kid, and all those experiences that you couldn't process as a child – like traumatic events and feelings that were just too big to cope with – they go into your child self, and that is what governs you in times of stress.

Do you advise clients who snoop on their partner's phone to tell them they've snooped?

Not necessarily, no. There's this weird Hollywood idea that we all have to be radically honest with each other and totally vulnerable all the time. I don't think radical honesty is the way to go in a relationship at all. In fact I think it's complete rubbish. Can't we just be with each other and accept that there are parts of each other that we will never know completely? Then when you do disclose something, it actually has real meaning and it can actually further the relationship and increase the intimacy. There's this assumption that we should all be intimate all the time, which is not the case at all. If you're sharing everything and being intimate with everyone all the time, then that's not real intimacy.

So how do you accept this secret world that your partner has?

There is a part of you that is known only to yourself, and your partner has a part of them that is known only to themselves, and you have to allow them to have that, otherwise you risk the quality of the relationship. This has always been present in relationships, but at the moment the internet allows you to 'look into a person', supposedly, as if their search history or their text messages say anything about who they are. Your sexuality is your most personal part of you, and if you want to be a complete individual, that part of you is yours, and it's no one's business what you do with that part – as long as you are in an adult consensual relationship where you have agreed what the boundaries are in some way.

How do you set boundaries?

I think we're worse off if we don't have that conversation and we just assume that we're going to be in this absolutely monogamous relationship without defining what that means for us two specifically. Do you look at porn? And am I okay with that? You can decide what the boundaries are, what you're okay with and what you're not okay with. I don't think you can say what's normal and what isn't normal. To have a part of you that is flirtatious or texts other people on the side or even meets other people on the side, or even has sex outside the relationship, that doesn't always break the bond, it just depends on the boundaries you agreed upon. We are really changing as a society in terms of what we feel is appropriate or monogamous. But it's hard to get to that place in this culture because very strict monogamy, i.e. 'don't look at other people, don't desire other people', is still the norm. And it just fuels anxiety.

Why do we make up stories and fill in blanks for things we don't know?

You can't help but do it. Narratives or 'scripts' are how you interact with yourself; it's how you make sense of everything in your life. Maybe the narrative is 'I am always abandoned', and therefore you always look for clues that will help you confirm that you will definitely be abandoned. So that's what you see – and that's all you see. There's loads of research looking at how people react to external stimuli – visual, audio, everything – and the results show that you only let things in that fit your narrative; you will literally see what you expect to see.

The main function of therapy is becoming aware of what your rigid narrative is, and then slowly, as you develop a relationship with a therapist, they can help you make connections and realise, 'Hey, maybe I don't always get abandoned.' You develop some flexibility. And then, after that, a whole part of the narrative gets replaced with a new one. In a safe therapy environment, you can actively rewrite this script for yourself – you have the capacity to do that. It can be the therapeutic relationship, but for some people what rewrites that narrative is just a secure attachment that they happen to have with someone who is more secure than them. I think it was Freud who said that love and psychotherapy are the only two things that can really change you.

In the 'Jealousy & Modern Relationships' talk I mentioned earlier, Esther Perel points out that the solution for some couples is simply not to be friends on social media: 'Some couples aren't friends on Facebook – and it goes very well. It's the same as "Should you be friends with your kids on Facebook?"'

Esther is of the same opinion as Barbara – that you must allow your partner to have a secret world and to retain their sexuality, even if it's not always about you, because that's what makes them an individual, and the same thoughts in your head are what make you an individual. In the talk, she says:

Trust is the ability to live with what you will not know. What you need to know is that your partner has a space of their own – it's called privacy. These days we don't have much of it. We have transparency and we have secrecy. We have bifurcated [meaning 'forked'] *this thing called privacy – an erotic space of their own – their own imagination, their own fantasies, their own memories, their own longings, their own associations, an interior life of their own.*

Accepting that your partner has a secret world that includes sexual thoughts relating to others, and that you have one too, is certainly an enlightening way to view monogamy in an age where every move can be scrutinised.

The idea of trying to hijack your partner's secret space reminds me of an analogy I heard in church once. The priest was attempting to make the Day of Judgement relatable, and asked us to imagine that, on the day we died, we found ourselves sitting in a cinema watching a film of our lives back in real time: everything we ever thought, everything we ever said, everything we ever did; the good, the bad and the ugly. The priest asked us to imagine the doors of the cinema room swinging open once the film finished, and all our friends and family coming in to take their seats for a second showing, where they would see and hear everything we ever thought about them, everything we ever said about them and everything we ever did against them in moments of anger or despondency. The thought is excruciating, isn't it? I would beg people not to watch my film. I would maybe throw myself into the burning fires of hell to stop it.

I think the priest's conclusion was that Jesus died on the cross to save our sins – that he popped into the cinema before everyone else was allowed in and signed away all the hurtful things we thought and said and did. After speaking to Barbara and listening to Esther Perel, I'm starting to realise that snooping on a partner's phone and sifting through their past online is like trying to watch your partner's film –

but a strange cut that omits anything that doesn't fit your script. It's like George Orwell's Thought Police in *Nineteen Eighty-Four*, a special force who read people's minds and punish them for their 'thought crimes' in an attempt to take away their individuality and free will.

When I told my friend Amelia I was writing a chapter on digital paranoia, she laughed and said, 'Should be an easy one for you.' Amelia is the least jealous person I know when it comes to relationships and, of course, I've always been jealous of that. She's also one of the biggest flirts I've ever met. Having been in a committed, monogamous relationship for the past few years, Amelia is the living embodiment of what Esther and Barbara are advocating: respect for a partner's erotic space in return for respect for her own.

Amelia Abraham, 27
Writer and author of *Queer Intentions*

Where do you think the line is when it comes to digital infidelity, i.e. not actually cheating physically, but likes and messages with other people online?

I think every relationship has its own rules. In my relationship the rules are quite slack about liking photos of hot people and stuff like that. Maybe because it's a gay relationship . . . I will quite often like pictures of hot girls who I don't know that well, but that's okay in our relationship. But if one of my really good [female] friends' boyfriends did that, they'd be livid; for them it's a deal-breaker.

Is it harmless to like photos of hot girls?

For me it's harmless. With a boy doing it to a girl, unless it's their best friend, I think it can only mean one thing. Whereas when I do it, there's more room for me to just be like, 'oh, it's just my friend on holiday' lol. Maybe it's not okay . . . The thing that actually does get me quite a lot is the search bar on Instagram, like when I go to show my girlfriend a picture of my cousin's baby and some hot girl I barely know comes up on my most searched – that's embarrassing. But I don't think it would make her feel threatened because we have a really stable relationship.

If anything, I think it would just make her feel a little bit sorry for me, like a bit embarrassed for me because it's just quite . . . pathetic.

Do you look at your exes online?

Yeah, sometimes. It's kind of like . . . looking up interesting celebrity news?! An ex of mine recently got married and I found a picture of it online and I saved it so I could show my friends without accidentally liking it. And we analysed the photo looking for, like, intel on her life. Which is maybe quite creepy . . . But it came from a nosy place more than anything. I'm not jealous that she's with someone else – I'm happy for her – but I am curious about what her life is like.

My exes aren't on social media, and I like that because it means I couldn't look even if I wanted to.

You say that, but one of my main exes doesn't have social media and that actually led to a much more embarrassing thing, which is that I found the person they're going out with now on social media, so I just look at their profile to see pictures of my ex's life, once removed. Actually, that's the worst thing that could come up if you're showing your current partner something on Instagram – and not even your ex's name, but your ex's new partner's name comes up. That's just so creepy and embarrassing.

It is so embarrassing . . . but why is it so embarrassing when so many people do it?

Because . . . you'll never know if someone is doing it to you. When you find out they are, you feel so validated. This ex I creep on through their current partner's Instagram page once accidentally liked a picture of mine really far down the grid. The reason all of this stuff is so embarrassing is because you can't see anyone else doing it.

Have you ever read a girlfriend's messages?

No.

Never?!

No. Sorry to be boring. I just don't want to see it. I'm very on board with the idea that you're happier not knowing. When I was 20, the girlfriend I was with left her emails open on my computer, and I could see the subject line was my name. I was tempted to click on it, but I just thought, 'Whatever is in there, she doesn't want you to see it.'

You didn't wonder about it afterwards?

No. It's strange, isn't it.

No. I guess that's the right way to be.

I don't think there's a right way to be.

Had you opened the email and found something you didn't like, do you think that experience would have encouraged you to read messages in another relationship?

No, I think it would have put me off doing it even more. The act of reading someone's messages is just as bad as whatever they've said about you.

IS IT?!

Yeah. Sorry to hit you personally [laughs], but it is.

Fine. Have you ever considered a polyamorous relationship?

Yes. I've repeatedly been told it would suit me because I don't get jealous. One of my exes said she thinks the reason I don't get jealous is because I think I'm so amazing that no one else could ever compare to me [laughs].

Do you think that?

Ummm ... no ... maybe a half-truth ... [laughs] Maybe it's one of the things at play. But to my knowledge – and again, bearing in mind I prefer not to know – nobody has ever cheated on me, so I haven't ever been given anything to worry about. I got a bit jealous once, or something close to it, when I opened up my relationship to have a threesome with my [then] girlfriend and a guy. We had the threesome, it was really nice, and then I fell asleep. While I was asleep, they had sex again next to me. I didn't wake up while this happened but she told me the next day and was apologetic about it. I was livid. Is that jealousy? Or is it just being annoyed with someone because they cheated on me while I was there, asleep? [laughs] Did they cheat in front of me while I was asleep, or is it not actually cheating because I was there? That's an interesting question.

That's the most rational form of jealousy I've ever heard!

Yeah. I think I view sex and love as very separate things. I'm a very romantic person; I really like the idea of having a life partner and spending my life with someone. Obviously if you're monogamous, that comes with the burden of never being able to sleep with anyone else ever again, which for me is a bit annoying. But if you were polyamorous, maybe you could have both. Actually, I don't think it would suit me to be 'polyamorous' because I don't want two girlfriends – the thought of that really stresses me out just in terms of admin. But I would like to be able to go to a party and get off with someone and it not be a big deal in my relationship. So more of an open relationship maybe?

Do you think polyamory will become more common in the future?

For a long time, polyamory has been quite a popular choice among gay men, and gay men have managed to come to agreements within their long-term relationships. But I am seeing more women and non-binary people trying out polyamory. I think that connects to the fact that we're seeing binary lines blur more generally: you're not either straight or gay, male or female, monogamous or polyamorous; you can explore the in between.

2. Digital Infidelity

Like that Mark Twain quote – 'I've had a lot of worries in my life, most of which never happened' – the majority of my digital paranoia turned out to be just that: paranoia. But a sliver of it turned out to be something. Like a game of Russian roulette, every once in a while there's a bullet that ruptures your stomach and begins a slow, painful bleed. My bullets have ranged from finding out that one boyfriend had slept with the girl he's now married to while we were together (by logging on to his Facebook account), to finding out another had repeatedly tried to snog his friend's sister on a night out (by looking at his laptop when he was in the shower). None of these digital revelations caused me to end the relationships at the time, but forcing myself to watch their foolish behaviour in drunken moments interfered with my soul and caused a butterfly effect where I retaliated to what I'd seen and did one worse.

The recently revived reality TV show *Temptation Island* took this idea of giving a person the opportunity to watch their partner's infidelities to the extreme. Criticised by religious groups for being 'immoral and sadistic', the premise of the show is that four straight couples go on a tropical island to put their relationships to the test. The girlfriends get sent to one part of the island, the boyfriends to another. Then 24 single men and women, specifically chosen to be the type of one of the boyfriends or girlfriends, arrive to tempt them away from their partners. Every few days, the girlfriends and boyfriends are given the opportunity to watch a short video clip of what their other half has been up to. The clips range from a boyfriend naked under the sheets with a hot single girl, to a girlfriend snogging a hot single in a steaming hot tub. Maybe one of the eight in the couple group decide not to watch the video, because they know it will mess with their heads, but the rest choose to watch – crying, commenting things like 'I feel sick' and 'This is torture, I'm being tortured'.

In the most recent series, three out of the four boyfriends and two out of the four girlfriends are caught cheating on film, and all of the relationships affected by cheating come to an end in a trashy but compelling bonfire finale. Most of the people in the couples say that the reason they cheated was because they saw their other half cheating first, or doing something incriminating on film which made it look like they intended to. Without this option to watch what the other was up to, we probably would have seen a different bonfire finale, with more of the couples choosing to remain together. But you can't unsee what you've seen, and in modern relationships it's often the image and the details of the infidelity that prove too difficult to recover from.

In the pre-internet, pre-text message days, signs of infidelity were lipstick on a shirt collar or a suspicious dinner receipt, and there was no way of finding out the intimate details unless you demanded them from one of the guilty parties – who, if they had any sense, would just disclose the bare minimum and coat it in sugar. You could try to go hunting, but you probably wouldn't get very far. But since text, email, internet history and social media came into our lives, there are hundreds of ways to 'catch' a person out and, like watching the videos in *Temptation Island*, to see all the intimate details of the affair on a

Has social media ever made you feel paranoid in a relationship?

I've been in relationships with people where their online behaviour and social media curation has made me feel paranoid. About ten years ago I found out my lover was married through Facebook, so social media has always been a triggering space for me in regards to relationships. We've got to a stage in contemporary communication where behaviour on social media is real, if my partner doesn't respect my online boundaries it can be a deal breaker. However, I think, ultimately, if you're in a secure and loving relationship offline that you should be able to talk through these boundaries without being gaslighted digitally.

SUZANNE PETTIGREW, ARTIST

screen: the jokes they shared, the pet names, the expressions of sexual desire, selfies she sent – every detail of her, who looks nothing like you, or looks a lot like you, with him.

'It's never been easier to cheat and it's never been more difficult to keep a secret,' says Esther Perel in her TED talk 'Rethinking Infidelity'. 'And never has infidelity exacted such a psychological toll.' Perel uses the case of one of her clients as an example, a woman named Helen who found out that her husband – the father of her children – was cheating on her when a message popped up on an iPad which was linked to his phone. Helen then went digitally digging and found hundreds of messages and pieces of photo evidence of a long-term affair. 'The vivid details of her husband's two-year affair unfolded in front of her in real time,' Perel comments. 'It made me think: affairs in the digital age are death by a thousand cuts.'

If digital paranoia is constructing an elaborate house of cards that exists only in your mind, then digital infidelity is watching those cards grow roots. It's so easy to find things online, and it's so easy for online things to find you. My friend Eve, 33, who until recently wasn't on social media and would never think to snoop, had a brutal digital awakening in her relationship. She'd been living with her boyfriend for two years in Spain when it was brought to her attention by a friend that her boyfriend had been on Tinder while she was visiting her parents in the UK. She confronted him, and after finally admitting that he had downloaded the app, he maintained he'd 'done nothing wrong', because he didn't meet up with anyone, it was just a game. After that, Eve felt she couldn't stay and decided to fly home again. He said he wanted to make it work and would visit as soon as he had time off work, and she agreed to see how things went long distance. But a few weeks later, Eve opened the Airbnb app on her phone, which he sometimes used when they travelled together, and found that he had tried to change her password and had updated her profile picture from a picture of them together to a picture of him with another girl. While Eve thought they were trialling long distance, he had abandoned that idea without telling her and moved on to another relationship. She later found out from Instagram that he'd gone on holiday with this girl two weeks after she had left. Referring to the AirBnb revelation, Eve said: 'It was such a shock finding out like that. Not only was he in a new relationship, but they were renting out the spare room of the house I shared with him just a month before – with the duvet cover my mum had bought us as a present still on the bed in the photos. They looked so happy. Seeing her like that, with my life, in my home, was worse than the betrayal, than the break-up, than having to leave and move back in with my parents. I was completely broken.' A display of digital intimacy she hadn't asked to see. Death by a thousand cuts.

In 2015, a group of hackers calling themselves 'The Impact Team' leaked the identities of 37 million people who had signed up to Ashley Madison, a website that facilitated extramarital affairs. The story went global fast, offering husbands and wives the opportunity to log on and see if their partners had signed up to the website. Several religious leaders and politicians were exposed in the scandal, and Twitter had a field day hanging out the accused to dry and delighting in this act of tech vigilantism. The Amazon documentary on the events, *Sex, Lies and Cyber Attacks*, contains an interview with a man who found out his wife had had six affairs through Ashley Madison. 'I threw up when I found it,' he says to camera, referring to all the messages, emails, videos and photos he found of his wife's affairs.

Like Eve, the victims of the leak hadn't really gone looking, they hadn't invaded their partner's privacy or read phones – instead they'd been confronted with the information just by being on the internet themselves. Eve happened to open the Airbnb app; the husbands and wives happened to see an article about Ashley Madison with a link to a public database. Digital media is so ingrained in our culture that it can be difficult to avoid 'spoilers' within your own life, even when you aren't looking for them.

With such a large group of people affected by the leak, it's likely that all outcomes played out across the world, and at least two suicides were linked to the case. One of those was 56-year-old American pastor John Gibson, highly thought of in his community, with a wife and two grown-up children. A few days after the leak, despite his wife not knowing he was a member of the site – having not thought to check the database – Gibson killed himself, revealing it in his suicide note. It reminded me of the film-watching analogy I heard in church: this well-respected man had found the threat of the exposure of his secret world to his wife and family too awful to bear.

For the last 20 years, technology has allowed us to see more and more of our partner's secret world, and to walk around in it. From the small, paper-cut events like seeing them happy with someone in the past or flirting with someone in their present, to the big, soul-crushing discoveries like the painful evidence of an affair, this particular by-product of the digital age is incredibly psychologically damaging. And we know it's damaging, but some of us go looking for it anyway,

Has social media ever made you feel paranoid in a relationship?

Yes definitely. In my current relationship I have come across my partner interacting with other women in a way that I find inappropriate. He's not on social media as much anymore, but it's something we've both had to work through and seek therapy for. I feel social media used in this way has made me a jealous crazy person at times, but it's also made me aware of how easy it is to 'wander' from your partner if you are seeking it.

BRIANNA LEE PRICE, 33
MUSIC PRODUCER, DJ, PRESENTER

because it's tempting and easy, because we're bored and want to play games, because we struggle to attach to our partners, because we've been burnt in the past, because we're confused by the changing goalposts of monogamy.

Our parents didn't have to answer the question 'Are you okay with your partner searching online for, and liking photos of hot women they vaguely know?' – in those days, infidelity was more black-and-white. Now there are so many extra rules and new spaces in which to test them. As a generation we're dealing with this shift in different ways: some are going with the flow, embracing polyamory and working out new ways to love; some are going mad with it, seeking help from therapists; some are getting along just fine until their partner changes their Airbnb profile picture to a photo of a new girl.

Since I learned about the 'secret world' theory of allowing your partner their fantasies and memories, and allowing yourself the same, I've stopped looking out of boredom and paranoia, and I try not to read into the things that make me wonder. I recently opened Facebook for the first time in a while and saw I had some new messages, so I clicked on them. I was initially confused by the name until I realised it was my partner's Facebook account; he must have been the last person to log in. The messages were from a girl I hadn't heard of, and I could see some messages had been deleted because the conversation was missing parts. I clicked on her profile and sighed when I realised she was a mega-babe, but since there was nothing incriminating in the messages that were visible, just a 'I'm living here and doing this, you?' type of catch-up, I decided not to pry or read into it and logged out. Either he deleted the messages by accident, or there was something he didn't want me to see, but even if it was the latter, I felt sure it was nothing serious. In the context of the experiment that Barbara outlined, where the anxious, insecure children appear calm when their mother leaves the room but are actually very distressed, it seems I've finally formed a secure attachment to my partner. I didn't feel anxious over the deleted messages as I would have done previously, I felt secure. Even if the worst turns out to be true, I've come to the conclusion that going looking for it causes too much hurt, and as Eve's experience and the Ashley Madison case proves, in this day and age, whatever it is will probably find you some other way. I'll exit hell with Eurydice behind me, never looking back, and if she feels like shooting me in the stomach once we're out then so be it.

VM SELVY ON THE RACIAL & GENERATIONAL DATING GAME

My parents only met once, about a month before they got married. After the wedding my father came back to the UK, where he was a student, and my mother completed her internship in Sri Lanka. The next time they saw each other was two years later, when my mother moved to the UK. Even by 1980s standards in Sri Lanka, this was considered somewhat archaic. Legally they are still married, which puts them in the category of one of the many arranged-marriage 'success' stories, except that, unsurprisingly, they found they had little in common and their decades-long union was incompatible with their respective happiness. They finally separated two years ago.

Despite being the breadwinner of the family, my mother – I expect still shackled by her culture and generation – was and still is reluctant to get divorced. Ironically, one of the main reasons given by my parents for their reluctance to separate over the years was that it would have implications on my own future marriage prospects, should I end up looking to settle down with a partner from the same background. By 'the same background' I assumed they meant someone who was also ethnically Tamil. But now that I'm older, this seems far too simplistic a definition of my background. I identify much more with the cliché of the second-generation immigrant: growing up constantly navigating between two cultures, uncertain as to where exactly I fit in.

Perhaps being the product of a fairly unromantic, contrived union puts me in good stead to embrace the formulaic modern-day equivalent of an arranged meeting. There are parallels between internet dating and the traditional arranged proposal. First you are presented with a portfolio of potential suitors and a few key demographics – age, name, location, plus some details of higher education and current job title – and then comes the perusal of a carefully curated selection of photos. Mutual matches exchange contact details, engage in some initial awkward chat as a means to an end (a meeting or date). Ironically, I always vowed I would never go through the arranged process, and yet it feels as though this has become the norm – whether through an online Tamil dating 'broker' or Match.com. My experiences of both the former and latter routes have been equally disheartening.

I should mention that my parents are fairly liberal by South Asian standards and would not object to my settling down with someone of a different ethnicity. Having said that, I suspect there is a part of them that would be relieved if I introduced them to a Tamil partner. I myself am beginning to understand this attitude too, as I continue to discover all the components of who I am and how I see myself. There is an undeniable ease to being with someone who understands exactly what your experience is and the 'otherness' that a person of colour falls into having grown up in 1980s and '90s Britain. This sense of otherness continues to make itself felt when I use online dating sites or apps.

I don't get all that many matches. While I suspect this is partly down to my own narrow set of criteria, I can't help but feel that it's more to do with not fulfilling Eurocentric ideals of physical attractiveness. As online dating is mostly based on an objective selection process – swiping photos – I don't think this is an unreasonable thing to think. Despite living in cosmopolitan London, I feel that most men, irrespective of their own ethnicity, desire a partner who looks Caucasian. Growing up, it was rare to see people who looked like me on TV, billboards or in the cinema. Is it surprising that in a society where for most of the century it has been normal for the universal experience to be white, that even in the context of mass immigration there remains a very narrow pool of what is deemed physically desirable? Unlike an accent, religion or specific sexual orientation, my otherness is always visible, juxtaposed against the invisibility of under-representation I felt growing up.

This might all sound like I have an unfounded chip on my shoulder, but a 2018 study by Cornell University found that online dating apps that allow users to filter their searches by race, or rely on algorithms that pair users with others of the same race, reinforcing racial divisions and biases. The research revealed that racial inequities in online dating are widespread – black men and women are 10 times more likely to message white people than white people are to message black people.

Colourism – often regarded as a post-imperialist sequela of the notion that 'lighter is righter' – has actually existed within many cultures prior to the arrival of European colonialists, and it still exists in non-white communities today. One of the questions on the South Asian dating website Shaadi.com pertains to describing your complexion: 'Fair/Wheatish/Dark'. Having a 'fair' complexion has equated to increased desirability among Tamils for generations, and I have had someone comment disdainfully that I appeared 'much brighter' in my dating profile photos. Exposure to this antiquated form of internalised bias among people of the same skin colour is pretty soul-destroying. That those with a lighter skin tone should benefit from a comparable privilege, through an approximation of whiteness, within their own ethnicity, has always baffled me.

It is during these encounters through the Tamil online dating route that I have felt I have very little in common with the person I am meeting other than my skin colour and mother tongue. There was a guy who had a problem with me drinking alcohol, a guy who had an issue with my working hours and whose mother said, 'How is she going to be able to cook for my son and look after children if her job is this busy?' and a guy who I couldn't even meet because his family said there was no point as our Hindu horoscopes were 'incompatible'. My reactions to these scenarios were pretty reflective of my being born and brought up in the UK. 'Do these people really give a fuck about this bud bud ding ding voodoo chart nonsense?!' I exclaimed in disbelief to my mother, my own internalised prejudice about my culture coming to the fore. (As they sing in *Avenue Q*, 'Everyone's a little bit racist'.)

Conversely, on the standard sites and dating apps I can feel fetishised because of my skin colour. The first thing someone on Tinder messaged me once was 'I love the colour of your skin lol'. When copper/caramel/chocolate-coloured is clumsily used in an attempt to compliment me, I just find it horribly derogatory and it prompts me to immediately unmatch myself from the perpetrator.

It often becomes apparent that most of the Caucasian men I match with just want a casual hook-up. I wonder if that's all I am in this internet era of instant gratification – Deliveroo to satiate your craving for Chinese food, and Bumble to deliver you an 'exotic' shag. This cynicism on my part has meant most of the men I've dated have been non-white. Of course, I don't want to generalise and say most men aren't interested in settling down with a woman of colour – this is obviously unfair and I have plenty of male friends and colleagues in relationships with women of a different background. But am I being totally unfair in branding the term 'fetishism' in this context? People can't help what they're attracted to, right?

After I politely rebuffed the previously mentioned Tinder guy whose opening line about my skin colour made me feel uneasy, he wouldn't take no for an answer, becoming increasingly irate and finishing with 'Ur a snake. Stupid Asian cunt. U all need putting down. N b4 u chat more crap to me about being busy. Or shall I translate that into curry, I have never met an Asian with a good character.' As well as displaying poor syntax, his reaction was paradoxical, but it brought to mind an anecdote by the comedian Hasan Minhaj about when he worked for *The Daily Show* in New York. He would see Fox News broadcasters – notorious for their xenophobic tirades against immigrants on air – leave their building at lunch time and line up for halal chicken and rice. 'Racist Randy just wants that red sauce!' he described it. 'Your brain can be racist, but your body will just betray you.'

Like I said, people can't help what they're physically attracted to.

I think the anonymity of internet dating facilitates more overt racism. At least via the arranged introduction there is some accountability, because people's families are aware of the match and, for the most part, basic codes of social etiquette are adhered to and 'ghosting' isn't possible.

I'm not sure which method suits me the best. I often feel too 'Westernised' for the traditional route, yet I'm not sure how suited my demographics are to sites and apps in terms of dating with a view to a long-term relationship. I'm not entirely convinced current algorithms and matching methods best serve people of colour, but I remain hopeful things will evolve to better reflect and represent our multicultural society.

I feel I can't write about my experience of online dating without a mention of the 'dick pic' phenomenon. I was having a pleasant WhatsApp chat with someone I matched with online and suddenly there it was, an image downloading in the conversation. 'Here we go,' I thought, somewhat resigned. But it was actually far worse than I'd imagined – it was a photo of his bathroom refurb.

The only thing more offensive than a dick pic is the assumption that I would be remotely interested in someone's home refurbishment. It's bad enough feigning interest in this type of thing when you actually know the person IRL. What a time to be alive.

VM Selvy is an NHS doctor who writes about identity and race in her spare time. Paradoxically, she likes both socialism, and when they clear your table crumbs with a mini dustpan and brush in restaurants.

Have you ever looked up somebody you've been romantically interested in on social media? How did it affect what you thought about them?

My boyfriend rarely posts on Instagram and has very few followers. His photos are often dimly lit, unedited and non-professional seeming. This is all very attractive to me.

TIERNEY FINSTER, 27, JOURNALIST, SCREENWRITER, ACTOR, MODEL, CASTING DIRECTOR

NAOMI
A Love Supreme

Last year, I got engaged to a man I met on Instagram. I had first laid eyes on him in the form of a tiny profile photo, underneath a headline for a story. The article covered an amazing community that I had never heard of. I felt deeply connected to the story, that felt like it had been relayed with so much heart. I lovingly inhaled it all and quickly scrolled back up to see who had written such beautiful prose. I examined the author's picture meticulously. Curiously. Who was this person? I couldn't deny that I felt an instant wave of attraction. His eyes seemed kind and warm. I somehow in that second felt truly convinced that I could see and feel the depth of his soul. All that from a tiny little thumbnail. I needed to know more. I took a mental note of his name and typed it into Google. An hour later, I was still sat on the edge of the kitchen counter, feet up on the stool, reading through other articles he had written. It felt to me like there was something in the way he wrote. Then I did what so many of us do in this day and age: I looked him up on Instagram.

I got back into bed with a big mug of coffee, put on my glasses and took the approach of a scientist in a lab, trying not to miss a single detail. What could I grasp from this tiled page of images? I instantly drew my own conclusions about him. First off, I could see that we had a few friends in common, which I took as a good sign. We also followed a lot of the same people, and I saw qualities in him through the photos he posted that made me feel like we were nothing short of kindred spirits. Social media can often be a place where we can easily create our own facades through the images and captions we post, a place where we often take images at face value instead of asking more questions. But when my eyes glossed over his profile page, he just felt different to me.

What I didn't yet understand was that a very primal instinct had taken over. There I was, sizing this total stranger up as a life partner. I was looking for and seeing things in these photos that ticked the internal checklist that I didn't even know I had, for a partner that I didn't even know I wanted. Smart – tick; strong – tick; attractive – tick; cool job – tick; looks kind – tick . . . Translation: Did he have potential? Could he protect me? Source my food? Provide shelter?

I took a deep breath and hit the 'Follow' button. I felt jittery and excited. I put my phone down.

Minutes later, my phone beeped. A notification said he had followed me back. Boom! A dopamine hit straight to the brain. I felt like it

overwhelming. After not having had a proper crush in a really long time, I found myself not liking the feeling of thinking about someone constantly, especially when it was someone I didn't even actually know.

The days flew by, and before I knew it, it was time to meet up with this person who had spent the summer living in the back of my mind. I was staying with a girlfriend while I was in the city. We often joked that she could have had a career as a super-spy. Social security number? Phone number? Yearbook photos? No problem! It was a hot NYC summer day, and my thighs stuck together as I sat on her couch letting the AC blow my hair into knots. We talked about my upcoming date. I told her that I wondered how tall he was. She quickly responded, 'Well, we can probably find out!' and started typing into Google. And just like that, I had fallen into the trap. He had been an athlete at university and she found his height out in two seconds flat. We decided it was debatable based on the height differences we tried to figure out from photos of him standing next to people. What to call this – was this a game? I knew we were doing something bad, but I also didn't want her to stop. We fell into the Google rabbit hole. We clicked on anything we could find on him. With hindsight, I was looking for reasons to talk myself down from the excitement I felt for a stranger, for fear of the reality not living up to how I had imagined it to be. I suddenly felt dirty. Like I had eaten two McDonald's meals at the airport while hungover and now felt terrible. I wished I could've gone back and unseen everything. I felt like I knew too much. Had anyone ever done this to me? Do we have access to too much information? As someone whose life is very much on the internet, the chances were, they probably had.

Is this what the reality of dating in the age of social media is – a messed-up game of espionage? But surely we've also been doing this since the dawn of time. Finding out about someone we don't really know through things such as word of mouth, books, the media and projecting our innermost desires onto them – that's not new, but now it's just the medium and thus the tools for engagement that have changed. The way we use social media to gather information on people sometimes makes me wonder how many potential relationships have been ruined before they've had a chance to even begin. How many times have we made assumptions about people based solely on their digital identity? If you're thinking about meeting up with someone, for your safety (especially as a woman), you just need to know more. The scrolling can be second nature, but it also sometimes feels necessary.

I had been in New York that week shooting a campaign and had planned to stay in town for a few extra days just so I could meet up with him. I pulled up at the bar where we planned to meet. The sunset was a deep pink, a welcome sight after a day of hot, torrential rain. We were in the middle of nowhere, in the industrial depths of Brooklyn, and I had picked this place for a reason. The spot was away from prying eyes; it required effort and dedication on his part in the form of a 40-minute subway ride followed by a 20-minute car ride from where he was staying in Midtown Manhattan. The dimly lit bar felt like a post-apocalyptic Cheers. Quiet, where everyone inside spoke to each other as if they were old friends. Big colourful paintings hung on the walls, while Ella Fitzgerald played softly in the background. Her voice was like sweet nectar welcoming us all in, asking us to stay a while. Having not eaten all day, I was on the brink of delirium, annoyed with myself for not having stopped at a corner bodega for an emergency banana. I was now hitting that edge where low blood sugar has kidnapped your good mood and replaced it with an inability to make good conversation. As I walked into the bar, everything felt like it kicked into slow motion. I saw his broad shoulders and the back of his athletic body. I knew immediately that it was him. He turned around and stood up to hug me hello. He had a pack of ruffled chips open, and pointed the open bag towards me and said. 'Are you hungry? Do you want a chip?' I just nodded, too weak from hunger and too taken aback by the gesture of the chips to speak. Then, a quiet 'yes' was all I could muster. I did want a chip. I wanted a chip more than anything. Did his voice sound like I had imagined it? I wanted to hear it again. I reached into the bag and grabbed as many chips as I thought I could fit into my mouth at once without looking like a total ravenous animal, and quickly dusted the crumbs off my face. He pulled out a bar stool, gesturing for me to take a seat. He asked me to sit down, sit down and tell him everything.

And so I did. In that moment in time, nothing seemed to matter other than the two of us sharing, connecting and discovering. We moved from the bar to an art opening to dinner in Manhattan. While we were eating, I made him laugh when I ate directly from a dish I'd kept on my lap – as we had ordered so much food there simply had been no room for it on the table. It started to rain as we walked out into the street. As we kept walking, I felt such a strong need to kiss him. I couldn't take another breath or walk another step without feeling what his lips were like. I stopped walking, he looked back at me and I pulled him into me, as the raindrops glistened on our faces, for our very first kiss.

I went home with him that night. As I lay next to him, I felt too scared to go to sleep in case I woke up and discovered it had all been a dream. I relayed my fear to him. He laughed at the face I pulled and drew me in closer and kissed my forehead ever so gently. Our bodies fit together like a jigsaw puzzle, like two lost pieces that had somehow, against all the odds, found their way home. It was beyond exhilarating to meet someone in real life that you had thought about for such a long time – for a fantasy to not only seemingly actualize but to seem even better than you could ever have imagined. To me, at the time, he was my 'perfect' build-a-boyfriend come to life, that being in his actual presence in that moment in time felt so powerful. 'This, has to be it,' I thought to myself. I quickly planned our future life in my head. Looking back, it's crazy to think how soon we both had the capacity to project all our desires onto each other without really knowing each other at all.

A few weeks later, I found myself in the southernmost tip of Italy. A job had brought me close to where he was on holiday, and I joined him for a few days before we both went back to work. A true escape from the real world, into each other's arms. Having fallen into an intense love – a love like nothing before – everything, felt different. Falling in love is a crazy thing. I thought it had happened to me before, but this time it was just so different. Was it that I was older? Or maybe I was more jaded, or I had less faith that I would find someone who would ever make me feel like this. We were locked away alone, in this beautiful place where there was no Wi-Fi, and the only distraction was the blue ocean in front of us. High on dopamine, we did what many other irrational couples struck by Cupid's bow have done in a moment of passion. We decided to seal our fate with the eternal imprint of a tattoo. We found a cute little tattoo parlour in the charming town we were staying in. Our tattooist didn't speak a word of English, but nevertheless we communicated what we wanted with a mix of hand signals and my sub-par Italian. He went first, and I looked at this man I was besotted with as he held my hand so tightly, like he was never going to let it go. His eyes were soft and trying to tell me something. He took a deep breath and whispered, 'I want to do this with you forever.' I stared blankly back at his face. Had I heard him right? 'I can't hear you properly, say it again,' I said. 'I'm trying to be with you forever,' he repeated. I felt like the word 'forever' was reverberating off his bottom lip that I never wanted to stop kissing. I felt intoxicated by 'forever'. I was absolutely drunk on it. I loved the way it sounded in his voice and I wanted him to keep saying it over and over. I smiled back with a smile that felt like it was radiating outwards from the deepest part of me. We swapped seats as it was now my turn in the chair. 'So, what are you asking me?' I said, not even feeling the pain being inflicted on me as the tattooist pressed the needle into my skin.

'So, are you trying to marry me or what?' he asked. I felt like I had gone slightly deaf in my left ear. I looked into his eyes and let his words ever so slowly wash over me. After a long moment that could have been one second or 60, I took a deep breath and ecstatically nodded 'yes'. And just like that we laughed, embraced and kissed in the name of eternity. In hindsight, I hadn't really asked enough questions about him or myself. But when you think the world is burning, believe that love somehow conquers all, and the person you think is your absolute dream partner asks to spend the rest of your life with you, you just say yes and hope for the best, right?

Tucked away in an Italian dreamland, this felt like it was everything I had ever wanted and more. So, of course I said yes. I said yes with my whole damn heart, to the person I'd found when I accidentally (and unknowingly) went shopping for a life partner on Instagram – a partner who I thought would be most suited for me.

We quickly planned what seemed like a very bright future. I would move to where he lived as soon as I could. Before then, he would come live with me in the meantime, as soon as we were done with our big work projects. After Italy, we returned to our homes. We spent half of our short relationship apart, with an ocean between us, but had plans to reunite in six weeks. That felt like the longest six weeks of my life. He quickly became the first person I spoke to when I woke up and I would fall asleep talking to him, my phone on speaker on the pillow next to me, letting his voice soothe me into a blissful sleep where I would dream of all the things we had to look forward to in our lives together.

With us, the time difference never seemed to be in an issue; we were somehow always available for the one we loved. We sent each other thousands of photos, wanting to introduce our worlds to each other, worlds that with time we'd soon be sharing. We were so convinced and proud of our union, we told everyone we could. Our families, friends, our exes and people we had been recently romantically linked with. Sometimes I couldn't even bear to FaceTime with him, as seeing him made me miss him so much that it physically pained me. He sent me videos of everyone important in his life, introducing me as his fiancée. They congratulated us, and spoke of how they couldn't wait to meet me. And I couldn't wait to meet them. I excitedly collected and packed gifts for them, I wanted to get to know them and of course, I wanted to make a good impression, I wanted them to like me as they were my new family after all! I could feel myself falling deeper and deeper in love. Every moment of every day felt soaked in bliss.

The day finally arrived where we were to be reunited. On the way to the airport, I sat in the cab and had this all-encompassing feeling that my life as I knew it was going to be different by the time I got off the plane. I felt calm but excited and ready for this new chapter. Soon, I would have a new family and a new city to start calling home. I thought of how safe and held I felt in his arms and his soft, gentle smile. In the time since we'd seen each other, with each passing day, I got more and more immersed in his world. Each time my phone buzzed, I could feel him drawing me in closer.

The plane touched down and I ran through customs as fast as my legs could carry me, hurling my luggage behind me, into those arms I had missed so much. On the roof of the airport parking lot, with the golden hour of sunset behind us, he slipped the most beautiful engagement ring onto my finger. I loved how it looked on my hand and how it felt as I tucked my hand in his. We moved into what would be our home for the next few weeks. Those first few days spent reconnecting were joyous. Filled with long walks and drives around town, introducing me to his life. I felt my body melt back into his. I felt like I had truly come home.

For a while it felt like the dreamiest time, but it wasn't very long before the cracks in the fantasy started to show. From a few photos – or a few weeks of passionate, never-felt-it-before love – you can't really know how things are going to turn out. Whether you meet someone online or in real life, that's the risk we take in the game of love. How many of us have fallen in love with the idea of someone? I hadn't even considered the possibility that, even though we spoke the same languages, the inherited, residual and lived traumas we both carried could trouble our ways of speaking to and understanding each other with honesty, care and compassion. We can't always see beyond the exteriors we all create to cope, to protect ourselves to survive.

After just a few days together, something started to feel different. We'd built our universe together so quickly that I don't think either of us could see there was a chasm opening up between us. I felt that the sweet man who'd once laughed with me was beginning to laugh at me. He'd make small comments about things that make me who I am. Comments that started out as seemingly harmless and humourous added up to become detrimental. I would sometimes wake up to him and wonder where he'd gone. It was becoming increasingly apparent that the ideas we had of each other weren't living up to the reality.

As the weeks went on the comments continued. He'd seem to criticise things that I had never noticed about myself and he seemed to take issue with things that were central to who I am as a person. I watched in real time as he had to contend with the fact that he was no longer dating my internet facade but the real me. I'd feel like he was questioning my intelligence and when I would explain that he'd hurt my feelings, he'd often go on to tell me that I was too 'sensitive'. Because of how brilliant I knew him to be, I quickly began to feel self-conscious about some of the things he said about me. When I would try to speak to him about how he was making me feel, he would tell me that no one had ever said these things to him, as if that made them unable to be true. I felt like any expression of my vulnerability to him was perceived as a sign of weakness. We were quite different, after all. It's true that I am soft, sensitive and empathetic. But I knew deep down that these weren't parts of myself that I wanted to relinquish to be worthy of his love.

In theory, everything should have felt great. I believed so wholeheartedly in this union. Technically speaking, we were still supposed to be in the 'honeymoon phase' of our relationship. We were supposed to just be head over heels. In those few months as well as spending time where he lived, we also travelled to other incredible places, doing so many fabulous things in the most breathtaking of landscapes. But at times the surrounding beauty, only seemed to magnify my feeling of utter isolation. There is no sense of loneliness like the loneliness one feels when the person you love seems to reject you. Something was wrong but I couldn't put my finger on it. I was in over my head. When I would try to talk to him about how his behaviour and his actions made me feel, he would tell me that I had just never been loved in such a way, and that my previous relationships must not have been as 'challenging'. When I would beg to be loved for who I am, I'd be met with what felt like excuses and more criticism. I felt like I was losing myself in his expectations. It seemed increasingly hard to communicate with him. At times I felt fearful, that I would never live up to how he wanted me to be. We would argue about my feelings, my opinions and my experience of the world. I often felt I was being studied, like I was a subject in one of his stories. I would try to talk back to him because I felt like I needed to be understood, I needed him to see me. But every time I did I felt shut down and belittled by him. I could feel myself shrinking under the pressure.

After two months travelling together, we went our separate ways again, back to our home cities. Even though there were moments on that trip that I had felt so hurt by him, leaving him inflicted a whole other kind

Have you ever looked up somebody you've been romantically interested in on social media?

My god, I think this is one of the most fundamental reasons social media exists at all! It was certainly part of Facebook's initial success and motivation. I have probably looked up every single person I have been romantically interested in to find out if they are single, remember what they look like and try to get a feel of their interests. It definitely has not affected how I feel about people I have met in life first (and I have never cold approached someone I have seen on social media). It is more a supplementary case of stalking. I was having this ongoing thing with someone in life, and we had a serious Whatsapp friendship. He then ghosted me for three months after almost a year of really close communication. I was really upset and would tell myself he was blanking me because he was busy working. When I saw him like other people's posts – admittedly rarely – I completely fell apart. I realised I had to mute him and his friends until I was less emotionally affected by a random meaningless like!

**FRANCESCA GAVIN,
WRITER AND CURATOR**

of pain. The panic of suddenly realizing I was going to be without him for another few weeks made me erupt and I started hysterically crying when it came to saying goodbye. To my surprise, he swiftly followed. His big back shook in my arms, tears flowing down his face. It was one of the few moments that I can clearly remember that he let himself be vulnerable with me. 'Wow, despite all the disagreements and bad feelings we'd had over the last few months, this must mean he actually really loves me,' I thought to myself. On the flight home at the end of our big trip together, I continued to sob for most of the 12-hour flight, putting on one sad movie after another so as to not panic the poor lady seated next to me who kept passing me extra tissues so lovingly. I couldn't deny I was mentally, emotionally and physically exhausted and was arriving back a shell of myself. I had never felt so misaligned. I was so confused at what I actually felt about our relationship now. How could I feel so much love, fear and pain all at once?

Even though I felt like I was constantly walking on eggshells around him, not sure of what would set him off, not being with him after having been with him every day for months felt like I had lost a limb. I reflected and wrote down all my fears and feelings, trying to explain to him how particular things that had happened in our months together had made me feel, trying to be clear about what my boundaries were, saying that I felt he was criticising me constantly, which hurt my feelings. I spent a week drafting an email so carefully, trying to word things in a way that would protect his ego. I took a deep breath and hit send. He called me back minutes later telling me that he had read my email and that he thought I had got a few details wrong. He jokingly asked me if this was a first draft, that he was hoping he could send me 'edits' to consider. He told me these were all my own insecurities. By refusing to acknowledge his part, I felt like he was denying my experience. I told him that I recognised that they were, but that I needed to talk about how he made me feel. This request seemed to be ignored. It felt like he refused to take me seriously. Our conversation ended there. I was hurt, but in that moment didn't really know how to absorb what had happened because I was too shocked by his reaction and embarrassed. So once again I just squashed the pain inside a box and buried it deeply within me.

While this was going on, I didn't really tell anyone – because I knew that what was happening wasn't okay but I just wasn't ready to accept the fact that my 'dream' fiancé could make me feel this way. These situations often have the capacity to shame us into complete secrecy and that secrecy encourages denial. We begin to police ourselves for having thoughts which interrogate unhealthy patterns of behaviour, to protect our partners but also ourselves.

Once I landed back in the UK, I went straight back into my busy life to cope. I moved into a new apartment and got back to work. After a few days of trying to acclimatize once again to the distance between us, we went back to talking and messaging as usual. It just seemed so much easier, so I forced myself to temporarily forget how unsafe I had felt after making myself so vulnerable with him, and instead we once again picked up the digital dance counting down the days until we would be back together again.

Aided by busyness, time went a lot quicker this time round and soon it was his turn to come to me. I made my new space a home for the both of us. I wanted us to have a solid base so we could start living like a real couple. We were both on deadlines, so mostly spent our days working from home, taking small breaks so that I could show him around at what a new life here could look like for us. There were days filled with laughs, dancing, cooking meals and nights where we woke up in the exact same position we had fallen asleep in, holding each other so tenderly. There were so many special things we shared that felt unique to us. But what also came back along with his presence were the demeaning comments and what felt like subtle, bullying behaviour. He sometimes began to justify his comments and criticisms by referring to my racial background. My father is Asian and my mother is white. I have grown up and lived between Asia, Europe and the States and that in itself has brought its own set of confusing connotations. I choose to identify as mixed-race and as a woman of colour. Despite being multi-racial himself, he would make ill-humoured comments that, I felt, negatively framed my racial identity. I thought that by being with someone who also presented as racially ambiguous, he would've had more compassion for my experience. Even though I understand the multi-racial experience is a complicated spectrum because of legacies of colonialism, slavery and contemporary forms of violence, by seemingly pitting our experiences against each other he seemed to miss the fact that we weren't on opposing teams, that we were meant to be teammates; that critiquing the nuances of my racial identity, and not from a place of kindness, only made our team weaker, not stronger.

On the last day of his visit, I was cooking breakfast for us and accidentally burned myself on the stove. Even though it wasn't a serious burn, I let out an instinctive yelp from the shock. He was seated at the dining table, next to me, reading something on his phone, but he didn't look up or say a word. My housemate, who was at the sink washing the dishes at the time, stopped to ask me if I was okay, and headed to the freezer to get me some ice. Still, my partner said nothing. We sat down and had breakfast in complete silence. I was weirded out by his complete lack of response and the silence that ensued. I wondered if he maybe just hadn't noticed. After eating I decided to ignore the weird vibe and went upstairs to start my day. Hours later, he asked me to come downstairs. I leaned over the bannister to respond to him. When I asked him what he wanted, he began speaking vaguely about what had happened at breakfast and how it was of interest to him. I asked him what he was talking about specifically and he said he was interested in talking about how I had handled burning my hand on the stove. A shiver rippled up my spine – a shiver that as I write this is still there, frozen in time. So he had seen. My jaw dropped. He kept going, saying that after I burnt my hand, he had observed that I had looked around the room as if I were a small child, deciding whether to cry or not depending on who had seen me fall. My heart stopped. I felt like I had been kicked in the stomach and the ground beneath me just disappeared. I felt like I couldn't breathe and my eyes began to well up with big tears. I was so shocked I could barely speak. 'Why would you ever say something like that to me?' escaped from my quivering lips. He coldly replied that he wasn't presenting criticism, but just an interesting bit of information. I was stunned. Why was the person I loved acting like he actually didn't care for me at all? There wasn't a moment in our exchange where he checked in to see if I was actually okay. His intellectualisation of what had happened seemed to take precedence over his capacity for care. How could I continue to love someone who spoke to me in what felt like such a manipulative way, as if I was some kind of anthropological research subject, like I wasn't a person?

We all yearn to be loved, but the truth of it is that so many of us don't know how to give or receive love properly in a healthy way. Author and cultural critic bell hooks, who has devoted her life to trying to understand the true nature of love, writes that part of the problem is that we grow up without having a clear definition of love: 'Affection is only one ingredient of love. That to truly love we must learn to mix various ingredients – care, affection, recognition, respect, commitment, and trust, as well as honest and open communication.' It's so easy to convince ourselves into thinking that we are receiving the love we need but love is a delicate dance between all these things, making it difficult terrain for most of us to navigate. If we're not careful, with no malicious intent, we can end up inflicting pain on the people we love, who love us, and we can end up pushing away the companionship and understanding that we want so much.

After that alarming experience, I spent our last day together in a muddled haze. I knew I was hurt and a boundary had been seriously crossed but I felt completely lost at what to do. I tried to bring it up before he left, but my feelings were once again dismissed as irrational, and my heart sank. I felt my body go numb. As I hugged him goodbye, I burst into tears as the car pulled away because, right in that moment, I wasn't sure if I was going to ever see him again.

As I write this, the relationship is very much over and we are no longer in contact. As a desperate last resort, I poured every ounce of my heart out into an email, because trying to speak to him wasn't getting me anywhere. Trying to wake him up to his behaviour. Begging him to understand how his actions made me feel. Trying to explain how his incapacity to be vulnerable blocked us from being able to fully connect. Trying to do the work of love. I told him that, after everything, I felt that he had still never acknowledged or simply apologised for any of his behaviour. That there had not even been so much as a hint of accountability, and without it we just couldn't move forward. A simple 'I'm sorry', which can go such a long way, can sometimes feel so inaccessible. I told him that I loved him deeply, but that his actions made me question what it even meant to be loved. At the time I didn't mean for it to be a final exchange between us; I was really hoping this was a way we could finally have a real conversation to try and save our relationship.

He wrote back to me, a few days later, as if we were strangers. His tone seemed so disconnected. Clinical, even. It seemed to me that he was clearly not ready to acknowledge what was happening, let alone apologise for any of his behaviour. Instead, he once again silenced me with his words, which stopped us from ever being able to communicate further. That was the final sign I needed to accept that he wasn't ready to be in a relationship with me. My boundaries had been repeatedly crossed and ignored, so I felt like I had no choice but to completely cut off contact. It was impossible to try and communicate further with someone who was completely shut down to any feedback. I needed to retreat and recover. As devastated as his reply made me feel, it was what I needed to find the strength within me to walk away.

It almost always reads true that when we cause pain it's mostly because we're suffering ourselves. With hindsight, I believe he had been giving me clues of his emotional well-being, but I was too caught up in the idea of him to see who he actually was. People give us signs and it's up to us to be open to seeing them. He was a human Rubik's Cube that I couldn't solve.

I felt that the values he put out into the world and his actions with me in private didn't align. I would read his work, which was always filled with so much softness, and I would wonder how to take this person off the page. I would ask myself why didn't he treat me with this same loving tenderness? What was blocking him? How could I break through? Was it even my place to try? Even though men are the chief beneficiaries of patriarchy, I can see how much they also suffer in the rhythm of its stifling beat. Patriarchy forces men to suppress the full spectrum of their emotionality, to discard their pain and perform success in accordance with facile capitalist signifiers of money, wealth and power. From the day they are born they are schooled in patterns of thinking that condition them to a life of performativity and emotional repression, damaging them whilst cruelly curating images of power, supposed happiness and success. For black and brown men, patriarchy can be even more cruel due to colonial legacies that impose destructive forms of masculinity on them, creating conditions, both internally and externally, which make it even more difficult for them to love themselves with tenderness.

We are living in an exciting age where, all around me, I see people talking and writing about vulnerability; a world where a woman like Brené Brown and her research on shame and vulnerability are becoming familiar to the general public. We see it in captions, tweets and long-read think pieces, which all tell us that acknowledging vulnerability is the key to real intimacy, personal freedom and true happiness. It's where all healing stems from. But we're at that point where we're still trying to learn how to put it into practice. Interpersonal vulnerability is different to public vulnerability. Writing a lengthy caption about mental health/pain/etc can be a lot easier than doing it in real life with the people we love. Brené herself says that 'vulnerability is not weakness … I define vulnerability as uncertainty, risk and emotional exposure'. To surrender to its will, and through that examine our shadow selves, is truly the most uncomfortable thing we can do.

Our shadow selves are far from pretty, but we all have them. Psychologist Dr Nicole Le Pera (@the.holistic.psychologist), who has built a huge community online through Instagram to explore mental health and how to heal ourselves, explains shadow work as 'the practice of returning to the authentic or highest self. Without awareness, we create an avatar of self. In the process we repress our deepest desires and emotions. Our fragile ego holds onto this version of self our entire lives. We've learned that part of ourselves must be hidden or we will not receive love. Until we do shadow work, we are viewing the world and every experience we have through the lens of our inner child.' Brown writes that 'vulnerability is the birthplace of innovation, creativity and change'. As human beings we are all flawed creatures, but we're often scared to confront our true selves because we're frightened that revealing our innermost secrets, thoughts and experiences will mean that the fragile world we have built around us collapses. But not being able to be vulnerable builds a wall around *that* world we're trying to get to – a world where we feel loved and cared for as we truly are. Unlearning these things is so far from easy, but how can we open ourselves up to love and being loved if we can't ever let ourselves be vulnerable? How do we (re)turn to love when there is no guide showing us how?

Our society tries very hard to make us forget about our internal worth and the importance of vulnerability and instead tries to make us value ourselves based on external things, like our work, wealth, beauty and status. We're so deeply conditioned to fall in love with the idea of someone, based on these external signifiers, as opposed to doing the labour of loving someone for the complexity of their inner world, taking the time to know and understand the nuances of who they are

I think we are often guilty of confusing external validation with love, but now I'm learning that no amount of external validation or prestige can replenish us in the way that our own self-love and deep connections with others can. When I started to think of a strong sense of ambition as something that can also be seen as a 'fear of failure' it really changed my perspective on everything. Every day I am reminded that fear holds us back from so many things we deeply crave as human beings, that when we operate from a place of scarcity we often miss out on everything that's already in our midst and takes us away from being able to be present. The capitalist messaging we are surrounded by every second of the day, every day of our lives, tells us that the cure for trauma is wealth: accumulation and consumption. That with the right schooling, job, holiday and money in our bank accounts, that's how you're going to heal, find peace and long-term happiness. To many people out there, work can sometimes take the place of love. And when work is predicated on our passions, it's so easy to conflate these things. But for me, it's just not the truth. External factors may help, but they will not heal the pain in our hearts. Choosing to love ourselves is one of the most radical things we can do. And loving ourselves is not about arriving at some kind of utopian peak of bliss, but about embarking on an unerring process of deep reflection, solitude and gratitude. I'm now constantly trying to check in with myself more now, and ask myself important questions: Is this what I actually want? Is this coming from me? Or is this a societal expectation that's been put on me that I'm adhering to?

The pull of adhering to societal norms can be hard to resist. We are part of a culture that is constantly projecting a message to women that no matter what we've achieved in our lives, unless it leads to a permanent partnership we are not valued in the eyes of our society. Because of this, there were moments when I questioned whether putting up with this behaviour, and how it made me feel, was still better than being alone. But I know deep down it's absolutely not. We should not have to tolerate any abuse to be loved. We cannot be in relationships where our self-esteem is being degraded. It makes me wonder about the stories that we tell ourselves about relationships. We've inherited myths from the various structures around us that we believe in despite them not serving us or helping us to see the abundant potential of love.

As much as I know it had to end, my heart still feels broken. Because despite all of this, I still see all the most beautiful parts of him. The ones I had fallen so deeply in love with, and those soft-hearted moments continue to haunt me in my sleep because they act as stirring reminders of the potential our love had. There were so many glimpses of the most gorgeous aspects of him that I loved so much, the tender and vulnerable pieces of his being which, to me, were trying to reach the surface. The pain of what felt like his complete emotional unavailability, lack of remorse and his unwillingness to salvage the relationship tore me up inside. While writing this, I am still in a place where I'm trying to heal from this whole experience. I know that all wounds heal over time and that I have to practise allowing myself to feel everything in the meantime, as if I suppress the sadness, the loss, the pain I know it will only catch up with me later on.

To try and do this, as the days go by I'm trying to sever my connections to the things that made me feel like I needed to be in this relationship. I'm mourning the idea of this person, who with hindsight, couldn't have been real because fantasies are fantasies for a reason. I'm mourning the life I thought we'd have together. I'm trying to let go the part of my ego that felt like I needed to be with a box-ticking 'relationship goals' partner who looked great not only paper but in photos too. I'm grieving for the part of me that feels ready to have a supportive, loving partner, that sometimes fears being alone forever.

I'm grieving for the children I thought we were going to have and mourning for the family that I wanted so desperately to be a part of. But most of all I'm grieving the love I think that deep down he has for me and I have for him that just can't be.

I archived (because I didn't have the strength to delete them) the few photos of him I had on my social media profile, the only public remnants of us ever having been together, because seeing him on my page was too triggering. He swiftly followed by deleting all the photos of me on his. The day I saw that he did that, even though I had done it first, felt like the real nail in the coffin, which I think he must've felt too. The erasure made me relive the break-up all over again. In the past I've never posted photos of the person I was dating – for this very reason – but I fell into the trap of the conventional Instagram trend and posted a handful of photos of him, because this time I'd thought it was going to be forever. I wanted to share the love I felt. Surely there was no risk in sharing a love that was going to be 'forever'? I had to eventually unfollow and block him, to protect myself and my energy, on the app on which I'd found him in the first place. The blocking part was really more for me than for him. To see him just going about his life as if nothing had happened, as if we hadn't planned to spend the rest of our lives together, was just too painful for me to deal with. It's strange how, just like that, someone you thought you were about to spend eternity with can just disappear – all by pressing a few buttons on your phone. Deleted off the 'gram and deleted from your life. But if only it was as easy to delete someone from your heart.

I was in two minds about writing about this whole experience. There was a part of me that felt a mixture of fear and shame. But at a time where the internet is shaping so many of our relationships, I have to remember that keeping those feelings secret, hiding them, fails to address the toxic behaviours that causes them in the first place. I wrote about it just in case it helps even one person to find the strength to recognise and to leave a situation that isn't beneficial to their growth. Because how can we ever begin to deal with something that we won't admit to?

There are always two sides to a story and no two people ever experience the same reality, so I wanted to write this story as honestly and compassionately as I could, because I still care for this person and I know it's been painful for the both of us. I want to insist that this isn't a call-out. This really isn't about him, or me; it is so much bigger than us. I'm not sharing this personal story for revenge or punishment, I am sharing it because I want us all to discuss long-term reform. I see different versions and scales of this story happening everywhere regardless of gender and see how it is not serving any of us. We need to talk about the reality of the need for control and domination and how patriarchal structures show up in our intimate spaces. To address them we need to open up the darkness of these experiences to the light so we can start to be more aware of how and why they happen in the first place. I felt the need to share this story because I understand that for us to transform as a society, we have to allow ourselves to be transformed as individuals and I'm not always sure that simply cancelling people makes things better in the long run. If we shift our focus slightly from the individual to the systemic, to dismantling the racist, sexist and imperialist structures which uphold and ingrain toxic patterns of behaviour in our intimate spaces and relationships, we can start to generate a new culture of intimacy and vulnerability that is rooted in love and justice.

I want this story to serve as a reminder to all of us that just talking online or calling people out regarding complex issues around trauma, gender, race and intimacy isn't doing the work. We have to question our own patterns of behaviour and work on healing ourselves. We have to approach these ideas with softness and compassion in our real lives – with the people we love – otherwise nothing changes. So many of us are carrying pain – pain that rears its head in lots of different ways, because pain in life is simply unavoidable. Without really being able to speak and listen to each other regarding these issues, we are in danger of perpetuating the harmful behaviours that can result from them, which hold us back from the love we seek and the love we all deserve.

But what does it mean to love at a time where people are claiming consciousness yet not embodying its power in their lives? What does it mean to love when 'woke'? What does 'woke' love even look like? 'Woke' as an adjective got added into the Oxford English Dictionary in 2017. The compilers explained the reasoning behind the addition as follows: 'In the past decade, that meaning has been catapulted into mainstream use with a particular nuance of "alert to racial or social discrimination and injustice"'. In a time where everyone on social media is 'woke', it becomes tricky ground to navigate. There were moments I experienced this in my own relationship. Part of why I was attracted to my ex-partner was that I felt like he represented a new kind of masculinity. But by having the language, we may remain blind to the fact that the very things we're speaking out against are deeply ingrained within us.

Wokeness gives us a powerful language with which to express

ourselves but it is not the only tool we need for true emancipation. Being conscious of the legacies of colonialism, racism and sexism is a point of departure into unfurling different dynamics of power, but what does dismantling the impact these systems have on our hearts involve?

Having the jargon, without embodying the nuanced essence of its meaning, we end up just performing the right things to say so that we don't get attacked. It becomes virtue signalling that fortifies the echo chambers we exist in, interrupting the need for dialogue and often uncomfortable conversation. I sometimes wonder if 'wokeness' and riding on the essentialist bandwagon of today has robbed us of our human compassion, particularly in private. By policing each other without kindness, without patience or empathy, are we actually making anything better? I feel like the idea of being 'woke' gets viewed as some kind of accessory when it should be more about a person's ability to learn and grow. In a post-#MeToo world where we are finally having important discussions around misogyny, sexual misconduct and the abuse of power, what does actually being an ally to women look like? Sometimes, I feel so overwhelmed and exhausted by the performative feminism the internet seems to be so full of. How do we not only talk the talk but walk the walk? What does it look like to be an ally to people of colour and people across the gender spectrum? What does genuine allyship look like offline, when we practise it behind closed doors?

I think this is the problem with internet buzzwords and terminology. We are schooled online to engage with these different conversations in a superficial way without developing a critical and well-grounded understanding of how we came to know what we know. We get too comfortable with it, thus becoming desensitised to its potency and how it lands. Take the term 'toxic masculinity', for example. It merely describes one version of masculinity that is endorsed by different realms of power, hence has become a dominant practice of masculinity yet, importantly, it does not really explain what it is to be a man. Mark Greene, author of *Remaking Manhood: Stories from the Front Lines of Change*, writes:

> *Language that critiques men's culture (toxic culture of masculinity) is received differently than language that critiques men's personal sense of self (toxic masculinity) . . . A term like toxic masculinity, even if we sense some truth in it, doesn't invite us to distinguish between ourselves as individuals and the culture we are caught up in.*

By talking about 'masculinity' as if it's something singular only holds us back from an actual shift in culture and behaviour. Alternative visions of masculinity exist but are suppressed by the obstructing culture of toxic masculinity. And it is this culture that (re)produces trauma. I don't want to live in a world where we cancel men; that notion, as much as I sometimes feel like I want to, just isn't conducive to the cultural shift we need to happen.

So, what have I learned from this whole experience? I mean, I can definitely say, hand on heart, that I'm not going to vow to marry someone I don't know, ever again. Obviously with hindsight that was a totally insane decision that was bound to have consequences down the line, but I can't deny that there were so many lessons in it for me, and despite the fact it was such a tough way to learn, I wouldn't change a thing. It's helped me find a new sense of empathy for other people who have been in similar situations. I used to think that I would and could never end up in a position like this, in a relationship like this. But this kind of behaviour can happen so subtly and so quickly. I turned away from it because I didn't want to get stuck in a life that I knew ultimately wouldn't help me grow and would stop me from evolving into the woman I'm supposed to be.

I don't want to be ashamed about being seduced by the myths of romantic love that we have been conditioned to believe in all our lives. I'm not ashamed for not wanting to be alone and for believing I deserve to be happy in a relationship. For believing I deserve to be loved, because even a fragment of real companionship felt so powerful. I often wonder if social media adds to that, because in so many ways we are so connected, but it can sometimes only magnify how much we yearn to seek deeper connections of the kind that can be found only in loving intimate relationships.

I'm reluctant to even say that I'm never going to speak to someone I might possibly be interested in romantically on social media, because that's realistically how most of us communicate with each other now, but I will definitely be going into it with a lot more awareness than before. I see now that this short-lived relationship served a long-lasting purpose: by stepping out of it, I learned what it meant to practise self-love. I decided that I was worth taking care of. Maybe he was what I needed to understand how to truly accept myself as I am. And that is a great gift, one I am so thankful for. Sometimes I catch myself running my fingers over the tattoo that I got with him and feel a pang of deep sadness, but then I tell myself that it's there to serve as a reminder of my capacity and yearning to love – and not just to love another, but to love myself, as I deserve to be loved.

But above all, the overriding lesson I have learned from this is that we have to have to pause, recognise and understand how much we internalise dominating power structures like capitalism, patriarchy, sexism and racism in our lives. These are the things that hold us back and block us from love. For us to have the love we desire, one that feeds our highest selves, there is a collective un-learning process that has to happen. I don't want to live in a loveless world that stops us from giving and receiving the love that we all deserve.

But love takes work. We need to do the work of undoing these myths of love, unravelling the normalisation of patriarchally inscribed ways of loving, creating new ways of relating to each other. By doing this work we can stretch love to do the work of real transformation, so we can begin to reframe the way we see ourselves and each other. I know it takes serious discipline to fight these narratives that have become hyper-normalised in the fabric of our society, but we have to try.

My beautiful friend and teacher, Aditi Jaganathan, sent me a message that, to me, sums up everything left to say about this for now:

Life shows us many lessons and it really often is a gift which we can learn and grow from and through. The shadows are hard to be still in, but if we persevere, they yield so much light and beauty. Loving in a capitalist, patriarchal and colonialist world can be so hard because of all the trauma we carry, but I truly believe that love is love and if we let it into our hearts and allow it to deconstruct all of the bullshit we've internalised, then we can finally be free.

It felt crucial to tell this story because so many of us are connecting romantically online. We are walking into relationships that begin with digital impressions, with ideas and projections and fantasies of curated lifestyles and edited versions of ourselves that leave out our innately human complexities. How can that lead to anything but confusion, hurt and disappointment? How can any of us live up to the high expectations we have for each other? I now know that any future relationships I may have need to be rooted in a love that stems from an acceptance of reality and not a projected digital fantasy, which maybe means a love that starts a little slower and a little steadier, because I understand it really takes time to build love and trust. Because we are all flawed as humans and all have our own traumas and pain to bring to the table, we have to try to learn how to be accountable and emotionally aware about how these things show up. My heart is still open, I'm still hopeful. We took a chance on love and for that I have no regrets. By risking a broken heart, I choose to live; and sometimes the pain of heartbreak is where our stories really begin.

Have you ever had a relationship with someone you've met online? In your mind, was it successful?

Yes, I have had few love affairs that began on social media. I don't regret a single one. For me, social media helped me to feel less alone and it helped me to love myself a little harder.

KIMBERLY DREW, 29, WRITER, CURATOR AND ACTIVIST

PAULINA PINSKY ON THE SWIPE RIGHT STATE OF MIND

When caught in a lull in any and all conversations, I feign engagement as I unlock my phone without even looking down. I swipe past the home page to where I have unsuccessfully 'hidden' Tinder. Placing my finger on the flame, I open the app to find another interaction: a match.

I'm addicted to Tinder. I swipe when I'm happy, I swipe when I'm sad; winter or fall, spring or summer. The rhythm my fingers fall into – left, right, left, left, left – helps me fall asleep at night, even if my phone's blue light does not. Dopamine floods my system, match after match. I swipe, and swipe, and swipe, chasing after an archaic fantasy made modern: finding The One.

Why not just be in the moment? I've tried, but then I find myself at a bar after last call, talking to someone whose breath makes me queasy. I look around, spotting two close-to viable options within arm's reach. Bleak. I promptly give up and turn to the screen in my hand to find the one for the night – or, hopefully, a lifetime.

I've dabbled with every major dating interface available, and each one presents its own problems. Bumble masquerades as the feminist dating app, since women message first, but I have been scarred and censored by it: 10 minutes after I downloaded it, I was sent three unsolicited dick pics; after that, one of my pictures was deemed 'inappropriate' and removed, because I was wearing a bikini under a mesh bodysuit.

Hinge, the next viable option, uses your Facebook mutual friends to find potential suitors, which creates the illusion of security. My one Hinge romance ended poorly. The app reminds me of my heartbreak, so I no longer use it. Plus, I find the questions they make you answer stupid. OkCupid is quite simply everyone's last resort. And finally, my favourite: Tinder. Presented with a few pictures and a few lines of text, there are as many swipes as the app will allow. (Which, after swiping for hours on end, is less than you would think – they start demanding that you wait 12 hours or shell out dough.) Tinder doesn't hide the fact that the interaction is based on a split-second superficial assessment. And because of that radical transparency, I appreciate Tinder.

But then there are the days when the endless options and split-second assessments feel mind-numbing. I swipe past faces that I will never remember, only to match with people who I will never message. Although I am on Tinder for the prospect of love, most of the people I encounter are not. To most of the men I match with, I am simply something – not someone – to fuck. I get more matches if my bio is empty; fewer words, more potential to project anything and everything onto me. On those days, I feel myself avoiding coming to terms with the fact that I, too, am just a face to swipe past. An idea, rather than a person.

At times, Tinder can be straight-up abusive. Countless men have thought it was 'funny' to send lewd first messages because they don't understand the onslaught of misogynistic sentiments and statements that women regularly face. I have received real messages like 'Are you a prostitute?', 'Are those boobs real?' and 'Suck my dick'. I take the time to lecture them, telling myself I'm making a difference, which has never yielded a positive response: I've been unmatched, scolded and harassed. But I tell myself that if I can change one man, if I can keep him from speaking that way to anyone else, then that is a win in my book – even if I skim a few years off my life in the process. But that's just a self-important false justification to keep someone's attention for a few minutes.

Then there are times when I use my better judgement and swipe left quickly on profiles that boast things like 'I like skinny girls with big butts, but I don't really care'. There are people who match with me and tell me they want to fuck me, but when I don't respond (or take the time to lecture them), they call me 'fat' or 'ugly' or 'fugly bitch' before promptly unmatching. I can see the fragility of their egos, but I am left feeling bruised. Responding, not responding – I put myself in harm's way. Which leads to the days when I simply delete the app from my phone, only to download it a few days later.

How I swipe directly correlates to my self-esteem. When I feel bad about myself, I swipe right without thinking. Despite the influx of matches, I don't feel much better. But on the days when I fully appreciate my bounty, I am more discerning. Although I get fewer new matches, my integrity and self-worth are left intact. And, of course, those are the days when I press 'Unmatch' liberally. Send me a lewd message? I'm reporting. On a second glance, not interested? When the app asks why I unmatched, I select 'No Reason'.

The more hours I rack up, the more matches. The more matches, the more messages for me to field. The more messages to field, the less interested I am by a simple 'hey' or 'hi' or 'sup'. But then I get one message that piques my interest. We message. We forget. More hours, more matches. More messages, until I find myself having a good conversation. We decide to meet. The date is fine. We go home. We never speak again.

Despite all the head and heart aches, I have found what I am looking for: a connection, good or bad. The bad needs to be taken care of. I can only hope that Tinder strengthens security so that people don't feel degraded, debased or abused. I also need to help weed out the losers by protecting myself. Report, report, report. As for the good, I may not have met The One, but I have found so much more. In pursuit of an archaic fantasy, I have found friends and romantic partners; book and running-shoe recommendations; boredom and elation; tour guides and lovers. I continue swiping because who knows what else I will find.

Paulina Pinsky is a writer and teacher living in Brooklyn with her cat Jack. She aspires to move to Hawaii.

When I'm with people IRL, I'm aware that I need other skills such as listening, feeling and body language; these are the ways we're able to get beyond the masks we wear and into vulnerability, which is the basis for real connection. I'm also sensitive to the expectation of mechanical 'efficiency' that can bleed into my IRL relationships; my patience is used to the time needed to wait, listen and relax enough to let myself and the person I'm with truly open up. I get caught up in the instant nature of digital communication, but real people, myself included, take a minute to land on the mutual ground of a relationship.

**MARGOT BOWMAN, 30
DIRECTOR, GRAPHIC ARTIST**

SOCIAL MEDIA +

COMMUNITY

♡ ◯ ◁

'We have to come together and speak honestly about what the barriers are within our community – and then tear them down. It's really that simple.'

TARANA BURKE

SARAH

Social media is a land of extremes – the far right and the far left; the most progressive politics of a generation alongside the most insufferable narcissism – and it all exists in a big tangled pile on the same feed, sometimes in the same photo contained within a peculiar digital format: the 'activist selfie'. When it's done right, this subgenre can be an effective communication tool. At the constructive end of the spectrum, there's Laverne Cox posting a selfie video protesting Trump's ban on trans people serving in the military. At the destructive end, there's Mischa Barton in a bikini on a yacht holding a glass of rosé, hair blowing in the wind, with a caption about the tragedy of Alton Sterling, a victim of racially motivated police brutality. Somewhere in the middle is me choosing the photo where I look best at the Women's March to post online.

We slide along this spectrum of admiration, disgust and egotism, struggling to absorb the good of social media without the bad, and to hold on to the good before it gets bastardised into a trend or a selfie excuse that we then feel compelled to contribute to in order to prove to our peers that we care about reproductive rights. My friend Sadhbh, the social media manager, brought up the self-care hashtag as an example of this – of how activism for the common good can quickly get twisted into individualism online:

The self-care movement used to be about activism – about self-preservation in order to continue fighting, from civil rights activist Audre Lorde's quote about self-care being an act of warfare. Now it's about bubble baths and spoiling yourself after just doing your job. That's happened with the majority of movements online; it's become about individuals who think, 'Self-care is for me. Self-love is for me. Body satisfaction is for me.' Understanding that it's not just for you has been completely lost.

I really want to believe in social media's power for good, as a vehicle for collective justice riding high above the chitter-chatter of selfies and personal goals. I want to know that it works as a network, connecting isolated individuals who are seeking a sense of community online. As an editor in digital media, where I've been most aware of this happening is in #MeToo, in trans awareness and in mental health awareness. Each of these movements has made rapid progress online that far outruns the progress in society, which at first sounds like a compelling argument in social media's favour, but once you scratch below the surface, it's also the strongest counterargument.

I've spoken a lot about the negative effects of social media on mental health, but the other side of the story is that, in the last five years, the internet has significantly reduced the stigma around mental illness in the UK. Online communities such as Big White Wall, which is recommended by NHS doctors, provide 24-hour support via text, audio or video to people feeling desperately alone. Multimedia support that doesn't require a depressed person to get out of bed and actually go to the doctor's surgery can be a lifeline.

After finding her TEDx talk titled 'What you don't see about depression' on YouTube, I interviewed Jayne Hardy, a mother and author who in 2011 founded an online support network called the Blurt Foundation for those affected by depression. When I asked Jayne how members of the Blurt community support each other online, she replied: 'In such a way that it continues to boost my faith in humanity. The Blurt community never fail to show kindness, support, encouragement and empathy for one another. When we take into consideration how unwell and low people in our community sometimes are, they still shine the light for others, and we can't underestimate the power of that.'

Jayne described social media during her periods of depression as 'my window into the outside world. It connected me with people who understood what I was going through and were incredibly kind. I was able to use their hindsight as my foresight and learned more about depression from their experiences of it than I had read in any book.'

I felt the same way reading people's five-word descriptions of their mental health on Twitter under the hashtag #MyMentalHealthIn5Words for Mental Health Awareness Day in 2017. @mattttmillerrrr summarised his as 'Hello Darkness, my old friend'; @forglutenssake said 'Much improved since quitting Facebook'; and @hellofelicia14 wrote 'Suffers with too little sleep'. I kept checking the hashtag all day, retweeting the statements I resonated with most.

Social media exacerbates anxieties about the self, causing all sorts of weird addictions and insecurities that didn't exist 20 years ago, but it simultaneously offers the type of unconventional support that helps to address them. Memes, YouTube videos, honest tweets and comment sections might sound surface-level, but they can provide a valuable boost in the moment.

I have a friend who is a scientist and who does a job I don't understand, alongside studying for a PhD in something I don't understand. She also struggles with depression, and recently sent me an illustrated quote by @bymariandrew (1.1 million followers) which was liked by 45,000 people. It said:

I was clinging to my wounds because I thought my pain was the source of my creativity, empathy, and wisdom. Until I started healing and realised that my soul is the source of my creativity, empathy, and wisdom. And it does a much better job of all 3 when healed.

It took me by surprise because this scientist is not an emotional-quote type of person, but somehow these words on Instagram resonated with her and she decided to share them with me. And what I took from reading the quote was that her emotional state was changing into a more hopeful one. It helped her, and then by her sharing it, it helped me understand what helps her.

Another friend who struggles with depression says watching dog videos and interacting with other dog lovers on Instagram really boosts her mood. Dogs have long been thought to improve the well-being and happiness of elderly people who are socially isolated, as well as providing emotional support to those with anxiety and depression; and studies show that watching cute dog videos online triggers hormones like oxytocin, the 'cuddle chemical', in our brains. Oxytocin is associated with empathy, trust and social behaviour, and triggering it is considered helpful as a treatment for some mental health disorders. As Seattle scholar Joshua Dale put it, cute stuff is 'not a real medicine … but it can make you feel better because it releases those chemicals in the brain that actually make you feel better.'

I follow @mytherapistsays, along with 3.6 million others. They post funny memes about not wanting to get out of bed, not wanting to socialise apart from with dogs; about insecurity, loneliness and the great lengths people go to in order to hide how they're really feeling. Though the topics are pretty heavy, it's laugh-out-loud funny. I sometimes feel panicked about the fact my friends are having babies and I'm not, and then I see a meme saying 'People my age be on baby number 3 and I'm still on mambo number 5' and it makes me laugh and feel a lot lighter about it. And when I'm feeling as if I just can't keep pretending I'm fine, I see one that says, 'Where's my Oscar for acting like my life isn't falling apart?' and I remember loads of other people are feeling the same way. It's dumb, but it helps.

The founders of the account are two friends in their twenties, Nicole Argiris and Lola Tash, and they draw on their own experiences with anxiety and having therapy. 'Having this account has definitely helped us laugh at some of our more questionable moments in our mental health history,' the girls told me over email. 'We're so incredibly grateful to the people who relate, reach out, and live out our memes with us. It's always a nice reminder to know you're not alone.'

Professional treatment is usually something you undergo on your own – a doctor prescribing medication, a therapist providing one-to-one care – but as a helping hand to that care, social media offers a community of millions who have a shared experience. Dog videos, tweets and memes don't treat mental health disorders, but they can have a walk-on part in the play.

Personally, I've found huge comfort in watching ASMR videos on YouTube to help with anxiety and insomnia. ASMR stands for 'autonomous sensory meridian response', a complicated term for a nice, relaxing, tingly feeling running down your body – the kind of feeling you get if someone draws on your back or plays with your hair. A curious form of vlogging, ASMRtists (as they are referred to in the community) record videos from their bedrooms as they whisper gently into very sensitive microphones and make soothing sounds with glass or wooden objects or a ballpoint pen on a piece of paper, in an attempt to make viewers feel calm. The ASMRtists also do role-play and 'personal attention' videos, in which they pretend to give the viewer a facial or a haircut. I watch these videos for an hour most nights, to stop my mind racing with anxious thoughts and lull me to sleep. In the comments sections I connect with other anxious souls around the world, who are also lying in bed using the videos to feel calm, and we laugh at ourselves for watching a woman ironing shirts and whispering

Are there communities on the internet that have made you feel less alone in the world?

Yes, now it feels like there is a constant stream of conversation that one can look at. I often stumble across something that I can relate to despite never having said it out loud. It's reassuring.

CELIA BURTON, 29, MAKE UP ARTIST

about her technique for 50 minutes. The community is constantly growing, with more ASMRtists starting channels and their videos getting upwards of 10 million views.

My family and friends think it's so weird that I'm into it, because they don't get the same feeling I do watching the videos; they just feel creeped out. But research released in 2018 by Sheffield University presents evidence to suggest it does work. Reporting from a sample of 1,000 people, those who claimed to get 'the feeling' had a lower heart rate watching the videos and reported 'increased levels of calmness and decreased levels of stress and sadness'. Dr Giulia Poerio, a psychologist at Sheffield who worked on the study, commented: 'What's interesting is that the average reductions in heart rate experienced by our ASMR participants was comparable to other research findings on the physiological effects of stress-reduction techniques such as music and mindfulness.'

Assistant professor of psychology at the Center for the Treatment and Study of Anxiety at the University of Pennsylvania, Lily Brown, commented: 'There may be something to having these videos as part of a patient's treatment. When dealing with emotional dysregulation, having a suite of activities or behaviours at the ready is very important. I can easily see ASMR videos fitting into that package for people who feel relaxed while watching them.' Brown went on to say that: 'Overwhelmingly, patients report that they like the idea of therapy, but real or perceived barriers may lead them to choose something easier and more accessible.' Social media can fill in a few gaps, providing temporary relief in the moment.

While waiting for therapy after a car accident that had left her with post-traumatic stress disorder, Emma Smith found ASMR videos online. Now she's the UK's most well-known ASMRtist, going by the name of WhispersRed. I interviewed Emma at the UK's first live ASMR experience in London. 'I went looking for nature sounds or something relaxing, but found ASMR videos and it was amazing,' she told me. 'I couldn't believe there was a name for this feeling I'd felt for as long as I can remember. I started talking to people in my local community about it and I was met with the same reaction I used to get when I was little: "What are you talking about?" So I just stopped talking about it, but carried on watching the videos.' Emma then started a UK Facebook group for ASMR fans, but didn't actually consider making a video herself until she read about an ASMR meet-up that stipulated you had to be a content creator in order to attend. So she put aside her shyness and made a video. 'I had one subscriber when I turned up to the meet!' she said, laughing. 'But I loved it, it was amazing to meet the community in real life.'

Emma now travels the world meeting fellow ASMRtists and is working on further research into the psychological benefits of ASMR with the team at Sheffield, as well as looking at ways to take the online community offline via live events and weekend trips. 'I grew up without the internet, so for me it's been so amazing to connect with all of these people,' she said. 'Now it's about bringing them all together in real life.'

I felt such a bond with Emma; we got along like a house on fire. 'You know when you meet someone and think, "They are an ASMR person,"' she said halfway through the conversation, and I nodded, feeling extratingly. Like Emma, I experienced the feeling of ASMR as a child in certain situations, such as having my feet measured for new school shoes or getting books out from the library where the librarian scans all the books and stamps them with a date mark. I never knew what that feeling was until I found an ASMR video on YouTube in 2014. I couldn't believe there was a name for it, and that people were making videos targeted at all the millions of other people who got the same feeling.

It makes me laugh because, as a journalist, the online space I should feel most comfortable in is Twitter – that's where 'my people' are supposed to congregate and share jokes and ideas and get into spats, but I never know what to say on Twitter, whereas I know exactly what to say on an ASMR forum because that, in fact, is my community, and I feel and think the same way that other ASMR watchers do. My online community has nothing to do with the things that define me in real life – my work, my interests, my beliefs, my politics, my social life. It's a sanctuary away from all that, where I go to relax with a million strangers – none of whom can see each other. I used to feel incredibly frustrated and lonely at 4 a.m. when I couldn't sleep, and my mind would wander to dark places, but now I load up an ASMR video, interact with others who have the same sensitivities as me, and it's instantly soothing.

The problem, a potentially fatal one, arises when the community you seek online doesn't support you in a positive way; when the memes and videos you find aren't about healing pain, but about inflicting further pain. There's been a lot of debate about negative communities forming on social media in the mental health space, specifically relating to hashtags like #selfharm. The *British Medical Journal* states that the UK has one of the highest self-harm rates in Europe, and one widely referenced study using data from GPs reported a 68 per cent rise in self-harm among girls aged 13–16 between 2011 and 2014.

Anna, mother to three teenage daughters, two of whom self-harm, told me she thinks it's '100 per cent related to social media. I don't know how else to say this, because I know it's a cry for help, but posting about how suicidal you are seems like ... a trend among my daughters' friends. Some of the content I see on their feeds about self-harm is really disturbing. My youngest daughter [aged 13] attempted suicide and posted a photo of herself on social media from hospital. I don't remember it being like this when I was at school. It's terrifying.'

Dr Steven, a GP who works in a low-income area in the UK, says self-harm is a big problem for teenage girls, and that he has patients as young as 10, still in primary school, who are self-harming. 'Their mums tell me they watch self-harm songs on YouTube and sing along,' he told me over the phone. 'Awareness of self-harm – and sharing methods of self-harm on the internet – is a big issue. They get ideas for using specific household items to hurt themselves with. Online self-harm communities provide negative emotional support from other self-harmers.'

When I asked him why he thinks girls are searching for this type of content online, he answered: 'I think it gives them an identity. I see girls who are 13 and 14 years old who desperately want to be on antidepressants. I tell them I don't think it's a good idea and refer them to their local psychology services, but they just keep coming back and asking for medication. I think they see being on antidepressants as validation for how they're feeling.'

In response to the dramatic increase in self-harm in this age group, and growing concern among parents, Instagram recently started removing self-harm posts identified as having graphic content. The app also introduced a blocker page, whereby when you search #selfharm a window pops up offering help with numbers to call or text in your area for support. At that point, you can still choose to 'See posts anyway' – and when I click that, the majority of posts that come up are healed scars and positive messages like 'Don't give up' and 'Life gets better', which is reassuring. But there are also posts encouraging suicide, such as 'If you wanna go ... I want you to know it's ok ... I understand'.

News coverage on the subject implies self-harm hashtags are having an overwhelmingly negative effect on teenagers, but a 2019 study by the *British Medical Journal* analysing images tagged with #selfharm rated just 6 per cent of the images as 'severe', which they defined as showing bleeding or serious wounds. 'None of the images we captured specifically encouraged self-harm or suicide,' the authors of the study wrote. 'Many posters also captioned their images with discussion points or questions suggesting that one of the functions was to connect with others who perhaps shared their experiences.'

But those using the hashtag to post negative messages are determined to preserve the community they belong to, and a little bit of censorship won't stop them. Once Instagram started policing #selfharm, people just added another 'm' to make it 'selfharmm' in order to get around the censor. Then when #selfharmm got rumbled, they added another 'm'. On another hack hashtag – #ehtilb – I find lots of graphic self-harm images and very few 'Life gets better' captions. On Twitter, no warnings pop up with support numbers when you search for these hashtags, and I quickly find a video of a young woman about to jump off a bypass, with police trying to talk her down; and another young girl with multiple posts on the hashtag about wanting to end her life. This young girl's entire feed is about self-harm and suicide, and the bio where people usually write a few defining characteristics about themselves reads '29 #suicide attempts – [most] recent 21/04/19 and my next suicide attempt will be successful'. There are even photos of her cut-up forearms taken from hospital. It makes me wince looking at this girl's open profile. It's obvious that she is very unwell and that this account is her cry for help, but I don't know how I would perceive it if I were a mentally ill teenage girl and this was the first thing that came up on a self-harm search.

At the time of writing (May 2019), the British government is in talks with the major social media companies – as well as the Samaritans – to improve the censoring of self-harm and suicide content. The chief executive of the Samaritans, Ruth Sutherland, has highlighted that while much faster and tighter censoring needs to take place to stop young people being exposed to distressing imagery and destructive captions, the positive support that online communities are offering must be allowed to remain: 'We need to work together with tech platforms to identify and remove harmful content while being extremely mindful that sharing certain content can be an important source of support for some.'

If the answer were simple, it would have happened by now. The latest figures from Hootsuite estimate that users post more than 3 billion Snaps per day and 500 million Tweets, and because the line between a positive post and a negative one is so fine, you can't just flick a switch and turn off the bad stuff. It's a flawed community, offering critical healing support to some and destructive pathways to others. Social media platforms aren't equipped to monitor communities of this size, which have evolved at a much faster rate than the technology that is needed to support them. The only solution I can think of is an implausible one: to have a psychologist present when a teenager is either posting or viewing these hashtags, to help them process the content and understand the impact. Perhaps this is where artificial intelligence in the form of therapy bots could operate in the future.

The question of how to maintain the positive aspects of community while avoiding the negative repercussions is keeping the internet up at night. It's an issue the leading voices of #MeToo are also wrestling with. Tarana Burke is the woman who started Me Too as a grassroots movement in 2006 to support survivors of sexual assault in underprivileged areas. Ten years later, Hollywood actress Alyssa Milano turned the movement into a hashtag, asking women who had suffered sexual harassment and assault to tweet #MeToo. With over 19 million replies worldwide, the hashtag highlighted the scale of the problem, creating an overnight community of millions whose collective voice gave power and support to the individual voices that had previously struggled to break through. In an interview with the *New York Times*, Burke expressed concerns over whether the hashtag had lost sight of the movement's original goal. Speaking about her current project – creating a digital hub for Me Too to connect survivors with practical resources – Burke commented:

We don't believe in collecting stories of people's trauma because I don't think the trauma should be curated. We believe in sharing people's stories of healing. When you start talking about what you've done to cope and how you have developed practices around healing, that's something that people need to see ... It's hard because the idea of sharing your story has become so popularized. We are in a time where the more you share about yourself, the more people like you; the more likes you get, the more attention you get on social media. So things are framed so that they have to be public and they have to be popular in order to be valid.

This is something I've struggled with as an online editor deciding which stories will work best on the internet. One major criticism of #MeToo is that the cases which have gained traction are predominantly from high-profile white women. Later in this chapter is an interview with Juno Roche, a trans writer living with HIV. When we spoke, she was researching for a keynote speech about how you challenge the invisibility of marginalised groups. Our conversation turned to #MeToo:

Beneath the point of invisibility are a bunch of people doing everything that they can just to survive. They haven't got the time to try and make themselves more visible to you. I came across these horrific stats that say in certain parts of Africa, a third of girls' first sexual experience is forced. They say 'forced', but it's rape. But people aren't interested in that story; what they're interested in is the single woman who fits the Hollywood description of what a '#MeToo woman' looks like and sounds like.

Annie Lennox OBE expressed a similar concern when I interviewed her for a piece on her NGO, The Circle, which champions women's rights. 'Girls and women living in the developing world are faced with lives that we cannot, as Western women, even begin to imagine,' she said. 'This is not mythology, this is happening right now, every single day, and this is the darkest of the dark side of abuse by men against children. It's so dark that I'm afraid even mentioning it. But the world needs to talk about this, the world needs to know about this. It's not only happening in Hollywood with the top executives, it's not only happening in industry in corporate offices.'

For many women and girls around the world, who live in countries or in situations where women's rights are savagely denied, social media activism doesn't do much – if anything. Either it's not safely accessible or it just doesn't reach people.

In researching how #MeToo translated around the globe, I came across the Chinese branch of the movement. Despite being one of the most technologically and economically advanced countries in the world, China's government is quick to censor any online content it deems a threat to society (which, incidentally, includes ASMR). #MeToo appeared on Chinese social media in 2017, initially used just to report on the highly publicised Hollywood cases, but as soon as the movement spread and Chinese women started using the hashtag to share their personal experiences of sexual harassment and assault, #MeToo was banned by state censors. What happened next was one of the most satisfying hacks of the technological era: Chinese girls started using other hashtags on Weibo (Chinese Twitter), such as #WoYeShi (Chinese for 'me too') and a bowl of rice emoji (a bowl of rice is pronounced mi) next to a bunny rabbit emoji (pronounced tu).

In the past, Chinese youth have used other hacks such as 'river crab', which signals the fact something is being censored, and 'grass mud horse', which in Chinese sounds like 'fuck your mother' and is used to avoid censorship on vulgar content. As the *China Digital Times*, a website based in LA delivering uncensored news from China to the world, explains: 'The Communist Party is often described as the "mother" of the people, so saying "fuck your mother" also suggests "fuck the Party".'

On the WeChat messaging service, Chinese activists started screenshotting sexual harassment stories before they got taken down, and reposted them upside down in order to confuse the censoring system. It's thrilling to know that technology can be used in this fundamental way in order to connect people and lead them to the truth, but the stakes are frighteningly high.

One of China's #MeToo heroines is Yue Xin, a 22-year-old graduate of Peking University in Beijing who helped uncover the (still 'alleged') rape of a former student named Gao Yan, who committed suicide in 1998. Yue Xin was part of a group that wrote an open letter to the university requesting information on the investigation into Gao Yan's death. The alleged rapist, a professor at the university, had been acquitted at the time and given little more than a slap on the wrist by the institution. Shortly after the request letter was submitted, Yue Xin published a second open letter outlining the intimidation and threats she and the other students who sent the first letter had received from the Office of Student Affairs, including being woken up late at night by her school adviser entering her dorm room and insisting she 'delete all data related to the freedom of information request from my phone and computer'. Yue Xin's second letter was quickly removed, but her supporters screenshotted it and posted it online using secure blockchain technology, meaning the letter is protected online and cannot be tampered with or censored. As journalist Li Jing pointed out on Twitter, this might have been the first time blockchain technology was used to fight censorship in China.

According to *The News Lens*, there's evidence to suggest that Yue Xin's name is now also a censored term on WeChat. After posting another open letter on another social-justice issue in 2018 regarding factory workers, Yue Xin was arrested by Chinese authorities along with dozens of other activists. As the *China Digital Times* reported, some activists were 'violently "kidnapped" from public university campuses by thugs'. Yue Xin has not been seen since August 2018 and is listed as a 'disappeared' person on the Chinese Human Rights Defenders website. She made a powerful contribution to the community, but at what cost? Gao Yan's alleged rapist is still at large, and #MeToo is still an underground movement in China. The community is there if you look for it – using technology in innovative ways to protect information – but that protection is limited to the online world.

#MeToo started a community, but did it empower individuals? Or leave them more vulnerable? This is the question I put to Rahila Gupta – author, lifelong activist, patron of Peace in Kurdistan and part of

How do you feel about the #metoo movement now?

I have mixed feelings. I feel like, to a lot of people, it is just a hashtag. I hate hashtags. I can't even begin to tell you how many men while travelling overseas say things like 'So, how do you feel about the #MeToo movement?'. They just look at it as this pop culture trend. It makes me want to scream.

JESS, 28, MUSICIAN

the management committee at Southall Black Sisters, a not-for-profit organisation established in 1979 to support black and minority ethnic women in the fight against gender violence.

Rahila Gupta, 63
author, activist

#MeToo succeeded in raising awareness and mobilising people, but do you think it failed to support the individual?

#MeToo felt important and like a real turning point because the sheer number of women who signed up to it forced a crack in that culture of disbelief that women have faced to date. The universality and prevalence of sexual violence helped to normalise it to such an extent that individual women who dared to complain, to fight back, were portrayed as deviant. But #MeToo turned that into a tsunami of common experiences which punctured the myth of deviance. The paradox of anonymity and visibility that Twitter, for example, can give you encouraged women to join up without personal risk, if they so wished. Of course there were brave individuals who took a risk, but they could choose the degree to which they wanted their real identity exposed.

The actions of individuals have transformed our collective consciousness. But the problem you point out with the #MeToo movement – that it started something and then failed to support those who joined up – is contained in the hashtag. The 'me' points to the individual experience and the 'too' may be a gesture outwards to others, but it remains a collection of individuals. So the system remains in place. That's the paradox of how change happens under neoliberalism: it operates at an individual level [but] individual challenges are accommodated and absorbed by the system – and the #MeToo movement is a victim of that. It is only when the system is toppled that the individual is really supported. But what the #MeToo movement did was validate the individual experience. We cannot underestimate the confidence boost it provided to individual women to be believed, and that belief came from the sheer number of women who put their heads above the parapet.

Did #MeToo give hope to the women at Southall Black Sisters?

Some people have argued that the #MeToo resistance to sexual violence connects women across race, culture and class, because of its global nature. But it has also divided women. How we talk about/analyse the massive and widespread abuse of girls by Asian men in towns up and down the UK has divided black women, for example. There are class divisions too. The women who come to Southall Black Sisters have all faced sexual violence and harassment, but they have not all heard of #MeToo. They recognise the hurt but not the hashtag. As you know, less than 20 per cent of the UK's population use Twitter.

As an activist, do you feel a sense of community on social media?

I belong to the old school of activism, which has seen change being brought about and awareness raised by hard graft, wearing out our shoe leather, pounding the streets in marches and demonstrations, stretching our vocal cords to chant slogans or make speeches, taking direct action, putting ourselves at risk and inconveniencing everybody else, hanging around in the corridors of power till somebody with power deigns to hear you out. (In fact, the model followed recently by Extinction Rebellion but without the same numbers.) To that extent I approached social media activism with a fair amount of cynicism. Somehow the very ease with which you could draw attention to your cause on social media invalidated it. In time, I began to see that it can and does complement real-world activism, but I am not convinced that it should be an end in itself. Therein sectarianism lies. When I and Ritu Mahendru organised the demonstration outside the Indian High Commission in January 2013 on behalf of Southall Black Sisters on the infamous Delhi rape case, we set up a Facebook page to publicise it and over 1,200 people said they would attend. Everyone said about 10 per cent of those who say they are coming will turn up, but in fact more than 1,000 people turned up which was incredible. There was a real anger about sexual violence which needed an outlet. We provided it with the physical demo, and social media helped spread the message far and wide with relative ease – as compared to the old days when we would have had to print leaflets and distribute them at various meetings.

I do like the feeling of belonging to an online community but it also feels insubstantial and superficial. It is extremely hard to judge the level of loyalty and commitment to the cause from the 'likes' that you acquire. How many of them are carelessly ticked? The ones that feel most substantial are from those people you know in the real (offline) world. [Though] I don't like to say 'offline' because it is defined by 'online', and sounds secondary to it.

Do you think activism should be separated from personal life on social media? Should we be separating the personal from the political in order to protect ourselves?

My answer is probably typical of my generation. We thought that the generation before us was too tight-lipped and they probably thought that we leaked too much, but I feel much the same way about this generation – that it overshares, that it appears to have no concern for privacy and then complains when that privacy is infringed. I never agree to befriend someone on Facebook that I have not met in real life, for example. In real life, we tend to compartmentalise: we share our personal secrets with some, we talk about politics with others, we share certain hobbies with some people and so on. Facebook has recognised that by allowing us to post selectively, to set up groups, and those of us who are clever about it might use that option; but generally the whole point of social media is to amplify your voice, and that amplification only happens if you have a large number of followers or friends. So the inbuilt bias is to talk to more rather than fewer people – even your online status is determined by the number of followers. Given that capitalism is about targeting new customers and generating demand for goods, it's not surprising that it has developed the technical knowhow to mine our online presence to sell us goods – and now political positions. The role that Facebook played in providing personal data to Trump's election campaign and the Leave campaign in the Brexit referendum has become the stuff of scandal, but without sounding too laid-back about it, it confirms that politics too is a commodity. Governments may try to regulate the infringements by introducing various kinds of firewalls, but I fear that the horse has bolted.

I'm struck by the visual of Rahila's generation of activists 'hanging around in corridors of power till somebody with power deigns to hear you out'. That's a powerful voice – the one that's waiting around in a corridor ready to say what needs to be said out loud to a person who probably disagrees, and to stand there and take the response, and then fight back again with words. I guess that's what Twitter is: a corridor of people trying to get the attention of the people in power and engage them in debate. #MeToo is a force, still active and thriving, recognising its shortcomings, regrouping and trying to find a way forward. The same could be said of all movements online: mental health awareness, body positivity, trans awareness – in each there are divisions, successes, failures, things to work on, to-do lists, campaigns, break-out communities. Social media feels like hundreds of interconnecting corridors with millions of people in each saying what needs to be said. And on every corner, capitalism lurks, hoping to take over the debate, slap its values on a can of Pepsi and sell it back to the people in the corridors – who are thirsty.

Amidst these mighty waves of community spirit and community breakdown, the individual can go under. In my conversation with Sadhbh, we spoke about the impact of movements on the individual in relation to the LGBTQ+ community, who have suffered a huge amount of abuse online in the last few years. 'You fight to become visible and then they try and use that visibility against you,' she said. 'I imagine that's the hardest part – managing to survive that.' It reminded me of something the author, journalist and trans woman Juno Dawson said in her speech at the Mind Media Awards in 2018.

It's precisely one year since I told everybody gathered at the Mind Media Awards that there was a need as an industry to stop debating transgender lives,' she began, receiving applause from the audience. 'I'm delighted to report that one year on, things have greatly improved! . . . Just kidding, things have gotten so much worse.

Dawson went on to talk about the power of online communities in the mental health space, and how helpful they have been in 'highlighting coping mechanisms and strategies'. She urged people to continue sharing their experiences online so that we all feel less alone. But her first statement about people debating transgender lives, and about how it had only gotten much worse between 2017 and 2018, made me wonder again about the impact on the individual. Trans awareness, like mental health awareness, like #MeToo, is a big talking point on the internet, and generally we think of that as a good thing – forcing those in power to put trans rights on the agenda, as well as educating the public about what it is to be trans. But, as Dawson says, being the person whose identity is constantly debated in public is exhausting.

For the last few years, I've worked with another Juno – Juno Roche, a writer and activist in her fifties who transitioned later in life. I've commissioned her to write dozens of pieces online about her experiences as a trans woman living with HIV, and I've watched in horror as some of those profound pieces that opened my mind to so many new ideas have been trolled on Twitter and in comments by people intent not just on expressing their opinion, but on inflicting as much hurt on her as they can. Like Rahila, Juno is someone I feel very privileged to be in a position to learn from. I asked her what it's like to be on the receiving end of extremely personal online abuse, and whether she feels a sense of community online.

Juno Roche, 55
writer, activist, patron of CliniQ, a community
interest company providing counselling and sexual health
services for trans people and their partners

How do you think your experience would have changed if you'd had social media when you were a teenager?

I was born before there was even the word 'technology'. Technology for my generation meant that you could walk around the room with your telephone cord. People would make mixtapes with notes stuck to the front of the tape box, and you'd listen on a Walkman the size of a small book and you'd think, 'Oh, they get me a bit, they understand me a bit, because they put this song on halfway through.' We didn't have smartphones, but I think we had our own version of social media. There were programmes on the television aimed at the youth market about fashion and clubbing, like *The Clothes Show*. And there were magazines like The Face and i-D, where you could find a whole plethora of stuff related to the LGBT community – well, back then, it would have been LG, and mainly G, but these magazines were beginning to tie people together as groups. I worked in the sex industry for quite a long time – I did phone-porn sex and then I did sex work – and there was this whole range of stuff that started to open up that enabled you to access different communities. Was it in any way, shape or form as effective as social media? No! Social media cuts through everything in a second – through time, space, concepts, taste, style, intention, it cuts through all of that, which is why people get it wrong so often because they go, 'oh that's not what I meant' because it all happens so fast that there's a lot of room for miscommunication and misunderstanding. Our own version of social media did exist. I suppose if it existed in the way it does now, I could have easily met other trans people, but trans people were a new phenomenon that weren't even allowed to exist then, so that might not have been possible anyway given the context of the time.

You told me last year that you've stopped writing so much for online publications, why is that?

I don't write articles so much anymore because of the flak I get online. I just write books now, and that's really fun. I started to feel like I was being curated by a whole set of people, not just from one group. People were really unhappy about me using words like 'woman' or 'vagina' or 'empowered'. If I used any word that didn't make me out to be this unhappy, tragic trans person, people would jump on those words and attack me. I could write about the problems that trans people were having in relation to a medicalised model and in relation to a societal model that treated us badly; if I was problem-solving while not trying to be empowered or ballsy, I could pass under the radar. But if I stepped out of that script, I would be jumped on.

What did you write that stepped out of that script?

I'd write about my vagina and about using dating apps and about my longing for motherhood. People attacked me viciously on Twitter for the motherhood piece, saying, 'you're mentally insane, you don't have a womb, why would you write this piece', and they used it as a case study to say, 'See, trans people are mad, this one thinks they could have had a baby!' The magazine had to release a statement defending the fact they had employed me to write it. It was a stark reminder of my economic status. At that point I was a freelancer, I needed to earn money. It reminded me of trying to transition as a teacher and being marched off the premises. How do we really bring other people down?

We threaten their economic or their physical safety; we go for that angle really quickly. People want to extinguish or silence the potential of somebody else that they don't agree with. Trolls always call you 'he' – they'd never call you 'she'. So they misgendered me and said 'HE used to be a teacher . . . HE should never be allowed to teach again'. People say, 'oh, just block trolls', but if you're getting lots of tweets that say you're mentally ill or that you shouldn't be allowed near children, that has an effect. It's not good for my mental health that my phone beeps all night letting me know there are 1,000 people saying I shouldn't be writing this article. Last year I wrote a piece for the women's section of the *i*, and that got loads of stick with people saying what was I doing in the women's section in the *i* because clearly I wasn't a woman. Most of the time now I say I'm not interested in being a woman, I'm interested in being me and I define myself as trans. I like that as a destination.

Why?

Because if you occupy the word 'trans', then you are really breaking down societal norms and expectations. The whole world is fed up with gender – from #MeToo to young men committing suicide because they don't feel like they're male enough. We need to reshape this whole debate. It's still a broken, rotten model.

Do you respond to trolls?

No, because I've worked out that if you do respond to them, it just piles on. After my book *Queer Sex* came out last year, I got a lot of horrible trolling. Somebody set up a web page called 'Who does Juno Roche think she is?' Somebody found out my mum's address somehow and sent her gay porn. My mum's a feisty old south London woman so she wasn't fussed, but I was fussed, it terrified me that they'd found her address. There's nothing rational about people piling on you online. What I take away from it is that I still have a platform. However people attack me or ignore me, my books are doing well, and that gives me great hope. If the trolls got together and wrote a book of essays about why they don't like trans women – well, it would probably be a really good read! And a really good basis for a set of arguments! But they won't do that because they don't believe in their words enough.

Did you inherit your mum's feisty spirit, and does that help in dealing with trolls?

Absolutely. I'm from Peckham. You wouldn't bring this to my door. You'd be really silly to bring it to my door, not because I want to be tough, I have no interest in being tough, but simply because I wouldn't put up with it. I wouldn't put up with somebody flinging gay porn in my 80-year-old mum's house; I would chase them down the street and batter them with the porn.

What do you think the positives of social media are for you, or for the trans community more widely?

I think it's amazing. I have been so isolated my whole life as a trans person living with HIV. Social media put me in contact with people and somehow it allowed me to become a trustee and then a patron of CliniQ. That would never have happened without social media. The ability to step into a space that can then become a physical space or an emotional space or a mental space or a practical space – that's immense. I wrote a series of articles for Refinery29, commissioned by you, that really got to an awful lot of people, like the piece about body hair. I often think: we're going to change the world not by big deep conceptual things, but by dealing with how we look at hair! What do we think hair is? Do we think it really demarcates attractiveness or gender or butchness or femininity? So many people contacted me after that article saying they related to it.

Social media allows these great connections in communities that are really fractured. Somebody tried to add me the other day – I'm always slightly concerned when somebody adds me because I never know if it's going to be somebody that's going to attack me, but I accepted them and they sent me a photograph of their feet in the grass with my book and the message said, 'I got hold of your book secretly, I'm a little queer in my garden in the outback of Australia and I'm loving reading it.' Social media didn't allow for that to happen, but it allowed me to know that it happened. And it was priceless. It just made me think even more that I don't care about the trolls, I'm going to carry on, and in my next book I'm going to be even braver.

Does social media provide a sense of community for you?

No, not really. I live in a 200-year-old schoolhouse in a tiny village in the mountains in Spain, where there's five houses and two of those are farm buildings. It's not glamorous but I love it. I won't see a soul today – I could stand outside my front door naked and it wouldn't matter, the postman comes every other week. I like being here because it's so dramatically different to my life when I come to London and do book readings and go to meetings. I don't really do social media over here; I post photographs of lemons and my dogs because I love my dogs, I'm obsessed with them. People who run dog accounts with 60,000 followers on Instagram for their pug follow me, and that's the truth of social media really. When you're in a city and you're in amongst it, it takes over, it becomes its own network. I think we've bought into the 'Matrix' idea that social media is another layer of the world that we can never step out of. But you can close it up like a book and walk away. I'm really happy just to sit under my tree. I don't want to spoil my tree by opening up social media and seeing lots of arguments. When I'm in London, I don't have such a good handle on social media because I feel like somehow I'm back in the Matrix and like I need to get with the programme. I start thinking things like, 'God, my wardrobe is not very capsule, I need to get smarter!' Right now I'm in my schoolhouse and I've got on a floral blouse and old green tracksuit bottoms and really cheap polka-dot slippers. I look raggedy, and happily raggedy. My life is so different here, but when I land at Heathrow, I get off the plane and I just think, 'Oh fuck! Do something! Buy a handbag! Make this better!' We have a duty to try and make social media a better space, because it's currently walking in the opposite direction of stuff that's good.

My issues with social media have to do with the pressures it exerts on the individual – to look good, to have the type of success that looks good, to be seen as popular, fun, socially conscious and well-travelled. I try to tick all of these boxes and then feel like a fraud for trying because I'm not sure how much I'm doing these things because I want to versus because I want to be seen to. Approaching social media as an individual seeking individual gain presents a wealth of problems and resentments, but I can't ever say that it's bad – no one can, because all the bad stuff takes place on the same platforms as the good stuff;

it's just the algorithms that make it seem more weighted in the bad stuff's favour.

As Juno said, we have a duty to try to make social media a better space. How? That's the million-dollar question. I don't have the answers on how #MeToo can be more effective, or how to stop trolls or prevent dangerous self-harm content from circulating, but I can personally try to move from a position of 'I' to 'we' online – which, granted, is very difficult when the whole thing is designed to reward 'I'. That's not to say everyone needs to become an activist, but it is to say don't post an activist selfie unless you're doing something to contribute to the cause besides being there and looking nice.

I've benefited from the support of the mental health community online, and that's the space I think I could contribute more to as an individual – not by posting positive affirmation quotes on Instagram, but by writing more articles as a journalist about this community and researching how developers are tackling the gaping holes in the system. My hope is that an almighty new technology comes out, like an AI therapy bot attached to every social network, designed to coach users through the dark side of the social media experience. In the meantime, I think it's worth following Juno's model of self-care when the negative feelings start to stir: close social media up like a book and sit under a tree.

Are there communities on the internet that have made you feel less alone in the world?

NAOMI

My colourful world is what it is because it's been greatly aided by the fact that I follow an incredible array of individuals that make up so many different interweaving larger communities on social media. Thanks to social media I don't feel like I have to choose to be part of just one community, but that I get to be a part of so many that each feed a different part of my soul and being, and allow me to relinquish and soak up all the things that make me, me. Whether they post things that are related to art, music, travel, food, fashion, healing, social justice etc, these communities can often serve as teachers who have helped me form my own distinct perspective on the world. Even through times when I feel overwhelmed by the sheer volume of activity and voices on the internet and feel the need to take breaks and distance myself from it, the thought of ever completely stepping away from it feels unimaginable. I think I would feel very lost, as, after all, I am a child of the internet. I still want to be a person of the world, I just want to be able to be more aware about how much and who I give my attention to.

Accounts of different people who identify as multiracial and social media movements like #ImNotAlone have been at times a helpful source to help me think about my own nuanced identity as a multiracial person who didn't quite fit in anywhere while they were growing up. Movements such as this have helped me see my multi-racialness as something multi-dimensional, something to be truly celebrated. It's taught me the power of belonging in my own essence, and helped me see and understand that the mixed race experience is so complex, that there are such nuances with every single mixed person, that with us there is no simple 'other' box to check and it has helped me to see the beauty in that. I feel optimistic and believe that there is a way that social media can help us garner a sense of openness and lots of wisdom to expand the minds of others and maybe even at best helps us to heal the racial divide in this world.

Online communities have reminded me of the power of coming together and they've only invigorated me to try to keep creating strong communities offline as well. That's what this whole book is about, feelings that start online, to have conversations and thoughts about, offline. That so many ideas are birthed online but we need to be together and share communal space to make things real sometimes. I don't want to just care about my online communities; I want to care about my local communities, where I can play a real tangible part in being a member. I don't want to live in a way where I don't introduce myself or not have some kind of rapport with people I see every day. I want to care about my neighbours and care about the state of my local businesses, schools and parks. I try to be part of the community that I'm actually surrounded by on a day to day basis.

My friend Kate is the hot water bottle version of a friend. Someone that always makes you feel better in times of need, a seemingly old soul combined with the most youthful fresh perspective on so many things. They are one of my very best friends. They've housed me and taken care of me in a way that helped bring me back to life through some of the most difficult times.

Our love of colour and rainbow dispositions runs through every aspect of our lives and continues to bind us together in a special way. I wanted to speak to Kate because not only do they live and breathe the internet; they now identify as non-binary, and as a close friend I saw first-hand the huge effect social media had on them exploring their own identity through finding and connecting to other non-binary and trans communities online.

Kate Moross, 33
art director, illustrator and graphic designer

How did you feel about your body when you were a child?

I think we're all most at home between the ages of about 7 and

11? Because I think you haven't got as many of the stigmas – well, maybe some – but you probably haven't hit puberty yet, I probably hit puberty when I was about 12/13. I guess then I just dressed how I liked. I was lucky enough to have parents that were super relaxed with how I wanted to behave or present or anything like that. So I was super confident in general. And then I think I hit puberty and that was confusing – I think it's confusing for everyone. Not just puberty, but all the gender stereotypes that come at you, around who you should be or whatever.

I was a really hairy kid. I used to get teased for being hairy. And that was really hard. And because I dressed like a boy – I don't like that phrase – but because I wore jeans and a t-shirt, I didn't wear what's traditionally associated with what girls wear, I guess people thought I was a boy all the time and it didn't really bother me, I used to think it was interesting as opposed to being upset by it. My mum used to tell me that my little brother used to get asked if he was a girl. So it was kind of like 'adults are stupid'. It wasn't strange for it to be confusing. So I think I was really privileged as a kid to have that freedom. I know my mum had this ideal of me in dresses and things, but she didn't hold on to it for very long. I just was like, 'nope'. And puberty was challenging for loads of reasons. I think when you're growing up, all the intersections of your identity start to blur a bit, because you don't really understand how to differentiate one thing from another. I definitely went through different phases of exploring hyper-femininity and then rebelling against that and becoming covered in piercings and tattoos and shaving my head and just being very alternative, I guess? But apparently that's also quite common later on in trans identity, like you go through different experimentations, because the identity of a goth or a punk or whatever is quite gender non-conforming. So to have a mohawk wasn't out of place.

But it was still kind of a way of expressing some kind of difference?

Yeah, gender queerness without being within a subset where that is what a girl does in the punk world. I don't know. It was interesting and playful and I enjoyed experimenting with how I looked. As for my body, I think my relationship with my body is confusing in itself anyway. I used to have very strange feelings when I saw women with flat chests. I didn't know how to process it – it's really strange even thinking about it now, I'm just kind of like – it used to like, shock me I think. But there also would be this strange element of jealousy.

How old were you when you were getting these feelings?

Not sure, probably when I was about 18.

So it was a jealousy from wishing that you could be flat-chested too?

Yeah. I don't think I knew that's what it was at the time – it's only now that I understand it. To have that feeling of desire for myself. I don't even know what I thought it was, I just remember them now as feelings. And then I think I have been suppressing my chest for years, probably in one way or another since I was about 19. I stopped wearing any sorts of clothing that made my chest look bigger, and started wearing as much as I could to make it smaller. Very tight crop tops in an extra-extra small. And I did that unknowingly, really, just kind of through my preference. You don't really understand it at the time, but then over time you go deeper and deeper into the things that make you feel comfortable.

How old were you when you started to develop a relationship to the internet?

Oh god, I mean I had the internet in my bedroom when I was 11. So a long time ago.

Was there a certain point where you felt like, using social media, you found people that you felt connected to?

Yeah, I think it's very strange to understand something that is so fundamental to yourself at such an young age. So I think because I didn't have those incredibly binary feelings that some trans people do of rebelling, or rejecting against the entirety of your gender, or the gender that's assigned to you, because I was allowed to express myself how I wanted to, I didn't have the same pushback against it. So I was quite happy being a very gender-nonconforming person basically my whole life, and not much about that has changed – I look at pictures of myself, and apart from like a blip in my teens, I've been the same person, and I've expressed myself since I was a kid. I think I remember very vividly listening to a podcast – I don't even know what podcast it was to be honest – about someone who was non-binary and they were talking about how they wanted to have top surgery, and I was like, 'God I didn't know that was a thing?'. Because firstly I didn't know I was trans or that how I felt even existed as a thing, and that other people felt like that and the internet has changed that for a lot of people. So that was interesting, and I was raising money for these trans organisations and getting involved with all these organisations because without realising I was curious about them for myself. You need to look deeper into these feelings that you have - this affinity for these people who have, you know, maybe there is something there. So I did a bit more exploring.

When I think about for whom social media has been the most beneficial, I definitely think about the communities that it's created so much awareness for, especially when it comes to shedding light on the trans community and trans issues. Do you think it's been a powerful resource? Was it a massive influence in you starting to think of yourself as a non-binary person?

Of course. I think it has so many benefits to people, and I think more than anything it's not just a resource for people to understand something but also for people to see it from the millions of different points of view. To understand that there is a thing, but that thing is different for every person and how they experience it. I think for a long time was only one understanding of what trans identities were, and that was through the medical profession and that was very binary, and it still is unfortunately that way in how legal and medical and how our cultural systems interact with trans people.

But in terms of within the community there's a much more broad understanding of what's under the trans umbrella. So I think I just started to slowly talk to people in real life, and also online, and watch videos, and understand what was possible from various Youtubers and social media accounts.

Did you have a lot of trans people in your life already?

No, I didn't.

Did you ever meet people online and then meet people in real life?

Yeah, I did that a lot, and that was a big part of me understanding that my identity was making friends with people all over the world who were non-binary and trans from various walks of life, and finding a really close-knit group of trans friends that I didn't have before, that I've only really met in the last few years, that I've been able to talk to about things that I couldn't talk to my cis friends about. So that's been really integral. I mean the trans community online is – of course there are deviations to that and there is some toxicity and bad stuff – but on the whole it's a powerfully strong and supportive community of people who are genuinely looking out for each other and supporting each other. But that did help a lot –and the internet has been a big part of that.

As a friend and as a person who's known you before and throughout this process, being able to watch you blossom during this time and really sitting into yourself has been such a beautiful thing to see. What made you decide to share your journey on social media?

I think the really difficult part of it all is the constant conflict of all of these weird perspectives on gender, from this cisnormative point of view. This is actually a genuinely normal human story that has been around since humans have existed, but the world thinks that you're an outlier and you're strange to science. And then actually, I think there are your own personal feelings and your history and the culture that you're within that you have to fight, but there is also a layer of that from how the general world looks at you. And I have been blessed to have had people in my life who are open and positive and very supportive, but there is still so much that needs to be done. I think that I'm privileged as a trans person who is accepted within my family, and my world, and my career, more or less. Of course there's still a tonne of work to be improved on, but that's what I decided to talk more about on the internet, because although yes it's a private thing, I felt like I had the capacity to do it, so I could maybe help some people who couldn't do it. As a white person, I have a lot of privilege in that respect on the internet. I run my own company and I have financial stability and other things that aren't afforded to other people, so why not. I can take the unfollows and the harassment, which is really minor to be honest, compared to other people.

You have documented many aspects of your journey and even shared images of your gender non-confirming top surgery on your social channels, what kind of feedback did you generally receive from people?

My family were freaked out by it. They found that very difficult and couldn't really understand why I felt the need to talk about it on the internet. I think that, generally, it stems from the fear we have of bodies, or people sharing their bodies or on the internet. Like for me, I basically never took my shirt off in front of anyone for 10/15 years of my life. This was exhilarating for me because I felt like I finally could. And that's not because I was ashamed, or felt suppressed because I had a female component of my body, but just because I felt like it wasn't mine? It didn't feel like me, and now I do feel like me.

When you first sent me that photo, my first reaction was like, 'oh that's what you're supposed to look like'

If you look at every photo of me that I like of myself, you wouldn't know the difference. Because I spent my whole life unknowingly trying to hide a part of my body that I felt incredibly uncomfortable about. You know, people would be all, 'You got the best tits in the world!' And I'd be like, 'I wish they weren't there!' Thanks, but no thanks.

How do you feel about your body now?

Great, I feel so at home, like just being. Before that I wasn't really sure, I felt uncomfortable. I've never experienced any kind of issues around my body size or weight. I did about being hairy; and that's another tragedy, I spent years of my life paying thousands of pounds to have laser hair removal, and now all I want is a moustache. You know, I think, apart from that, which I slowly learned to accept. But I remember another weird memory, being at summer camp as a kid and seeing someone's mum and she had hairy legs. I nearly jumped out of my own skin! I don't think I'd ever seen a woman with hairy legs in my whole life, and also, isn't that wild that something so small can give such a visceral reaction to a 7 year old child?

I kind of have memories of that too actually - being so unfamiliar because you're so used to seeing women hairless.

Yeah. I shaved my legs and bleached my arms because I was bullied so much that my mum helped me to navigate it.

That makes me so sad!

Isn't that unfortunate to think that a percentage of people who have or haven't got body hair purely because society says should or shouldn't have body hair? It's so huge.

We're asking everyone in this book this one last question - what do you wish for the future of social media?

I really hope that the balance between access to information and communities isn't offset by access to harassment and the spread of lies and really damaging materials. I think that's the biggest challenge, as a trans person, that I'm navigating, and that this community is navigating. But really it's not just the internet, it's also the press! I think it's a really challenging time to be online. But there are so many positive things that come from access to the web, but also a lot of very difficult things too. I hope the tools that we use to do it become safer and easier to moderate, because everyone is different and they should be able to moderate the tools that they use for themselves. I hope they become more customisable and better-run. I think that would be good.

TAHMINA BEGUM ON LEADING A DOUBLE LIFE ONLINE

I have 68 accounts blocked on Instagram. Some are spam accounts that won't leave me alone; some are people I've had to 'cancel' in real life; and some are external family members.

Now, you may wonder what the last bunch could've done to be blocked online. For the most part, they've done nothing wrong. But this kind of blocking isn't unusual, and I know I'm definitely not the only one who has been affected. In fact, for many Muslim girls online, members of their family are blocked. Some girls are one step ahead, and have a private account or even a separate account for friends, away from the one that's open to anyone and everyone.

For Sunayah Arshad, senior editor at *Azeema* magazine, a publication exploring the lives of women from the MENASA region of the world, it took moving to London from her hometown of Nottingham for her to share her life online and even have an 'open' Instagram account.

'I used to say to family, "Please don't follow me, I'm not going to accept you anyway," because I didn't want any whisperings about my life. My dad used to always remind me, "You know how Asian families can be nosy, and I don't want anyone judging you".

For both Sunayah and me, social media is imperative to the projects we work on as creatives; we need it for promotion. But navigating what we share online is an even more conscious decision than it is for others. 'Oh my god, aren't you worried who will see and tell your parents?' is a very common direct message I get from South Asian and Muslim teenage girls whenever I share a photo showing too much skin or talking about taboo subjects such as sex before marriage in the South Asian Muslim community. What they're really asking is 'How Muslim are you?', and how much I'm willing to show the less-than-picture-perfect image than the one we have all in one way or another been trained to hold up.

You may ask what the big deal is, and what makes my content so scandalous when it's literally just magazine features I've written, outfit snaps, book recommendations and dinners my friends have cooked for me. But for much of the world, in both the East and the West, it's a Muslim woman living her life on her own terms. And this is seen to be an improper way to act, as Muslim women are supposed to be the nurturers for others. Their lives aren't meant to be their own.

Following this line of thinking, because I am free in many ways I therefore must be wild. As my mother always says, 'Isn't holding on to your roots really just understanding what lines to stay behind?' Hence the occasional argument between us, when a distant relative calls her to tell her what her daughter has been wearing (and posting on Instagram) – or worse, who she's been seen out with.

The problem I see with Muslim girls censoring themselves online, or essentially leading double lives, is that it promotes this false image society has of us already. That we don't drink occasionally. Or date people who are bad for us. Or have shit mental health days. Or be queer or non-binary. Or have several boyfriends without our mahraam present. That we don't fuck up sometimes.

This disparity between 'good Muslim girls' and 'bad Muslim girls' widens. Fake-woke but still misogynistic 'halal bros' make it their mission online to pit women (who are also active across social media) against each other. They make Muslim women feel as though they can only be one way, when there is no one cookie cut out for Muslim men. I don't think I've ever seen Muslim women make YouTube videos on the rules Muslim men aren't following.

And frankly, this behaviour is never for the benefit of Muslim women's lives. It's just an easy way for the minority of barbaric and sexist Muslim men to work out who is worthy of being a wife. You don't want to marry the one who shares a selfie wearing a short skirt or too much makeup – who is she trying to attract with all that?

Muslim women leading a double life online also means we sometimes feel like we can't be a part of certain conversations across social media – though we're definitely discussing them in our group chats or in person. I don't implore Muslim women – or anyone – to share their whole lives on the internet, but I can't stand the idea that being cautious of who may be watching our social media accounts is yet another thing Muslim women have to think and worry about.

There's also the idea that you have to present the 'best Muslim' to the world as Islamophobia continues to rise. It's another filter on what you're posting online, but this particular mask is largely held up by 'not wanting to get a bad reputation'. Whether that means for the lives of all Muslims or so your family doesn't get a 'bad name'.

But sometimes, it's not that deep. Sunayah and I spoke about how we select what we post from our holiday pictures, as there's no point in our parents being grilled for having daughters that enjoy a bikini or two. The hassle isn't worth it. But for those whose identities are at odds with the path that feels marked out for many Muslim women (university, marriage and babies, but mostly the last two) – whether that be having a girlfriend, being transgender or simply not wanting to go down the traditional route – leading a double life can be exhausting.

And it can be harmful too. Muslim women like Qandeel Baloch have been killed by their families because of how sexually liberated they've been online. Influential Muslim women like Dina Tokio are hounded on Instagram for deciding to take their hijab off.

There's no point in technology progressing and social media evolving if our minds, and how we see Muslim women, aren't also moving ahead.

Tahmina Begum is the editor of XXY Magazine, and a journalist focusing on culture and communities. She attended 29 weddings in 2012.

Are there communities on the internet that have made you feel less alone in the world?

I have definitely benefited from the access of seeing the global black female community active on Instagram. It's validated my existence in ways I don't think I would have ever been able to fathom without constant reminders from women I admire on social media.

**LYNETTE NYLANDER, 29
WRITER, EDITOR AND CREATIVE**

AMANDA HARRIS WILLIAMS ON BROWNING UP YOUR FEED

Images are instructive. They take real sensory space, and a good one can trigger endless interwoven thoughts and ideas. Those thoughts and ideas spur feelings. Some of those feelings lead to actions. I think often about the state of our world and the actions that need to be taken. We need to save our planet, we need to fight fascism, we need to feed the world and ensure that everyone has access to medical care; we need to honour history and indigenous cultures from around the globe. At least, that's the future I wish to see.

Prominent in that future, and every likely iteration of the future, is social media. My mission at this moment is to brainstorm and create community: what user actions can we take as responsible digital citizens to ensure that social media is a space that represents and extends our politics and values and expresses our deepest wishes for the world? And specific to my favourite platform, Instagram, what sorts of images and accompanying text (that we create and share, and that we pay attention to and like) spur ideas, feelings and actions that can lead us to a more just world?

The first step, of course, is to acknowledge that images carry loaded meanings, that they are rich with symbolism – whether that's in a photo of a person at the Louvre next to the Mona Lisa, or a text saying 'Keep Calm and Carry On'. Example number one suggests luxury, access to foreign lands, art knowledge and belonging in the art world, and whatever the subject wears in the photo might suggest a cultural or social membership. (It goes without saying that race and gender matter in how we interpret people.) Example two states the message of course, but also a bit of Anglophilia and a certain middle-of-the-road coping mechanism of self-care and stoicism. Changing the font or background colour affects the experience and meaning of the text. As a coarse example, adding a pink background and putting the letters in cursive would make the image more 'feminine'.

Art historians have long analysed the meaning and function of images and art objects in society. Similarly, we can analyse the images that everyday people make. Social media is not mere documentation; it is more frequently intentional expression.

A second step is that we have to normalise having politics and values. We have to sit down with our understanding of history and culture, and decide what kind of world we want to live in, and what feels right and wrong and fair and unfair. We have to think about this in terms of both overarching structures and micro-structures. I think about how people are utilising the hashtag #BlackLivesMatter but not documenting any black lives that matter to them, and not following and liking black people's content or sharing images that help to spur thoughts and actions that materially improve black lives. And it begs the question: Why are your social values and your social media so misaligned?

My own politics and values were born from deep curiosity and study around the legacy of the transatlantic slave trade and what happened to the descendants of these groups. I have observed that at no point in time has Western culture appropriately atoned for its atrocities of empire and slavery. I have learned of tremendous cultural fortitude and innovation despite this lack of atonement. To that end, on my social media I create and highlight these slave descendants, and use the platform to build community around the goals of this identity group and to build alliances with people who have common needs.

As a consumer, this means supporting (liking and following and reposting) those who are slave-descended, while avoiding media that appropriates from these groups. I build alliances by engaging with content from people who are similarly under-acknowledged in popular media, and who as a result fail to conscript to Western sympathies such that they may gain equal rights. In my captions, I challenge well-worn media narratives that present people descended from slaves share a similar appearance as those slaves. I call this project #BrownUpYourFeed, and I encourage you to join me.

As part of #BrownUpMyFeed, I investigate the roles that black people were meant to play on screen. I think about whether we've really been able to move past sassy dark-skin bit characters, sexualised women of mixed descent, and servile, invisible helpers – even in the media we create for ourselves. I think back to the first moments we were on screen: *The Birth of a Nation*, the first-ever long-running feature film, which follows the insatiable appetite of black men (played by white men in blackface) for white women. I consider *Gone with the Wind* and Hattie McDaniel's pleasant servitude. I consider women like Halle Berry and Viola Davis, who won Oscars for portraying a sexual object and a maid respectively.

I make and share media that contrasts to those stereotypes: black women reading or thinking deeply; black women as beautiful, not just because of their sexual availability for white men; black women who rewrite and offer new options to others. These are women I see as deserving representation and self-determined narration. And although black femininity is at the centre of my practice, I also feature those whose struggles and curiosities overlap with ours, or deepen our understanding of life on and beyond the media margins. #BrownUpYourFeed looks queer, fat, Native, disabled and intellectual too.

Think about how much time you spend on your phone, and how many images you process unknowingly. Think about how much news you consume on social media. Think about how powerful sites such as Facebook and 4chan were in recent elections. Think about what constitutes a tragedy and how you understand it as such.

Images are instructive. Images make us feel and act. We get stuck using social media only to express interests and hobbies, style and aesthetics – elements of our awareness that directly or indirectly can be monetised by corporations who want to advertise on our feeds. Values-based social media simply cannot sell as many ads; this takeover, therefore, is somewhat hostile.

I think back to when I first joined Instagram, and how every time I would search for hairstyles and care tips for hair that was kinky like mine, I would get suggestions to follow people with hair slightly more 'acceptable' than mine, as though if I were to follow the regimen and buy their products, I might have a looser (more European and desirable) curl pattern. Social media, just like any sphere that is intent on driving us to spend, has a vested interest in making me feel as though I'm not good enough.

What began as a peer-to-peer photo-sharing site has ballooned into a new platform for celebrity, work opportunity, political and social influence. But without our intentional infusion of something meaningful, it will fall to the advertisers – whose goal is to make us feel that the perfect self is slightly out of reach unless we buy their products.

I will not compare and despair, though, and nor will I give up on what I feel is an incredible opportunity to connect with like-minded friends around the globe. I've thought intentionally about how to use social media as a window to the world I wish to see, and I've built an incredible community exploring how I might belong to that world. I'm hopeful that our generation remains wise and intentional, and that we use these powerful platforms to create the visual language that gets us all the love that we deserve.

Amanda Harris Williams is a theorist, multimedia conceptual artist, writer, educator, host and internet community academic living in Los Angeles. At her Manhattan pre-school interview, she got asked what time it was and she responded 'Hammer Time'. She got in.

Are there communities on the internet that have made you feel less alone in the world?

I've spoken to other girls who haven't felt like they've been able to fit in anywhere or other 'fat girls' who feel like there was no space where they could see fat girl imagery anywhere before the internet.

Sometimes it's not even notable people, sometimes it's just people who comment on my pictures and I'll randomly click on one, and I'll look at their Instagram and they'll post something really cute and I'm so tickled by it, I'm so lucky to be able to see that.

Are there any messages you have received that have stuck with you?

People really don't have any sense of boundaries. So I'm really appreciative of people who understand the amount of – I hate saying emotional labour but it's really what it is – the labour that goes into existing as a visible person online.

SANAM, 28, CREATIVE DIRECTOR

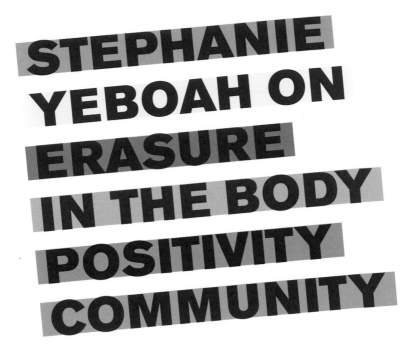

STEPHANIE YEBOAH ON ERASURE IN THE BODY POSITIVITY COMMUNITY

'Weren't you on yesterday's episode of *Planet Earth*? The gorilla episode, wasn't it?' The two white businessmen laughed to each other as they walked away from me towards Marylebone. I had just wrapped up an event at a nearby venue and was making my way to Great Portland Street station when I'd accidently bumped into one of the pair. I was greeted with that casual bit of racist, fatphobic abuse as a result. I continued on my path to the station, and immediately shrugged off the encounter. Unfortunately, existing in this darker-skinned, black fat body has made me almost numb to this kind of treatment.

Navigating society as a darker-skinned, black fat woman in the UK can sometimes feel like an extreme sport; existing within so many intersections has had a detrimental effect on my well-being and mental health. From being fetishised by men to not having the plus-size representation I needed to see within the media, it's always been a bit of a struggle to develop self-love and respect for my body, which is why I was so grateful that the body positivity community appeared in my life when it did — even if I don't feel this way anymore.

In fact, having to navigate through society in this body has sometimes felt like a prison sentence. I taught myself how to reject amazing career opportunities for fear of being ridiculed or tokenised. I trained myself to remain emotionally indifferent to men for fear of being rejected or mocked. To me, my body was a cesspit – a life sentence I had to serve for a crime I don't remember committing. Being fat, as well as darker-skinned, automatically rendered me invisible, and it stayed that way for many years. I discovered the body positivity community back in 2014. At the time, it was still a somewhat diverse, social media-based community celebrating self-love and radical self-acceptance of fat bodies of all races. But this inclusion was a given, seeing as the re-emergence of this important movement stemmed from predominantly black plus-size women in the US. In recent years, however, the movement has become more commodified. Body positivity is now a 'free-for-all' movement, monetised and politicised by brands and public figures in ways that often result in individuals above a certain size being left out of the conversation.

Who 'invented' body positivity anyway? It's important that the foundations of the movement are known and understood in order for the movement to progress in a more intersectional and inclusive way. The body positive movement originated with the fat acceptance movement of the 1960s, which aimed to combat anti-fat discrimination and to celebrate and inspire the validity and acceptance of fat bodies. In the US, this resulted in the creation of the National Association to Advance Fat Acceptance, a charity organisation dedicated to combating size discrimination. The movement – as well as the general ideology of 'body positivity' – experienced a quiet period from the 1970s to the early noughties, as we entered the era of the 'supermodel' in which we saw the likes of pioneering models such as Kate Moss, Naomi Campbell, Christy Turlington and Linda Evangelista spearhead the 'waif chic' trend that was rampant throughout the 1990s. Body positivity experienced a resurgence in the late noughties, as an increasing number of black and POC plus-size activists began to use online social platforms such as Tumblr, LiveJournal and BlackPlanet to create safe online minicommunities in which fat women could celebrate and appreciate their bodies without fear of judgement. These communities were accessible via the use of the #FatAcceptance hashtag, which then later graduated to #BodyPositivity, as some fat women were still a bit unsure about self-identifying as 'fat'. These up-and-coming communities provided us with a forum to discuss the complexities of marginalisation, and to celebrate diversity in all its forms, whether that be physical, sexual or racial. At first, I would observe and read the stories of the many women who had found their way onto the self-love train. I would be inspired by their vulnerabilities and strength, and eventually I decided that I would start posting too.

The day I decided to start the journey to loving my body, I was on a beach in Spain for my birthday. It was the first time I had ever been on a beach, and to prepare for it I had decided to lose weight so I could attain the 'beach body' that I so desperately felt I deserved. For me, this involved starving myself, using laxatives and illegal diet pills bought online, and throwing up after I ate. I ended up losing four stone, but the toll it took on my physical and mental health was unbearable. I felt constantly weak and tired, and I hated myself more than ever. I hated that I had put my body through so much stress and strain, when all it had ever tried to do was keep me alive. That was the day I told myself that I had to start loving my body at all costs. As the body positivity community grew and became more mainstream, I noticed that the conversations were now most often centred around white women, whereas before they had been centred around women of all ethnic backgrounds and sizes. The black and ethnic voices that had once dominated the discussion had now been marginalised in favour of what was palatable to brands and publications. And as more and more publications began to pick up on the 'body positive' trend, the voices of black and POC people slowly subsided to the comments sections of social media posts, while the photos and stories of beautiful, white, slightly chubby women were pushed onto the billboards and ad campaigns for the masses.

The current prioritisation of the perspectives and visibility of white, able-bodied, cisgender women with hourglass-shaped or smaller bodies is problematic. Slimmer white people can love themselves loudly, quietly or not at all, but they will almost always be seen as 'normal' in the eyes of society at large; they already fall well within society's accepted standards of beauty. They will likely not experience overt or covert discrimination based on their size, and neither will they face ongoing pressure to lose weight in order to be accepted.

Of course, all bodies are equally important, and I hope that everyone reading this – whether they are a size 6 or a size 26 – feels good about themselves. But body positivity is not about boosting the confidence of people with conventionally attractive and 'acceptable' figures. The world already does that for them. The world affords certain privileges to people whose bodies fit within the standards of beauty that society dictates we should have in order to be seen as 'normal'. By dismissing the movement by claiming 'all bodies matter', it glosses over the abuse, marginalisation and othering of unprivileged bodies that fall outside the scope of what is seen as 'beautiful'. Body positivity should be a social movement aimed at removing the prejudices that make us value some bodies more than others. It is incredibly political, something that should not be overlooked or forgotten. And, like feminism, any approach to body positivity that refuses to acknowledge hierarchies of privilege, that refuses to learn from those who are more oppressed and that neglects to fight for those more marginalised, is missing something crucial.

I could go on and on about all the 'well-intentioned but ultimately failed' body positive campaigns built on the backs of black women. Recent situations include: The online body-shaming of black comedian Leslie Jones and the lack of defence from her white co-stars. The public shaming and negative treatment surrounding Gabourey Sidibe as a visibly larger, fat black actress, in stark comparison to white actress Rebel Wilson, who seems to be universally admired. The #RealBeauty campaign created by skincare brand Dove, and their failure to include plus-size women and women of colour. The constant inclusion of plus-size women of colour in TV and movies who only serve as 'sassy' accomplices to help uplift the central white character, and who often have no character arc of their own.... You catch my drift, right? The truth is, body positivity as it currently exists is for white women. White female bodies being safe is paramount to maintaining white supremacy. Accordingly, white female feminists who claim to be here for all women instead play favourites with whose bodies they covet and uphold and whose body-shaming is worth reviling. And so while people within the body positivity community have to deal with gender equality and size equality, black women have to deal with race equality and colourism as well. Which means it's even more important to include all bodies – regardless of colour – and to give a voice to those who are not represented fairly.

Here's hoping that, one day in the future, the community and those outside the body positive movement will see us as a collective, and not marginalised within a group that is already in itself pretty marginalised. There are so many different experiences, thoughts and perspectives, and everyone deserves to be heard and represented – not just the thoughts and experiences of those with privilege. Black women matter. Fat women matter. Black fat women matter. It's important that the body positivity movement includes, engages with and better understands the experiences of black women, to ensure it becomes a truly inclusive movement that breaks beauty standards in all its forms.

Stephanie Yeboah is as plus size style blogger, freelance writer and author. She is a huge Jason Momoa enthusiast and is the treasurer of his South London fan club.

ERIN NOVAKOWSKI ON INCLUSIVITY IN SOCIAL MEDIA ACTIVISM

I spend a lot of time on my phone. This is common in my generation, much to the dismay of our parents and various older relatives who, "back in their day," spent time outside and actually socialized with people. I understand the disconnect, and realize that it can seem as though scrolling through Twitter or snapping a picture for Instagram is futile. However, as a disabled teenager with an ardent passion for politics, social justice, and learning, my phone is my lifeline. Social media has the astounding ability to connect individuals across the world in an instant, and share information at a never-before-seen rate.

Recently, as I was scrolling through Facebook (are you surprised?), I came across an image that an acquaintance of mine had shared. The image featured a man feigning shock and standing next to a sign which read: IMAGINE THEY DELETE FACEBOOK AND INSTAGRAM, AND BOOM! YOU'RE NOT AN ACTIVIST ANYMORE. My first impulse was to explain just how wrong this sentiment was, likely shouting into a void of internet dwellers who had no interest in what I had to say. I decided that rather than waste my frustration on a Facebook comment, I'd use my inherent anger to contemplate what exactly it was about this image that made me so upset.

At first, I was confused as to what exactly the creator of the statement wanted from people. I understood quickly that the message was likely referring to people who share activist content, maybe cutesy images with a statistic about sea turtles dying or quick read articles on social justice, without doing anything further. I supposed that the creator wanted people to attend protests and marches, or maybe chain themselves to a tree.' I still couldn't fully understand why this message, undermining the effectiveness of online activism, was popular enough to be shared. Thanks to the many years I've spent online and the invaluable lessons I've learned from activists just like me, I eventually figured it out. This message, that activism which doesn't involve a physical presence is 'lazy,' is inherently ableist. The sentiment presented made me upset because the activism it is advocating for is inaccessible to me, and the message behind it is suggesting that I can never do enough.

Social activism has come a long way, and it still has a long way to go. The many intersections of social justice are not yet perfectly overlapped, and many groups of people are prevented from contributing in the ways they may wish to. Social media has created the largest, most accessible community for activists and like-minded individuals to come together, whether in an effort to teach, celebrate, protest, or advocate. Is sharing a post or creating content that educates others easier than attending a march? Maybe. Is it not just as, if not, more effective? Absolutely.

By utilizing platforms such as Twitter, Instagram, and Facebook, a voice is given to every individual who has something to say. Protests, marches, and parades are more often than not completely inaccessible. To wheelchair users, to those with mobility aids, to those with sensory difficulties- these events are simply not inclusive. Social media gives disabled people a method of having their voice heard by countless people, in a decidedly meaningful way, without sacrificing health, safety, or comfort. I do not know why the creator of this image believes everything must be a competition, but I know that I do not agree. Activism of any kind is activism, and truly, the most miniscule amount of 'effort' is still creating change. If one person sees a post, reads an article, or engages in conversation, progress is being made. I hope to dedicate my life to creating positive change, educating others on the things I am passionate about, and offering my unique perspective to the greatest amount of people possible. I know that social media will be a substantial part of my attempts. I love my phone, I love social media, and I love the opportunities they present to me. I cherish the fact that I can connect with others across the globe and participate in movements that mean so much to me. I will continue to spend a lot of time on my phone, because my phone is my voice, my most important tool, and my ticket to becoming the activist I aspire to be.

Erin Novakowski is a 17-year-old writer and activist living in Canada. She is a power wheelchair user with Spinal Muscular Atrophy and a political science student. Alongside writing, Erin enjoys spending her money on anything that comes in pink.

SOCIAL MEDIA +

THE FUTURE

♡ ◯ ◁

I hope that our conversations around social media continue to get more sophisticated and dynamic as we mature alongside this technology. I hope social media offers more than a way to showcase our lives; I also hope social media offers a way to examine our lives and our relationships to each other, and raise awareness that these tools have the power to reshape our sense of self – and possibly our humanity. Our lives have been irrevocably changed by social media in many ways, most of which are good. But we are also the insatiable repeat customers of a highly addictive product, and we will need all of our resources and wits about us to ensure that logic, compassion and empathy influence how much power these services have over us.

JENNA WORTHAM, 36, WRITER, THINKER, REIKI PRACTITIONER, HERBALIST

What do you wish for the future of social media?

I want Facetune to go bankrupt. I want tighter controls for under 21s until people have some sense of who they are and what they want to present to the online world, if anything. I want a social media that has all the positive messages and useful information and connection capabilities but no dark user pathways. I want someone to tell me that that's possible even though I know it isn't because good can't exist without evil in either the online or the offline world. In the very least, I want the 'no likes' experiment in Canada to be enforced worldwide and 100 more large scale 'no like' style experiments to be introduced, if only to show us that someone somewhere cares and is taking action to make these platforms better. I want all the components to be separated and seen clearly for what they are; I want there to be a dedicated space where people brag about their success at work, a dedicated space where people post selfies, a separate platform for influencers, a fitness space, a travel space, a feel good place for funny memes, inspirational quotes and dog videos, and a different app for activism. You could say this is already in place — that LinkedIn is the answer to the work objective, Instagram to the selfie need and Twitter to the activism space, but it all gets tangled up on a feed and I think that's what makes social media so addictive and so anxiety inducing. Maybe if it was divided up into categories like this, people would be more conscious of what they post and more honest about their intentions in doing so. I think if we all called a spade a spade on social media, there might be less negative social comparison and less overall anxiety. I think… but nobody knows.

SARAH RAPHAEL, 32

What do you wish for the future of social media?

I feel like so much of our world is exploitative, whether we're exploiting people to make more or exploiting people to sell products or ideas. There is just so much exploitation - I hope we find ways to make it less exploitative.

MONA CHALABI, 32, DATA JOURNALIST

That it makes people feel better, not worse when they are on it. And that it stops becoming so embedded in culture that people don't have an option not to participate.

**LYNETTE NYLANDER, 29
WRITER, EDITOR AND CREATIVE**

What do you wish for the future of social media?

I hope people become more true to others. I hope they stop downgrading others because of how they look and how they dress. I hope influencer culture stops being so much about flex and starts being more motivational. I just want it to be a more welcoming environment.

LESLEY, 18, STUDENT

I wish that it would encourage unique voices and connect them with real people, rather than pushing everyone towards homogeneous alienation.

MARTINE SYMS, 31, ARTIST

What do you wish for the future of social media?

The internet can offer so much comfort and community that, for some people, it outweighs the negatives. I suspect the answer [to a happy future] lies in the middle ground and within each individual's own comfort zone – and especially in remembering that we have agency in setting our own boundaries between the spheres of our lives.

But while we figure it out, all I can say is: find your people. They are out there, and the internet will help you with that. Make sure you show up for their real-life hugs, and make sure you show up for the sunshine. They are both medicinal.

MARTA BAUSELLS, 31
WRITER AND LITERARY EDITOR

What do you wish for the future of social media?

I think we should remove visible likes. I think they create a sense of unneeded competition and can have severe effects on people's mental health. Shouldn't social media be a space for creative and political expression, rather than a game where we create gladiatorial winners who have somehow 'won' compared to others? People get angry, sad and even suicidal over likes. I would like a more level playing field. I would also like far more thorough input in the creation of algorithms by women and people of colour and by different identities and genders. What you see is no longer just a timeline, but about what social media companies think will help sell advertising-based products and manipulate us. I would also love to have advertising removed from social spaces altogether – even if this means paying a small subscription fee to remove them. Ads should muted.

FRANCESCA GAVIN,
WRITER AND CURATOR

What do you wish for the future of social media?

I want social media to be a place where we're allowed to make mistakes. I think so many of us are afraid to express ourselves as we are because we are afraid of being policed and judged. Social media often feels like it lacks room to ask questions and thus room for growth. We don't know everything and that's totally okay! When we have to constantly define ourselves it infringes on how we can really be. Social media that is based on individualism and personal branding is a result of that. I'm yearning for more sensitive platforms that can support more layered encounters and differences where we can integrate all the different parts of who we are.

I want more IRL community-based internet experiences that encourage us more to act locally with the world immediately around us. I want to really know what's going on in my community and how to be involved in smaller projects that can make small differences that lead to big ones.

Going forward I want social media to be something our lives don't totally revolve around. Even if it's something we're actively using with more awareness. How we manage our time around it feels like a key thing to be looking at in the future.

NAOMI SHIMADA

What do you wish for the future of social media?

I hope we open up more conversations around the idea of normality. I hope people stop projecting false realities and I hope that other people stop taking these false projections at face value. And I hope I can dial in to call my friend and appear in holographic form so I can invite myself to dinners.

KEZ COO, 27, FILM MAKER

What do you wish for the future of social media?

I think social media can be a powerful tool for honest conversations, change, and personal and creative growth. I guess it is about examining what we use it for and how we use it: how can we shift the focus from appearances or material gain or material comfort in a way that still feels accessible and relatable?

AMANI AL KI, 27, JEWELLER AND MAKER

What do you wish for the future of social media?

I hope for the sake of our children, that the importance of it passes or at least, that the apps come with better content management. As individuals, we need to look at the messages we're putting out and preempt the various interpretations. The 'influencers' must be monitored better to make sure that the influence they have is positive.

CELIA BURTON, 29, MAKE UP ARTIST

What do you wish for the future of social media?

I wish for even more real life transparency and for people to take responsibility for what they post and for their words.

BRIANNA LEE PRICE, 33
MUSIC PRODUCER, DJ, PRESENTER

What do you wish for the future of social media?

It's disheartening to see people with a platform who are peddling useless ideas and products. I hope for more 'influencers' who actually have something to say.

PAULINA PINSKY, 26
WRITER AND TEACHER

ACKNOWLEDGEMENTS

SARAH

Thanks to everyone who has bought and read this book or just read the parts they could relate to, that's sort of how we imagined it.

Thanks to our most wonderful, reassuring editor Susannah Otter; you've got the eyes of an eagle and the courage of a lion. Thanks to everybody at Quadrille – Katherine, Ruth, the Lauras. Thanks to our literary agent Niki Chang, whose own star I'm really enjoying watching ascend and who is admirably dedicated to making the publishing industry more diverse.

Thanks to Naomi for giving me monthly TEDx style speeches on life and making peace with myself, and for always seeing the big picture. Thanks to Tom Rasmussen, Amelia Abraham, Barbara Volkar, Sadhbh O'Sullivan, Roxie Odoyo, Claire Byrne, Rahila Gupta, Juno Roche, Ariane Mason and Charisse Chikwiri for agreeing to be interviewed and for adding so much charm, heart and experience. Those interviews really changed my perspective. As did the contributed essays by established and emerging writers who I'm proud to be on the same spine as; they are really the currency of this book. Thanks to the group of teenage girls in Brixton who lifted my spirits every Thursday – Lesley, Vanessa, Ikhlas, Nya, Million, Freya, Berenice, Sophia – and opened my eyes to the on and offline issues young girls are facing in the UK today.

Thanks to my Pulitzer prize-winning husband-to-be, Dominic, who is my favourite distraction and who I know will be so kind and supportive if anyone says anything mean about me on Twitter. To my dad, who is indescribably hilarious and should be an influencer, I'm trying to make it happen on #nabschat. When I read him my bodies essay he said 'Fantastic. Just one question, what is Kardashian?'. To my equally hilarious mum, who has just sent us all an email with the subject line 'INSTAGRAM - NO PRIVACY' asking if we know whether Instagram is public and advising we watch what we post. To my various chapter readers, most notably my brilliant sister Claire who wrote a medical textbook on hearts in half the time I took to write this book, and who edits like Ezra Pound; also to Rose and Nadia who sometimes sent me detailed edit notes and other times drunk voice notes saying IT'S FINE STOP WORRYING. Thanks to my brother Steven for helping me to turn my worry into laughter for 32 years. Thanks also to my later readers Tess and Alice. To Kate and Gillian and everyone at Refinery29 for believing that every woman's story should be told and for supporting me in every possible way as an editor. And finally to my therapist, who could read between all the lines in my essays and tell you a totally different story.

NAOMI

A friend once told me 'The moon is just a mere reflection of her sun', so everything you see and connect to in this book resides in you and your spirit too – thank you for taking the time out to read this. By doing so you are actively making a choice. A choice to be curious to other ways of living online and to be curious about unmasking the social media profile.

When I was a kid, as the eldest of 4, my parents favourite phrase that they drilled into us (probably with the help of Barney the Purple Dinosaur who made a catchy-ass song about it) that 'sharing is caring'. This is a phrase I've held close, that's only continued to evolve in my adult life, and unintentionally has become my modus operandi. Sharing not just in tangible forms with the things we own/have but sharing feelings, ideas, learnings and our stories. I really believe that sharing is such a powerful way of showing care. There were moments that I felt scared about being so honest but I feel so loved and held by my IRL and online communities, so you made it feel safe to do so. Thank you for making me brave.

This book would never have happened if it wasn't for my inner circle with whom we shared our collective stories of struggle at my dining table. To everyone whose conversations I overheard and eavesdropped into, speaking about so many similar experiences. You were a constant reminder as why we had to keep going. I was adamant when we started this project that it had to be open and honest. Social media is already often a place of pretence and projections so we needed this book to be soft and vulnerable. A space to be real about their experiences. So thank you to all our contributors who did exactly that. We are so grateful.

To Sarah, I can't imagine having done this journey with anyone else. All the phone calls, messages, tears, 3am ideas. This is only the beginning, I'm so proud of you <3

To Susannah Otter and everyone on the team @ Quadrille, bless your kind souls – thank you for your soft ear, patience and your generosity. I was so scared of doing this project and you helped make it less scary.

To my literary agent Niki Chang @ The Good Literary Agency who slid into my DMs, so many years ago – thank you for coming to me and making me believe that I could do this. Thank you to my team @Storm for looking after me.

To Mama, Luka, Taro + Enzo. You are my rocks. We are a beautiful mess and I wouldn't have it any other way. Ride or dies forever <.3

To Papa, I feel you by my side everyday – I love you, we did it!

To Kimberly, Ruth, Harriet, Tara, Aditi – who kindly looked over my work and supported me when I needed it the most. There are not enough words, I love you so much. To Darcy & Joe – who gave me the physical and thus the mental space for this project to have been able to come into fruition. To Joel – who stopped me from completely losing my mind. Thank you for just being there, for the endless cups of coffee, the much needed megan thee stallion breaks and for not judging me when you find me constantly talking to myself. To Kate, Matthew, Samantha, Em, Linda, Yumna, Maia, Anita, Jonathan, Melati, Donna, Georgia, Mark – my angels. Eternal love. Thank you for holding me down.

Thank you to the people I follow and the followers. To everyone who has ever written to me over so many years on Instagram. Thank you for sharing your stories with me. Your words of encouragement, your vulnerability and love – made me see this project through. This is for you!

While I was writing this book we lost my beloved grandmother Marion Sheila Cinnamon. She was the true matriarch of our family and my first ever pen pal. She encouraged me to read and write more than anyone and always spoke honestly, from the heart no matter how difficult the subject matter. She would've loved this book.

And last but not least thank you to life's many teachers who come to us in so many different ways and forms.

Naomi Shimada is a host, writer and model with over 75k followers on Instagram. She has been featured in *Vogue*, *Elle*, *The Observer* and starred in campaigns for Nike, H&M and the Gap. Her writing has been featured in *Elle*, *i-D* and Refinery29. Naomi developed her platform speaking out against oppressive practices and unrealistic beauty standards in the fashion industry. Now, she's using her influence to push the needle on conversations about humanity with the hopes of encouraging others to step out of their comfort zones.

Sarah Raphael is a digital journalist and editor. Her previous longstanding roles included Editorial Director of Refinery29, the leading global digital media company for women, and Digital Editor of *i-D* Magazine, part of Vice Media Group. She has written for numerous publications including *The Guardian*, *Dazed*, *Vice*, *Vogue* and *Elle*. Sarah has also lectured in digital journalism at the London College of Fashion, is a youth volunteer at a girls' empowerment charity, and regularly speaks on the representation of women in the media at industry events.